HEROES
OF THE
HOLOCAUST

'Goodness, like evil, often begins in small steps...

Heroes evolve: they aren't born'

Ervin Staub

HEROES
OF THE
HOLOCAUST

Ordinary Britons

who risked their lives

to make a difference

LYN SMITH

1

Ebury Press, an imprint of Ebury Publishing,
20 Vauxhall Bridge Road,
London SW1V 2SA

Ebury Press is part of the Penguin Random House group of companies whose
addresses can be found at global.penguinrandomhouse.com

Copyright © Lyn Smith 2012

Lyn Smith has asserted her right to be identified as the author of this Work in
accordance with the Copyright, Designs and Patents Act 1988

First published by Ebury Press in 2012
This edition published by Ebury Press in 2021

www.penguin.co.uk

A CIP catalogue record for this book is available from the British Library

ISBN 9781529107470

Printed and bound in Great Britain by Clays Ltd, Elcograf S.p.A.

The authorised representative in the EEA is Penguin Random House Ireland,
Morrison Chambers, 32 Nassau Street, Dublin D02 YH68.

Penguin Random House is committed to a sustainable future
for our business, our readers and our planet. This book is
made from Forest Stewardship Council® certified paper.

CONTENTS

ACKNOWLEDGEMENTS

I owe a great debt of thanks to the many institutions and individuals who have made this book possible.

At the Imperial War Museum, my thanks to Tony Richards and his team within the Department of Documents and Sound, with my appreciation to Simon Offord, Peter Hart, Richard McDonough and Richard Hughes for their valued support; also my appreciation to the staff at the Photographic Archive of the Museum. I am very grateful to the Holocaust Educational Trust which initiated the Heroes of the Holocaust concept, with special thanks to its chief executive Karen Pollock and to Paul Evans. I also wish to express my appreciation for the assistance given by: the Association of Jewish Refugees, the Department of Communities and Local Government, the Public Records Office, the Church of Scotland, the Daughters of Charity, the Society of Friends in London; the Channel Islands Occupation Society (Jersey) Ltd., Jersey Heritage and the United States Holocaust Memorial Museum in Washington DC.

I have particularly appreciated the pivotal works of the following writers: Denis Avey/Rob Broomby, Brenda Bailey, John Castle, (Senator) Freddie Cohen, Ida Cook, Muriel Emanuel and Vera Gissing, Agnes Grunwald-Spier, Louise London, Rev David McDougall/Ian Alexander, Sara Hannah Rigler, Paul Sanders, Michael Smith, Hugo Vickers and Sofka Zinovieff.

For their most generous help, I thank: Denis Avey, Dorothy Aalen, Liam Byrne MP, Terry Charman, Ian Chatterley, Sister Joan Conroy, Alain Cremieux, Patricia Dunstan, Ralph Emanuel, Christopher Forster, Norman Hutcheson, Anders Jay, Anita Lasker-Wallfisch,

Pam Lyes, Rick Medlock, Carly Medlock, Fiona McElroy, Dorothy McMonagle, Doreen Montgomery, Sally Ravenhall, Russell Brown MP, Rev Roger Ryan, Laura Sarti and Sir Nicholas Winton.

There are several people to whom I owe a huge debt for the time and effort they have taken in responding to my enquiries – my appreciation to: June Isobel Medlock, John Cook, Clare Haddad, (Senator) Freddie Cohen and Agnes Grunwald-Spier. It was a great pleasure to meet Sara Hannah Rigler on her last visit to London – my thanks to her for the interview she granted me, and for permitting full use of her writings, letters, and Willy Fisher's diary – with such a dearth of information on the ten British prisoners of war who saved her life, this proved of paramount importance. Especially, I must thank Michael Smith, who has been exceedingly generous in allowing me to share his impressive range of archive material on Frank Foley; this has been particularly appreciated given the current closure of the archive and files on the Righteous at Yad Vashem, the Holocaust martyrs' and heroes' remembrance authority in Jerusalem, as well as its inability to grant special arrangements for researchers.

I am grateful to Dr Ervin Staub, Professor of psychology at the University of Massachusetts, who has kindly given permission for the epigraph of this book.

At my publishers, Ebury, I thank Andrew Goodfellow, Liz Marvin, Caroline Newbury and Ellie Rankine. A considerable debt is owed my agent, Barbara Levy, who has given her usual encouragement and advice at key points throughout.

On a personal level, I am very grateful to my husband, Peter, who has been a patient and unflagging supporter throughout.

Finally, my thanks to copyright holders for granting permission for the use of recordings, documents and photographs. My apologies for any copyright holder I have failed to trace, with assurances that this will be rectified in future editions.

Lyn Smith, October 2011

PREFACE

Most Holocaust historians agree that the Germans could not have committed their crimes on such a huge and systematic scale without the collaboration or indifference of people in occupied countries. With notable exceptions such as Bulgaria and Denmark, this is true, not only in the eastern European states known traditionally for high levels of anti-Semitism, but also in western states like France, Holland and Norway. Even in the British Channel Islands, those who helped Jews, and Russian slave labourers being worked to death, were often frowned upon as 'rocking the boat' by the general populace.

But there were thousands of other non-Jews, living in relative safety, who endangered themselves and their families to save Jews and others persecuted by the Nazis. Until recently it was not known that some of these were British subjects.

This was remedied in March 2010 when 27 Britons who had sheltered or rescued Jews were formally recognised by the British Government as 'Heroes of the Holocaust', with their brave acts brought to the attention of the British public and the world. The silver medal, inscribed with the words 'In the Service of Humanity', was created to acknowledge the men and women whose 'selfless actions preserved life in the face of persecution'. The Prime Minister at the time, Gordon Brown, said, 'They are true British heroes and a source of national pride for all of us. They were shining beacons of hope in the midst of terrible evil because they were prepared to take a stand against prejudice, hatred and intolerance.'

Banners of the Nazi stormtroopers are held aloft as the 150,000 Nazi soldiers are reviewed by Adolf Hitler in the Luitpold Arena in Nuremberg, September 1938. Six of these massive Nazi propaganda rallies were held between 1933 and 1938. Each rally was given a title which related to recent national events. Because of the recent annexation of Austria to the German Reich, this huge event was called 'Rally of Greater Germany' (*Reichsparteitag Grossdeutschland*).

Few of those honoured spoke of what they had done to help or save Jews during their lifetimes. Nor did they even consider their actions to be remarkable or exceptional which is partly why it took so long for their stories to come to light and why the majority of the medals were awarded posthumously, with only two men – Denis Avey and Sir Nicholas Winton – able to receive them in person. After the end of the conflict, the prevailing mood was to put the war behind and get on with life. Also, at the time few people were interested, and those like Denis Avey who, as a POW had been interned in Auschwitz and forced to work alongside Jewish slave labourers, found that equivalences could not be found with which to convey the horror they had witnessed. It too has to be remembered that until the 1960s, the genocide against the Jews was conflated with the general Nazi barbarity and not recognised for what it was – the greatest human rights' crime of the 20th century.

It was the 1961 trial of Adolf Eichmann, one of the main architects of the Final Solution, in which many Holocaust survivors bore witness to the suffering they had seen and endured, that brought much information to light that had not previously been widely known or discussed. Since then, the Holocaust has become one of the most researched topics of all times. A study of its history is depressing, revealing a bleak, very dark picture with little relief. Aside from the inhumane treatment and murder of nearly six million Jews and countless others considered *Untermenschen* (sub-humans) by the Nazis and other perpetrators, possibly the most disturbing aspect of the Holocaust is that the majority of ordinary people remained bystanders to the brutal crimes against European Jews that often happened before their eyes.

Karen Pollock, who as chief executive of the Holocaust Educational Trust, began the initiative to raise awareness of these men and women which ultimately led to the creation of the Heroes of the Holocaust medal, reminds us, 'Unfortunately the sad truth of the Holocaust is that most people did turn a blind eye and most thought of themselves. That's the sad reality…The story of the Holocaust is about suffering, indifference and discrimination and that's what makes these people so exceptional.' Rabbi

Albert Friedlander reinforces this: 'So much evil in our time is the result of apathy rather than enthusiastic evil. The Nazis in Germany did not depend on total support for their actions; all they needed was apathy – and there was an abundance of it.' The historian Laurence Rees, in his book *Auschwitz*, tells us, 'In this history, suffering is almost never redemptive. Although there are, on very rare occasions, extraordinary people who act virtuously, for the most part it is a story of degradation.'

Against this depressing historical record, it is all the more important to remember the small but very significant number of Britons who stand in stark contrast with the overall record of the Holocaust.

During the 1930s in the run up to war, as the Nazis' intentions towards the Jews were becoming increasingly apparent, tens of thousands of endangered Jewish men, women and children were saved, primarily from Nazi Germany, Austria and Czechoslovakia. Frank Foley, for instance, a British spy, who worked under the cover of Passport Control in Berlin from the 1920s until forced to leave in 1939, cut yards of red tape and took huge risks bending the rules, issuing forged visas and other documents in order to help the 10,000 Jews it is estimated he saved; all this without diplomatic immunity. The indomitable Quaker, Bertha Bracey, worked tirelessly throughout the interwar years, criss-crossing occupied and the threatened countries of Europe right up to the outbreak of war to save thousands of Jews. An improbable pair of opera-buffs, the sisters Ida and Louise Cook, took it upon themselves during their opera visits to Austria and Germany to meet and organise the flight of Jews to Britain, gathering funds in all kinds of imaginative ways, collecting the necessary documentation, and even buying a London flat with their own earnings in which the refugees could find safe refuge until they could fend for themselves. Many of the pre-war rescuers, like Bertha Bracey and the Cook sisters, continued to care for the refugees during the war and returned to a devastated, chaotic Europe after war had ended, to help the millions of displaced persons, many of them Jews.

Although mainland Britain was not occupied during the war and the British population was not put to the full test of how they would have reacted to those persecuted within their shores, many Britons trapped in Nazi-occupied Europe were faced with this challenge. Despite being severely limited in their movements and actions, and often at huge risk, there was a whole gamut of help which they gave Jews and others persecuted by Hitler's regime. This ranged from simple kindnesses such as treating them as fellow human beings rather than despised outcasts, to the shining example of June Ravenhall who, living under Nazi house arrest in occupied Holland, with her husband incarcerated in a concentration camp, hid a Jewish youth in her home for several years risking not only her own life, but the lives of her three young children. And the ten very ordinary British prisoners of war who, with the war coming to an end and longed-for liberty and home in sight, risked everything to hide and tenderly care for a pitiful young Jewess, after she had escaped from a death march.

These are but a few of the outstandingly brave individuals who, in the face of great danger, ignored rules and regulations, often standing in opposition to public opinion, and stuck their necks out to do what their consciences told them was the right thing, when everything they saw and heard counselled caution and self-preservation. Unlike the great majority, they refused to be bystanders to the unfurling tragedy of the Holocaust, whatever the costs and dangers to themselves. As Jeremy Browne MP said in a House of Commons debate on 29 April 2009, 'The Holocaust is a reminder to us of mankind's ability for greatness, as well as mankind's ability for evil...'

Speaking with relatives, friends and others who knew the 27 'Heroes' one gains the impression that far from considering themselves 'heroes', they were modest, self-deprecating people who, when faced with a choice, decided 'this is not right' and did the decent thing, with no thought of personal gain. This silence meant that it was a total surprise for their families and friends when they heard of their extraordinary deeds and the risks they had taken during the war years.

Heroism suggests something glorious and emblematic and is usually associated with military endeavour, although it has to be said that in recent times the term is often applied to less serious events and behaviour. But the award 'Heroes of the Holocaust' places the accolade on quite another plane: the unique heroism of the weak and helpless. This was aptly expressed by Ron Ravenhall at the ceremony for his mother's posthumous award as 'Righteous Among the Nations'. Contrary to his late mother's modesty, he agreed that she fully deserved the accolade, suggesting that her actions were even more outstanding than those receiving the highest military decoration awarded for valour 'in the face of the enemy' – the Victoria Cross. For, unlike the VC, he argued, she had no defensive weapon to provide a chance of survival: 'She was an unarmed woman alone, with her husband in a Nazi concentration camp and three young children to protect, and her action was sustained and deliberate lasting for years, during any second of which there could have been rifle butts knocking on the door. She would be shot. Her death was certain.'

It is beyond the scope of this book to analyse the motives guiding these people whose actions are described within it. Religious women like Princess Alice, Sister Agnes and Jane Haining were no doubt inspired by Christian principles of goodness and charity. The fiery-tempered Denis Avey, as well as acting out of deep respect for the sanctity of human life, reacted instinctively out of sheer rage at the sadistic brutality he witnessed, eventually losing an eye as a result. What can be recognised as a common factor in this diverse group of people is their moral courage and sheer goodness. To put it simply, as Sara Hannah did when speaking of the British Tommies who saved her life, 'they were good, *good* people'.

Compelled to act and help those at the extremity of suffering, theirs is a story of hope and inspiration: they were ordinary men and women who acted out of the unquenchable spirit of humanity in providing glimmers of light in the darkness of the Holocaust. As Dr Julian Lewis MP said during the House of Commons' debate, 'It is hard to know why we have taken so long to recognise and acknowledge our own heroes.' But now they are known, they provide a reminder to us and to future generations, that the Holocaust is very much a part of Britain's Second World War history.

The rescue work for endangered Jews during the 1930s, and the humanitarian relief work carried out by British people in the devastated Europe of the war's aftermath, are perhaps better known. Less familiar is the story of Britons trapped in Nazi-occupied countries, who witnessed and suffered something of its darkness for the choices they made; some of whom, like Jane Haining and Louisa Gould, entering its ultimate depths when perishing in the gas chambers and crematoria of Auschwitz and Ravensbrück.

It is to these men and women, and others yet to be acknowledged, that I dedicate this book – shining examples to us all in challenging the racism, inhumanity and hatred all too evident in the world today.

Lyn Smith, October 2011

THE RISE OF HITLER
1920–1939

PERSECUTION

©AFP/Getty

Insulting anti-Semitic signs on a Jewish-owned shop in Germany. Graffiti and signs such as 'Jewish pig' on this shop were widespread in Germany from 1933.

The Holocaust – the genocide of nearly six million European Jews and more than 250,000 Sinti and Roma – was implemented between the summer of 1941 and Germany's defeat in May 1945. But Hitler's campaign against the Jews and other groups considered to be undesirable began well before this, even before the National Socialist Workers' Party – Nazi Party – came to power on 30 January 1933. Nazi ideology outlining the worldwide conflict between Aryans (Caucasians) and Jews was a major theme of Hitler's book *Mein Kampf* ('My Struggle', published in two volumes in 1925 and 1926). Jews, along with Communists, with whom they were closely identified, were regarded as threatening the very basis of German and Aryan culture, and Hitler's stated mission was to alert Germany and the world to this threat and to destroy it. With chilling prescience, he wrote, 'If at the beginning of the [1914–1918] War and during the War twelve or fifteen thousand of these Hebrew corrupters of the people had been held under poison gas, as happened to hundreds and thousands of our best German workers in the field, the sacrifice of millions at the front would not have been in vain.' For, 'There is no such thing as coming to an understanding with the Jews. It must be the hard-and-fast "Either–Or".'

Although Hitler and the Nazi Party were active from the early 1920s, it was only after Hitler's seizure of power in 1933 that the impact of anti-Jewish measures was felt. German Jews, increasingly isolated by Nazi anti-Semitic propaganda and segregated by various laws, were the main victims of his racism and hatred in the years 1933–1936. During this period, the violence against German Jewry was increasing but still of a relatively sporadic character compared with the mass campaigns which came later – although there were indications of what was to come. For instance, on 9 March 1933 the *Manchester Guardian* reported Jews beaten by Nazi stormtroopers (*Sturmabteilung*, the SA) until 'the blood streamed down their heads and faces… Many fainted and were left lying on the streets…' A few weeks later, on 1 April 1933, a one-day boycott of Jewish shops occurred, when windows were daubed with anti-Jewish slogans and armed stormtroopers prevented Aryan customers from entering Jewish shops. A purge of German Jewish, Communist and other books considered to be 'disruptive influences' was also undertaken, culminating in the mass book burnings of 10 May 1933 – both events organised by Joseph Goebbels, the Reich Minister for Propaganda, and his Nazi cohorts.

One of the first tasks the Nazi Party set itself on achieving power was to establish the concentration camp system. Dachau concentration camp was opened in March 1933, the first prisoners consisting mainly of Communists, Social Democrats and other political enemies of the Nazis. Sachsenhausen and other camps soon followed and by 1 September 1939 the concentration camp system had expanded to accommodate almost 25,000 inmates, the majority then Jews. It was during this early phase that legislation was formulated and implemented restricting economic and professional activity for anyone Jewish, as well as social contact with Aryans. On 11 April 1933, the publication of the Law for the Restoration of the Professional Civil Service and the law establishing a *numerus clausus* on Jews for admission into the legal profession was published. More than fifty other decrees were enacted between this date and September 1935, each of which covered a different profession, restricting entry to Jews, and eventually banning them altogether.

However, it was the so-called Nuremberg Laws passed on 15 September 1935, by a special sitting of the Reichstag during the massive, dramatic Nazi rally held in the city, that brought shockwaves to German and European Jewry. The Nuremberg Laws defined who was considered a

Jew and revoked what few rights, including that of citizenship, Jews still possessed. All these measures were backed up with an increasing vitriolic anti-Jewish and racial propaganda campaign by the Nazi-controlled media, led by Julius Streicher's rabidly anti-Semitic tabloid weekly, *Der Stürmer*. Throughout this time, Jews were encouraged to emigrate and, despite all the problems of gaining admission to safe havens, more than 35,000 Jews left for Palestine, Western Europe, Britain and the United States in 1933. The degree of anti-Semitism served as a reliable indicator of emigration: between 1933–1935, one quarter of Germany's Jewish population had emigrated.

British immigration policy towards European Jewry in the years 1933–1939 underwent several changes in response to the crises developing in the *Grossdeutsches Reich* (the greater German Reich, better known as the Third Reich). Britain was still clawing its way out of the effects of the depression of the mid 1930s with over a million unemployed in 1938. Also, at this time Britain had no refugee laws and had the freedom to grant or refuse entry as it chose. During the years 1933–1939 it continued a policy that had been established in The Aliens Registration Act of 1914 and extended in 1919 with new restrictions. It stated that Britain was not a country of immigration and settlement and operated mainly as a place of temporary refuge, which meant that entrants had to demonstrate prospects of re-emigration to be allowed in. With each phase of increased persecution of European Jewry the pressure for admission intensified, leading to adjustments to British immigration policy throughout the period, although the basic fact remained that large-scale Jewish immigration into Britain was not desired.

After 1938 the campaign in Germany to create a *Judenrein* – 'Jewish-cleansed' – economy started in earnest; further laws and decrees published between 1937 and 1939 led to an ever-increasing spiral of anti-Semitic violence, suffering and desperation among all sections of the Jewish community, destroying the very foundations of Jewish life. As a result of the strident anti-Semitic rhetoric spilling over the German borders, Jews in Germany's neighbouring countries were growing increasingly uneasy. The Nazi takeover (*Anschluss*) of Austria on 13 March 1938 intensified these fears. Whereas the process of discrimination and violence against the German Jews had been relatively gradual, the persecution of the Austrian Jews was immediate and devastating; overnight they were deprived of civil rights and subjected to extreme violence and humiliation, especially in Vienna.

In July 1938 an international conference regarding the future reception of refugees was opened at Evian in Switzerland. It was agreed to set up an intergovernmental agency to decide what could be done. In effect nothing was achieved, though for the governments attending it proved a reprieve from having to take action. As a refugee remarked at the end of the conference, 'Evian' was merely 'naive' spelled backwards. By this time more than 150,000 Jews from Germany and Austria had already been admitted to the United States, Britain, Palestine, Brazil, Bolivia, France, Belgium and the Scandinavian countries. But attitudes against refugees were clearly hardening as the numbers desperate to leave grew apace with restrictions imposed against them. Also, many would-be emigrants were without passports, outcasts stripped of nationality. These were Jews who had fled persecution in eastern Europe and had been naturalised as German between the end of the First World War and 30 January 1933.

The exodus of Jewish refugees following the terror unleashed against Austrian Jews after the *Anschluss* of 13 March 1938 caused the British government to rethink visa policy. Since 1927 passport holders in Britain, Germany and Austria had not required visas when travelling between each other's countries. But with the expectation of an influx of Austrians seeking refuge, as well as German Jewry increasingly worried with this latest demonstration of Hitler's intentions and far more anxious to emigrate, British government policy was quickly revised. Although detrimental to European Jewry, the government's revival of visas was facilitated by the support given to the Home Secretary by the Anglo–Jewish leaders, who feared increased immigration would fuel the growth of anti-Semitism in the country.

In the autumn of 1938, thousands of Polish Jews were forcibly expelled from Germany to the border areas between Germany and Poland. On 28 October of that year, for instance, some 17,000 German–Jewish citizens of Polish origin were stripped of their citizenship and dumped in no-man's-land on the border near the town of Zbaszyń. This outrage provoked Herschel Grynszpan, the son of one of the displaced, to assassinate Ernst vom Rath, the first secretary of the German embassy in Paris, which resulted in a wave of Nazi anti-Semitic attacks throughout Germany, Austria and the Sudetenland on the night of 9/10 November, the like of which had not been seen since the *pogroms* against Jews during the Russian civil war twenty years earlier. The outbreak of violence is known as *Kristallnacht* – the night of broken glass – when more than 7,500 Jewish shops were wrecked and many synagogues and precious religious artefacts were desecrated or destroyed. Following *Kristallnacht*, 30,000 German Jews were rounded up and imprisoned in concentration camps. As the camp population changed from 'undesirables' and 'criminals' to Jews, living conditions deteriorated to sub-human levels. *Kristallnacht* had enormous international repercussions and in Britain helped swing public opinion to a new awareness of the Nazi terror against European Jewry and against the policy of appeasement. Until then, only a minority had opposed Chamberlain's appeasement policy. After the First World War, a vibrant anti-war movement had gathered momentum and even non-pacifists, albeit with unease, supported the Munich Agreement. Peace was certainly more attractive than a war potentially even more calamitous than that which had ended only twenty years before.

The Munich Agreement of September 1938, which surrendered the Sudetenland to the Reich, convinced Hitler that Britain and France would not confront him over further expansion eastwards. But, after the Nazi occupation of the rest of Czechoslovakia in March 1939, both Britain and France guaranteed that they would go to the aid of Hitler's next likely victim, Poland, should her independence be threatened. As war approached, Jews desperately sought refuge from what was now a very obvious threat. Jewish parents were particularly anxious to find safe refuge for their children. In late 1938, after *Kristallnacht*, Britain agreed to take 10,000 Jewish children. In the event just over 9,000 arrived under the *Kindertransport* plan, the last group arriving on the very eve of war.

Despite the stringent immigration policies of potential host nations, emigration from the *Grossdeutsches Reich* increased dramatically throughout the autumn and winter of 1938–1939. Adolf Eichmann's Central Office for Jewish Emigration, based at first in Vienna and later in Berlin, began to drop its previous policy of persuasion for a new policy of intimidation, with Jews being subjected to humiliations, beatings, confinement in concentration camps and even death. These tough methods, along with the anti-Jewish laws, were extended to Czechoslovakia after the occupation of March 1939. By September 1939 about half of Germany's 500,000 Jews had left the country, along with 125,000 from Austria and 20,000 from the newly occupied Czech lands.

During the summer of 1939, Nazi threats against Poland increased, with demands for the Free City of Danzig and the Polish Corridor to be ceded to the Reich. On 23 August 1939, Hitler signed a non-aggression pact with the Russian leader Stalin which gave him the 'green light' to invade Poland. On 1 September 1939, German forces launched a *Blitzkrieg* – lightning war – against the Poles. The long agony of Poland was about to begin. On Sunday, 3 September 1939, following Hitler's refusal to withdraw his troops from Poland, Britain and France honoured their guarantees to the Poles and declared war on Germany.

During these turbulent years of Hitler's rise to power and the expansion of the Third Reich, there were a number of British men and women who witnessed at first hand the state-sanctioned persecution of European Jewry and who did their utmost not only to shake the impercipience of both the Baldwin and Chamberlain governments, but also took great risks to rescue endangered European Jewry.

FRANCIS 'FRANK' FOLEY
1884–1958

*'He was a very kind, religious man who felt it was the job
of every good human being to save people. Despite the British
policy of giving visas to only a few selected Jews, it was
known that he would do everything he could.'*

Frank Foley is remembered today as a 'British Schindler' for saving the lives of 10,000 Jews from the 1920s to the outbreak of the Second World War. In his role as Passport Control Officer attached to the British Embassy in Berlin he did this by cutting red tape and pushing through visa applications for those desperate to emigrate. As the persecution intensified, along with increasing immigration restrictions, Foley issued fake documents, entered concentration camps to deliver visas and hid Jews in his apartment.

These activities carried a great deal of risk. However, Foley was in yet more danger. His role in the Passport Control Office was in fact a cover for his work as a spy for the British government. Not only was he breaking British law and risking the displeasure of the Nazi Party with the help he offered the Jews, he was simultaneously passing information back to the British government about the Nazi war machine. Although he was part of the embassy's staff, the Foreign Office took a negative stance towards secret service work and refused to give Passport Control Officers diplomatic status; this meant that Foley was lacking diplomatic immunity, and therefore treading a fine line. Had he been arrested and the extent of his spying activities discovered, he would have been in a very difficult situation.

Born in the small Somerset town of Highbridge in 1884 of a relatively poor family, he gained a scholarship to the Jesuit Stonyhurst College in Lancashire. Having decided to become a priest, the young Foley studied for while in Poitiers, France before taking up an academic career. He was studying philosophy in Hamburg when the First World War broke out. After his distinguished service in the war as a second lieutenant, later a captain, in the Bedfordshire and Hertfordshire Regiment, Foley was posted to Berlin as foreign Secret Intelligence Service (better known as MI6) station head with the cover of director of passport control. With revolutionary Russia then perceived as the major threat, Foley was involved with monitoring the movements of Soviet agents and preventing them from entering Britain

Post-war Berlin, despite the dire economic situation and an atmosphere of unrest under the Weimar Republic, was a fascinating, uninhibited city, a major centre for both the arts and science, with a plethora of avant-garde nightclubs and bars which Foley frequented and enjoyed. He lived in a flat in Wilmersdort, a largely Jewish middle-class area in the west of the city. In 1921, he married Kay Lee, and the couple's daughter Ursula Margaret was born one year later. From the 1920s until the outbreak of war, he was well positioned in his dual role to observe the rise of Hitler and the Nazi Party. He was appalled by the moral and social depravity of the regime and horrified at the distress and desperation of the Jews as Nazi persecution against them increased.

John Silberman, a schoolboy from Berlin, gives some idea of what life was like for young Jews just after Hitler came to power in 1933:

'I had just started school a year before. There were warnings from parents and others not to get mixed up in fights with *Hitler Jugend* [Hitler Youth]... After 1933 it was just accepted that if you were a Jewish child you were liable to be beaten up, bullied or whatever else they chose to do with you. It was no use appealing to policemen or teachers because they were not supposed to interfere or even be interested in helping you because you were perceived to be an enemy of the state. That was fed into my mind as a matter of self-preservation... The bullying and verbal assault was not confined to German children: it was quite common if some adult, who was nothing more than an ignorant thug, called you names or

kicked you. It was bullying all down the line and that was totally accepted...

As time went on I became aware that business for my father seemed to be getting difficult. I didn't fully understand why, but there were pressures on customers not to buy from a Jewish manufacturer and pressures from suppliers to get higher prices, or not supply Jews... There was always this perpetual threat that if you didn't comply with non-Jewish requests, you could be reported to the Gestapo and be arrested. One always heard of people disappearing, or being arrested then coming back after a week or so having been beaten up or given hard labour, or occasionally, being killed – although the latter was much more common after 1937. But even in those early days, talk of the Gestapo was always rife... With the Nuremberg Laws it became quite evident that there was no future for Jews in Germany and that's when people seriously started to consider emigration...'

The mass emigrations of Jews between 1933–1935 created many problems for Foley in his role at the Passport Control Office, as his despatches to London reveal. On 29 March 1933, he wrote, 'This office is overwhelmed with applications from Jews to proceed to Palestine, to England, to anywhere in the British Empire...' By 1935 he was reporting, 'It has become increasingly apparent that the Party has not departed from its original intentions and that its ultimate aim remains the disappearance of the Jews from Germany, failing that, their relegation to a position of powerlessness and inferiority.' Responding to the announcement of two new anti-Jewish laws in September 1935, at the time of the huge Nuremberg rally, he presciently wrote, 'German policy is clearly to eliminate the Jew from German life, and the Nazis do not mind how this is accomplished. Mortality and emigration provide the means.'

Insulting, provocative anti-Semitic signs soon became commonplace on the streets of the city, signs on shops exhorting Berliners, *'Deutsche, kauft nicht von Juden, die Juden sind unser Unglück!'* – 'Germans, don't buy from Jews, the Jews are our misfortune!' Other notices urged Jews 'Go to Palestine', 'Go to Jerusalem'. As it happened, this is where thousands of Jews wished to go, seeing Palestine as a safe, secure long-term sanctuary. Foley agreed, considering it a more suitable destination than other countries where an influx of Jews might lead to anti-Semitism. But this was not so easy despite the British Mandate for Palestine of 26 September 1923 that had favoured 'The establishment of national home for the Jewish people, it being clearly understood that nothing should be done which might prejudice the civil and religious rights of existing non-Jewish communities in Palestine…'.

Throughout the 1920s the levels of immigration to Palestine were lower than expected, but the year after Hitler came to power, the Jewish exodus began. Of the 75,000 Jewish refugees who had left Germany by 1935, 30,000 had gone to Palestine. Palestinian Arabs became increasingly concerned that large-scale immigration would lead to the take-over of the country by the Jews. Serious rioting, aided by Nazi propaganda, began in 1933. The British government, alarmed with the turn in events, reviewed its immigration laws to stem the flow with restrictions on immigration numbers, despite the urgent need of a safe haven for Jews. It also meant that German Jews hoping to emigrate were required to have visas which had to be obtained from the British Passport Control Office in Berlin. This impacted hugely on Foley's time and energy; but he never failed to cooperate fully with Jewish welfare organisations which had been set up to help those suffering persecution.

In particular, Foley worked closely with the Assistance Organisation for German Jews, or *Hilfsverein der Deutschen Juden*. This organisation helped Jews to emigrate, giving advice regarding visas, finding sponsors and providing funds wherever necessary. Several of Foley's Jewish friends were members including Wilfred Israel, a prominent member. Another, Hubert Pollack, one of Foley's secret service agents, worked as his liaison with the *Hilfsverein* as well as providing reliable, often vital, intelligence for what was going on within the new regime. Together, the trio formed a very useful team, working the system while making full use of their particular skills and resources.

As Passport Control Officer, Foley was granted considerable discretion in interpreting rules and regulations and he took full advantage of this. For Palestine, Britain and the British Empire, immigration continued to be strictly limited. Foley used legal means wherever possible in his visa work but also exploited loopholes in British immigration laws. The only way that the majority of German Jews from the business and professional classes could gain entry to Palestine was through the so-called Capitalist Visa (*Kapitalisten-Zertifikat*) for which the payment of £1,000 was required. This was a huge sum at the time – £40,000 in real terms today – and unavailable to many wealthy Jews whose bank and other assets had been frozen by the Nazis. If potential emigrants possessed sufficient funds and could pay a 'flight tax' of 25 per cent of their capital, the remainder of their marks were then paid into a special blocked account within the *Reichsbank* which then transferred £1,000 pounds into the Templar Bank in Palestine. Only when this money was paid could they obtain their visas. But there were further complications as the money could only be withdrawn in Palestine, and visas couldn't be granted without ready money.

Foley bent the rules many times. He suggested, for instance, that a sponsor in Palestine wrote a letter guaranteeing the money, on the basis of which the visa could be granted. This worked in many cases although the promised money was seldom used. The prominent Jewish artist and sculptor Wolfgang Meyer-Michael, for instance, accepted his cousin's guarantee in writing that the sum would be paid once he had crossed the border into the safety of Holland en route to Palestine, without his cousin ever having to pay.

A further problem arose in 1934 and 1935 when the shortage of currency occurred and the *Reichsbank* was unable to transfer pounds into the Templar Bank. Waiting numbers were given to those depositing their £1,000; only when their number came up and the money transferred could the visa be issued. Although another paying-in system negotiated by the Jewish Agency was tried, this also dried up through lack of hard currency. Foley then started issuing Capitalist Visas with the capital on paper only. Foley was helped in this work by his *Hilfsverein* contact, Hubert Pollack, who informed him of endangered Jews desperate to get out.

The British Foreign Office meanwhile was receiving reliable details of the increasing persecution of Jews as well as warnings of another war, not only from Foley, but from diplomats like Robert Smallbones, the British Consul General in Frankfurt, and many other well-informed individuals, including journalists such as Norman Ebbutt, the Berlin correspondent of *The Times*, until his expulsion by the Nazis in 1937. But the Foreign Office took little notice; its main concerns continued to be the Bolshevik threat from Soviet Russia, as well as the appeasement of Hitler which continued despite the movement of German troops into the demilitarised Rhineland in March 1936, against the terms of the Locarno Treaty of 1925.

Throughout his years in Berlin, Foley was without diplomatic immunity; with increased spy mania from the mid 1930s and the ever-more vigilant Gestapo, he was very vulnerable, at great risk of arrest as a spy. But all accounts present him as continuing to act in his unflustered, determined way, never hesitating to confront the Gestapo when they appeared at the Passport Control Offices in *Tiergartenstrasse*, harassing the queues of terrified Jews seeking visas. Foley would courteously, but firmly, tell the bullying Nazis to join the queues if they wanted passports, or leave.

Alongside the increasing demands of his work, Foley continued with his secret service work, feeding valuable information back to Britain. This was obtained not only from his Jewish friends, but also from senior officials he had recruited from the German army as well as a *Luftwaffe* colonel who fed Foley information on the German air force's rapid expansion over the course of three years.

Meanwhile events were happening in Austria that were to have an enormous negative impact on European Jewry and were to present further challenges to Foley.

The annexation of Austria to the German Reich on 12 March 1938 was greeted by Austrian Nazis with immediate anti-Jewish violence which led to a frantic search by Austrian Jews for safe havens. In the autumn of that year, Adolf Eichmann's Central Office for Jewish Emigration was set up in Vienna, and adopted a carrot-and-stick approach, with the emphasis on the stick. As well as losing all civil, professional and social rights, Jews were now subject to public humiliation and arbitrary physical assaults, as John Lawrence experienced when being seized by a group of local Nazi thugs:

'I was taken to the local barracks. I was butted with a rifle and made to lie beneath a mattress on the springs of a bed and four of them jumped on the mattress. I was then taken up to the top floor – by which time they had stripped me to my underpants. They held me out of the window. "Shall we let him go now?" I was sixteen, for heaven's sake! Then they took me downstairs. "We've forgotten something, the lavatories need cleaning." So three of them held me, and the lavatories were cleaned with my head and my hair. It was dreadful, dreadful. If I told you in detail what happened to me in that barrack you wouldn't believe it! And they were all Austrians.'

With increased demands for immigration to Britain, from Austrians now as well as Germans, and under pressure from trade unions, business and professional organisations, many just recovering from the Depression, entry requirements increased in stringency. This is when the revival of visa policy between Britain, Germany and Austria occurred, the purpose being to further regulate the flow of refugees. The Passport Control Officers' task in Germany and Austria was to select from only 'desirable' categories: agricultural workers, domestic services, or those elites with international reputations in science, medicine or the arts, who were likely to be of benefit to Britain with their specialist expertise.

Just after Hitler had come to power, and in response to the drastic moves against academics by his regime, an Academic Assistance

Council (AAC) had been set up in Britain to help fund and find new positions for displaced scholars. William Beveridge, then director of the London School of Economics and Political Science, and other academics such as Lord Rutherford and A.V. Hill were among its leading figures. Many British scientists and academics subscribed to the AAC and went out of their way to help their persecuted German counterparts – who fell within the 'desirable' category. Hans Krebs (later knighted for his work), a young German biochemist, came to Britain in this way. He explained how important influential contacts were:

> 'I was somewhat surprised when I got a letter from a German colleague who worked in Cambridge, England telling me that people had heard that I was in difficulties. He told me that if I was interested in coming to Cambridge I should write to Hopkins (Sir Frederick Gowland Hopkins, OM, English bio-chemist) and I would be sure of a sympathetic response. So I wrote to Hopkins and got a reply which I found very touching because it began with the sentence, "I admire your work so much that I am anxious to help you…" I decided to emigrate…'

Among the 1,500 refugees assisted by the AAC in the 1930s were those that became part of the British team assembled at Los Alamos in the United States during the war, including refugee nuclear physicists such as Otto Frisch and (later Sir) Rudolf Peierls. These two German Jewish refugees went on to co-author the 'Frisch-Peierls Memorandum' in March 1940, which accurately detailed the exact calculations for an atomic bomb . Of those arriving under the AAC scheme, sixteen went on to win Nobel Prizes, eighteen received knighthoods, and over 100 were elected Fellows of the Royal Society and the British Academy; many more became leaders in their respective fields. They never forgot their gratitude to the AAC, as Hans Krebs later said, 'We often talk about the debt we owe your organisation.' In turn, the beneficiaries of the scheme made a valuable and lasting contribution to British society.

But in Germany this concern by the British authorities to accept only those considered 'desirables' undermined Foley's ability to issue visas. Few people who did not have relatives in Britain, or others willing to support them, could qualify for a visa. Despite the challenge this presented, he continued, in his determined but increasingly cavalier way, to do his utmost to get visas for those in need.

The anti-Semitic excesses occurring in Austria after the *Anschluss* accelerated those perpetrated on German Jewry. Foley reported the increased searches on Jewish premises, arrests and increasing detention in concentration camps, describing how 'it is no exaggeration to say that Jews have been hunted like rats in their homes, and for fear of arrest many have to sleep at a different address overnight'.

As the situation was building up for the Nazi takeover of the Sudetenland, and with the arrest and detention by the Gestapo of Captain Thomas Kendrick, Foley's counterpart in Vienna, the chief of the Secret Intelligence Service, Sir Hugh Sinclair, recalled Foley and his MI6 staff to London, fearing for their safety. The signing of the Munich Agreement on 29 September 1938 by Neville Chamberlain and French premier Édouard Daladier reduced the tension for a while, allowing Foley and his staff to return to Berlin to the increasingly difficult and time-consuming task of helping the Jews in an ever more restrictive immigration environment.

Both this work and his intelligence gathering were to increase dramatically following the *Kristallnacht* pogrom unleashed against the Jews on 9 and 10 November. In Berlin about 1,200 men were arrested and taken to Sachsenhausen concentration camp under 'protective custody'. Foreign diplomats noted and reported the destruction, physical injuries and fatalities throughout Germany and Austria. Foley witnessed the Berlin situation as he drove around the city, reporting back the terrible abuses towards Jews and Jewish property that he had seen and helping as many Jews as he could. Sir George Ogilvie-Forbes, Counsellor and Chargé d'Affaires at the British Embassy in Berlin, who had also helped a number of refugees escape from Germany, telegraphed to London

A youth prepares to clear up the broken window glass from a Jewish shop in Berlin on 10 November, the day after the *Kristallnacht* rampage, when Nazis set fire to hundreds of synagogues, looted thousands of Jewish businesses and homes and attacked Jews in Germany and Austria, incarcerating thousands in concentration camps.

details of the violence against Jews, 'I can find no words strong enough in condemnation of the disgusting treatment of so many innocent people and the civilised world is faced with the appalling sight of 500,000 people about to rot away in starvation.'

Berta Ollendorff, a niece of Leo Baeck, the chairman of the Association of Jewish Rabbis, witnessed the destruction of her family's shop,

'They smashed the windows of my father's shop. It was a corner shop so there were windows in the main street and windows in the side street and the middle was the entrance to the shop. They had smashed both and there were some bottles for show in the windows but they had no fluid in them so they had smashed the bottles, the windows, the lot. In the morning the police phoned my mother and said would she clear it up. My mother didn't want my father to go into the shop so she phoned me and asked if I'd come. I came and I had boxes and a broom and I started clearing up and the people in the main street stopped and watched me. I became so furious and full of hate that this had been done to my father and to us that I wasn't afraid any more. I was absolutely cold inside, full of hate and fury.'

Many ordinary Berliners, such as Gudrun Kübler, unlike those gawping at Berta clearing up the mess, were ashamed and appalled by the excesses of *Kristallnacht*:

'You were shocked that something like that could happen, and why? These were also human beings; you can't do that to somebody, just destroy everything rather than let them have synagogues and keep their own religion. The houses and shops! Some of them were attacked, windows smashed. In other words you could plainly see it; also the oppressed people, later with their Stars [the Star of David that Jews were ordered to wear] and suchlike. It was very noticeable.'

It was at this time that Foley began to take increased risks by hiding Jews in his home in *Lessingstrasse*, including Rabbi Leo Baeck. He also allowed certain foreign journalists, such as *The Daily Telegraph's* Berlin correspondent Hugh Carleton Greene, into his home for briefings with Leo Baeck. Through his Zionist links, Foley also made contact with *Mossad le Aliyah Bet*, a new organisation, related to secret service activity, set up to help Jews without visas escape to Palestine; the relationship also proved useful for the sharing of intelligence.

With the need for visas now desperate, Foley appealed to the Palestine Commissioner for Migration, Eric Mills, for additional blank visa certificates. These were quickly provided, together with 1,000 special *Youth Aliyah* certificates which enabled Jewish youngsters to leave, unaccompanied by their parents, for Palestine. Foley's response was a cable saying simply 'God bless you – Foley'. Arieh Handler, a German member of the *Youth Aliyah*, later recalled his gratitude for Foley's efforts, saying, 'He was a very kind, religious man who felt it was the job of every good human being to save people. Despite the British policy of giving visas to only a few selected Jews, it was known that he would do everything he could.'

With the vast increase in his workload, Foley appealed for extra assistance from London. Margaret Reid and another assistant from MI6 arrived and were able to give invaluable help over the coming months. By now long queues of Jews could be found day and night outside the British Embassy, many of them terrified German Jewish women. As Benno Cohn, co-chairman of the Zionist Organisation, explained, 'Thirty-two thousand men were held in concentration camps in those weeks and their wives besieged Captain Foley in order to effect the liberation of their husbands from the camps... in those days he revealed himself in all his humanity. Day and night he was at the disposal of those who sought help...'

Foley and his team worked relentlessly, dawn until dusk, to help them, issuing visas of all descriptions and in vast quantities which meant the release of many Jews from the camps. This is when his skills of organisation came to the fore. Acting always in a most kindly way, he kept order among the surging, desperate Jews, organising refreshments for them, pestering London for any visas held up there, and all the time continuing to provide the British authorities with reliable up-to-date information on what was happening in Germany. Many years later, in April 1961, a letter to *The Daily Telegraph* written by Robert Weltsch, former editor of the *Jüdische Rundschau* (*Jewish Review*), acknowledged Foley's efforts, '...Nobody who lived in Berlin during those days of horror will ever forget what an island of comfort Mr Foley's office was to thousands of harassed and suffering people; to some he appeared a saint...'.

There were also many cases where men awaiting visas had been interned before the visas arrived; Foley would take all measures to get the visas through from London and push for their release. When the visa arrived without a relative to present it to the camp authorities, Foley never hesitated to enter the camps himself making sure these men would have their chance to escape.

After *Kristallnacht* and the tightening of immigration restrictions, the only place in the world that Jews could enter without visas was the International Settlement in Shanghai. For many Jews this was their only chance and another great exodus occurred. The British Foreign Office urged the Passport Control Office in Berlin and elsewhere to discourage this. Foley, who fully understood the turmoil the city of Shanghai was in, with the Sino–Japanese war and the increasing levels of violence in the International Settlements, weighed this against the Jews' desperate plight and responded:

'...One has to remember that the declared wish of the N.S.D.A.P. [Nazi Party] is that Jews should 'verrecken' (die like a dog). If they have to 'verrecken' it is of minor importance to the Party where the process takes place, but it might be considered humane on our part not to interfere officially to prevent Jews from choosing their own graveyards. They would rather die as free men in Shanghai than as slaves in Dachau.'

Jews had lived in Shanghai since the opening of the Treaty Port in 1842 after the first Opium War. Among the International Settlements, they formed a distinct and vibrant community which was greatly expanded in the late 1930s when the Nazi persecutions increased in intensity and the Japanese, who had occupied the city in 1937, started to allow entry without visas or passports, regarding them as 'stateless persons'. Life, however, was far from easy for Jews, and became ever more difficult when, after November 1941, they were herded by the Japanese into crowded, insanitary conditions in Hongkou ghetto where they lived in a situation of near starvation. But at least Jews weren't particularly discriminated against, sharing the harsh conditions with Chinese people and European civilian internees. Most significantly, unlike millions of European Jewry, they nearly all survived the war – the Japanese were not anti-Semitic and refused Hitler's demands to hand them over.

In early 1939, the British government had put an upper limit of 100,000 Jews allowed entry to Palestine over the following five years. Despite his protestations to the Foreign Office regarding its reluctance to assist Jewish emigration to Shanghai, Foley knew that Palestine was a better alternative and when the Nazis began to charter ships to take refugees to Shanghai, charging each 1,000 marks for their passage, he appealed to the Foreign Office.

'Both on grounds of humanity and of wider British interests, it is an infinite pity that these unfortunate people are not allowed to emigrate to Palestine... They beseech us to allow them to join their children in Palestine. I have referred hundreds of cases to Palestine. If I am not sent hundreds of certificates in the near future, I fear they too will be dumped in Shanghai.'

At the end of January 1939, in an address to the Reichstag, Hitler made his position on the Jewish question clear, predicting their 'extermination' if they caused a world war. Not without grounds, he went on to challenge the major powers on their hypocritical attitudes towards the Jewish situation in Europe:

> 'If Britain, America and France believed that "such highly cultured people" were being so harshly treated, why were they so reluctant to allow them into their own countries? Why weren't they grateful for this magnificent gift that Germany was offering them? I believe this problem will be solved – and the sooner the better… Europe cannot find peace until the Jewish question is out of the way.'

It was just prior to this challenge that the British Cabinet decided to allow 10,000 German Jewish children to enter Britain on the *Kindertransport*, provided the refugee organisations would guarantee their maintenance. But at the same time it refused an appeal for an additional 21,000 Palestinian visa certificates from the Jewish Agency for Palestine.

One of the last visas Foley issued for Palestine was for Amelie Arian, the mother of Dr David Arian, whom Foley had assisted on his earlier emigration to Palestine. When his mother arrived safely in early July 1939, Dr Arian wrote to Foley thanking him and adding, '…whenever your name is mentioned – From Dan to Be'er Sheva – you are talked of with the greatest respect and devotion and that you and other persons effect a counterweight where the evils of the every day's politics suppress and destroy the faith in honesty and humanity'. Foley replied, '…Conditions are getting worse and worse here for the Jews. I dread to think of the misery and suffering they – especially the older people – will have to face next winter… the quota is a calamity, especially in these days of rabid persecution and permanent cold pogrom. The courage and fortitude of Jews are beyond praise, they have our profound admiration.'

In London, the Council for German Jewry had pressured the government to open Kitchener Camp, in Richborough, Kent, as a transit camp for those refugees who had stated that their intention was to move to another country – the United States preferred above all. Robert

Smallbones, the British Consul General in Frankfurt, was the instigator of the scheme. He had worked out details with Otto Schiff of the Jewish Relief organisation and an American official whereby the refugees-in-transit would be no burden on the British taxpayer and authorities and would eventually be admitted into the United States. It came to be known as the 'Smallbones Scheme'. Foley used it to the full, realising it was a golden opportunity to persuade the Home Office to allow Jews into Britain, even though he suspected that many would never re-emigrate.

The United States meanwhile, alarmed at the prospect of increasing numbers of immigrants arriving on its shores, made it clear that more refugees were not welcome, creating a difficult situation for the British government which was already faced with opposition to more immigrants. But whatever the difficulties, Smallbones, Foley and others in diplomatic circles continued to issue Home Office letters of temporary asylum pending re-emigration and the last group, some 300 men, arrived in Britain on the eve of war, 30 August 1939. It is estimated that tens of thousands of Jews entered Britain in this way. Once war started, many went on to undertake war work or join the British fighting forces.

Living and working in the oppressive atmosphere of Berlin as war approached, the strain began to tell on Foley. Not only was he dealing with the never-ending queues of would-be, ever more desperate emigrants and unremitting and frustrating negotiations with London urging haste with processing visas, he also had to process and despatch the vast amount of intelligence building up as Germany prepared for war, as well as organising his agents for the time when he departed. Although his wife, Kay, returned to England for much-need breaks, Foley rarely had the time for any respite, especially in late 1938 and 1939.

Doubts about Chamberlain's appeasement policy were finally confirmed when Hitler sent his troops in Bohemia and Moravia on 15 March 1939, thus greatly extending the *Grossdeutsches Reich*, which now included the whole of Czechoslovakia as well as Germany and Austria. But it was not until after the signing of the non-aggression treaty with the Soviet Union on 23 August 1939, which assured Hitler that he would not be fighting a war on two fronts, that the evacuation of the British Embassy in Berlin began. Even at this late stage Foley managed to save more young Jews, when, following a tip-off from the Gestapo, on 25 August he told one of his Jewish contacts, Hans Borchardt, that he ought to get out and that he should collect 80 permits for Britain, with another for himself.

After Foley had left Berlin to take up his new intelligence posting in Oslo, again under the cover of Chief Passport Control Officer, he continued to save hundreds of Jewish children, allowing them to escape to Palestine by issuing *Youth Aliyah* certificates via the American Embassy, which had remained operational in Berlin. During a brief stop in Bordeaux, on the retreat from Norway and Europe with civilians and troops, Foley continued to issue visas for Britain. Those who worked with Foley in Berlin reckon that at least 10,000 Jews were saved by his flexible interpretation of the rules and his daring activities from 1933–1939. As Hubert Pollack has written of the responsibility Foley took upon himself:

'What drove him to that was that nobility of origin, disposition and education which makes a man in such a post feel that power was given to him in order to help the helpless: noblesse oblige… The number of Jews saved from Germany would be smaller by tens of thousands of people – yes, that's right, tens of thousands – if instead of Captain Foley, a "diligent official" had sat in his position. There is no word of Jewish gratitude to this man that would be exaggerated.'

During the Second World War, as head of A1, the intelligence section that covered Norway and Germany, Foley was involved in a wide range of top-level intelligence work including the interrogation of Rudolf Hess, Hitler's close aide, who landed in Scotland in May 1941 hoping to strike a deal between Germany and Britain. Knowing the Nazi psyche well, Foley was also involved in many of the deception operations against Nazi Germany, particularly the double agent network – The Double Cross System – and was a member of the top-secret Twenty Committee where he helped develop deception into a fine art, with daring operations such as 'Operation Mincemeat' which persuaded the Germans that the allies would invade southern Europe through Sardinia and Greece rather than Sicily, the real target.

Foley also worked on 'Operation Bodyguard', the strategic deception plan for D-Day which led to the Germans concentrating their troop build-up on the Pas de Calais rather than in Normandy. Foley's last deception 'Operation Crossbow' was a part-successful attempt to counter the V1 flying bombs and V2 rocket attacks on London. At the end of the war, Foley's career came full circle, as he returned to Germany to lead the intelligence service's Special Branch hunt for Nazis. Foley himself noted the irony of the situation in a letter to Werner Senator, one of his former Jewish contacts in Berlin, 'We are reading and seeing photographs of those places the names of which were so well known to us in the years before the war. Now the people here really and finally believe that the stories of 1938–1939 were not exaggerated... Looking back I feel grateful that our little office in *Tiergartenstrasse* was able to assist some – far too few – to escape in time.'

In 1947, when the German authorities took over the task of searching out former Nazis, Foley was posted back to London. He retired from MI6 in 1949 and lived in anonymity with his family in the West Midlands town of Stourbridge until he died of a heart attack at the age of 74 in 1958. His great-niece Patricia Dunstan, who was often with him on family holidays in Burnham-on-Sea, Somerset, remembers him as a quiet, modest and very kind man; many other accounts confirm this impression. Patricia had no idea of his humanitarian service until years later when she was 'amazed to learn of what he did'. During his lifetime he had received several honours, mainly for his intelligence and wartime work, but few people knew of how this private man had saved the lives of thousands of Jews with such courage, energy and compassion. Nor were the majority of those he had helped to safety aware of his identity and the risks he took in saving them. Some of those survivors who had known Foley personally contributed to the planting of a grove of trees in Israel in 1959, as a memorial to him. In tributes paid to him at the small but moving ceremony, speakers expressed their gratitude in statements recalling Foley's 'simple humanity beyond the call of duty'.

Benno Cohn, one of the Jewish leaders who worked so closely with Foley during the difficult days of the 1930s, posed the question:

> 'What were the motives that stirred him to act like this? ...He told us that he was acting like a Christian and that he wanted to show us how little the Christians who were then in power in Germany had to do with real Christianity... Foley acted, however, also as a good Englishman. He saw all the crimes of the regime at closest quarters and therefore realised better than ministers in London that there could never be any real peace with these people... Through his endeavours, the British authorities received an accurate picture of what was currently going on in Germany.'

Cohn paid tribute to Foley in his evidence to the Eichmann trial of 1961, telling the court, 'There was one man who stood out above all others like a beacon... He rescued thousands of Jews from the jaws of death.' And yet it was not until 25 February 1999 that Foley was formally recognised by Israel as one of the 'Righteous Among the Nations', an accolade bestowed since 1963 by Yad Vashem, the Israeli martyrs' and heroes' memorial authority in Jerusalem, to non-Jews who risked their lives to save Jews during the Nazi period.

Michael Smith's book on Foley – *The Spy Who Saved 10,000 Jews* – published in the same year that Foley received his honour, revealed for the first time the full and fascinating story of this remarkable man, informing the world of his outstanding humanitarian efforts in saving such a vast section of German Jewry. Smith, supported by the Holocaust Educational Trust, can be credited for drawing Yad Vashem's attention to Foley's case. During the research for his book he had found solid documentary evidence within its archives. Having alerted the museum to this material for re-examination, and finding 'living witnesses' to support Foley's case, the accolade of 'Righteous Among the Nations' so richly deserved by Foley was finally granted. Smith's other aim of making Foley a national hero was achieved when he was posthumously granted the status of British 'Hero of the Holocaust' in March 2010.

Frank Foley would have been the first to draw attention to the fact that he was not the only British official who helped persecuted European Jewry. Scores of diplomats, consuls and other foreign officials – Sir George Ogilvie-Forbes in Berlin, Robert Smallbones and Arthur Dowden in Frankfurt, John Carvell in Munich and Sir Thomas Preston in Lithuania, to name but a few – with equal compassion and verve extended significant help to Jews seeking refuge abroad. Like Foley, bending the rules, they often stuck their necks out and disobeyed their own governments to issue documentation that allowed refugees to escape. On 28 November 2008, a plaque was unveiled at the Foreign Office in London by Jack Straw, the former British Foreign Secretary, to commemorate those British diplomats who helped rescue victims of Nazi persecution. It is a bronze relief by the sculptor Philip Jackson and depicts hands pulling apart barbed wire, with the words, 'Individuals of conscience can make a contribution to the safeguarding of humanity.'

The indomitable Bertha Bracey.

BERTHA BRACEY
1893–1989

'If more people had read Mein Kampf *they would have seen that the very regulations of the National Socialists contained its poison and its deepest poison was of course its anti-Semitism.'*

Bertha Bracey was an English Quaker whose work in Berlin overlapped with that of Frank Foley's. Although there is no evidence that they ever met, they had several mutual Jewish contacts and it is highly likely that they had at least heard of each other. Like Frank Foley, Bertha worked tirelessly to help rescue Jews and others persecuted by the Nazis. Her rescue work covered refugees from Austria, Poland and Czechoslovakia as well as Nazi Germany, as the Third Reich expanded during the years before the outbreak of the Second World War.

Bertha was not a Quaker by birth. She joined the Religious Society of Friends in 1912, at the age of 19. The Society, whose members are known as 'Friends', is noted for its peace testament of 1660 which states, 'We utterly deny all outwards wars and strife and fightings with outward weapons, for any end, or under any pretence whatsoever. And this is our testimony to the whole world...'. Friends are unusual in that they do not have a written creed. Over the centuries this has proved a great strength as it tends to prevent them being dogmatic or intolerant, inclining to inclusivity and open to change. They believe that there is something of God in every person and that everyone has good in them. The tenets they value are truth, peace, justice, equality, simplicity and community. In international affairs, Quakers always strive for balance and objectivity, thus avoiding direct political involvement; the development and spread of Nazism in Germany and Europe was to prove a real testing ground for those, like Bertha, with first-hand experience of Hitler's regime.

Bertha was born and grew up in Birmingham, a major centre of Quaker tradition. On graduating from Birmingham University, she spent five years teaching, leaving in 1921 to help with relief and reconstruction work at the Quaker Centre in post-war Vienna, where she also established and helped run a number of youth clubs. She then moved to Weimar Germany, working first in Nuremberg where she set up a warehouse where those in need could obtain food and clothing cheaply. Later, in 1926, she moved to Berlin doing similar work, all the while continuing to work with young people.

Post-war living conditions for ordinary people were bad enough in Austria, but in Germany the situation was desperate: food was lacking to the point of starvation, and what was available was often ersatz (made from substitutes) such as coffee from ground acorns; heating in most homes and workplaces was almost non-existent; unemployment was rife and inflation had started. Under the 1919 Treaty of Versailles, Germany was required to make reparations payments in gold-backed marks, and the country lost part of the production of the Ruhr and of the province of Upper Silesia. The Weimar Republic, formed in 1919, was politically fragile, and the hyperinflation that Germany experienced from 1921 to 1923 caused a social tragedy of huge dimensions. The cost of living rocketed. For instance, to buy a newspaper in April 1923 was 200 marks; by the beginning of September it rose to 500,000 marks, and by 8 November to 8,000 million – by that time, with one US dollar equal to one trillion marks, currency had lost all meaning. Stories of wages being paid twice daily and taken home in suitcases or handcarts were not exaggerated. *Die Inflation* caused destitution to masses of Germans.

It was into this dire situation that Bertha and other Quakers arrived to give their relief services. One of the most memorable parts of their work was the *Quaker-speisung*, the feeding of school children, which expanded until over a million were being fed daily. Many of the top Nazis had benefited from the programme when they were children, and their memory and gratitude of this often helped Quakers maintain their relief work in Germany during the difficult political years of the 1930s, as Bertha was to discover. Even today, *Quaker-speisung* is remembered in Germany, with Friends welcomed by, 'You fed me (or my mother or father) as a little child.'

The hardship and uncertainty experienced by ordinary Germans led to a bitter and resentful mood in the country, which Hitler was quick to exploit. Although the hyperinflation ended with the introduction of a new currency, the Rentenmark (Debt Security Mark) on 15 November 1923 (and the Weimar Republic itself lasted until 1933), it is widely believed to have contributed to the rise of the Nazi Party and support for its anti-Semitic activity. Jews were blamed, with Communists, not only for the 'stab in the back' – the defeat in the war – but also, being well represented in banking circles, for the hyperinflation and its resulting misery and social unrest.

As well as improving Bertha's German language, her work in Vienna and Germany provided valuable insight into the requirements of relief and welfare work. During this time she also made a large network of contacts that was later to prove vital in her work with Jewish refugees.

Although, like all Quakers, Bertha was not overtly political, she displayed a sound political and economic sense. She was concerned about the huge bill – £6.6 billion, equivalent to £217 billion today – for what she later described as the 'impractical and somewhat vindictive repayments' Germany was forced to make under the terms of the Treaty of Versailles and the crippling effect this had on the country and its people that she saw first-hand and tried to ameliorate with her welfare work. Like many others, she soon realised the connection between economic, political and social instability with the rise of Hitler and the National Socialists. Bertha and other Quakers in Germany were well aware of the pressures exerted on German Jewry before Hitler came to power in 1933, and regretted that his growing influence was not recognised more widely. As early as the Munich *putsch*, of November 1923, when Hitler and the Nazi Party attempted to seize the government of Bavaria and from there topple the Berlin government, Bertha noted how he was 'seen as a flash in the pan, there was no realisation then of the real threat… If more people had read *Mein Kampf* they would have seen that the very regulations of the National Socialists contained its poison and its deepest poison was of course its anti-Semitism'.

In 1929, Bertha, by then an experienced relief worker, was recalled to London as Administrative Secretary for the Friends in Germany and Holland. In this position she and her team endeavoured to put into practice the Quaker tenets for reconciliation and peace at a time of increasing political tension and violence in Germany. She was kept abreast of developments there by German Quakers and early Jewish émigrés who warned and updated British Quakers on the growing threat of National Socialism. The nature and pace of her work increased dramatically when Hitler came to power in January 1933. Returning from a visit to Frankfurt soon after Hitler's appointment, Bertha wrote in *Quaker World Service*, 1 May 1933:

'Anti-Semitism is a terrible canker which has been spreading its poison for decades in many Central European countries. It came to a head on April 1st, when Germany dropped back into the cruelty of the "Ghetto" psychology of the Middle Ages. The very yellow spots [Star of David] used to indicate Jewish business and houses is an old medieval symbol. Words are not adequate to tell of the anguish of some of my Jewish friends...'

She had attended a meeting of the German Friends Executive Committee on 9 April 1933 to discuss the disturbing events of 1 April when the boycott of Jewish shops had occurred. Many German Friends had ignored this, entering Jewish shops to buy goods, defying the stormtroopers trying to bar their way. At the meeting great concern was expressed about the 'Enabling Act' (*Ermächtigungsgesetz*) which had been passed the previous week, and gave the Cabinet authority to enact laws without the participation of the Reichstag, in effect establishing Hitler's dictatorship. Bertha, in her report, wrote sympathetically, and with great understanding, about the difficult position of German Friends and the dilemmas they faced as they strove to maintain their Quaker faith and objectivity alongside their knowledge of what Hitler stood for, advising them, 'Do not feel that you have to bear witness as Quakers, nor that as a Quaker you should shoulder burdens that are greater than you have strength to carry on your own.'

Corder Catchpool, a Quaker working in Berlin with his wife Gwen and their young family, was one of the Quakers arrested by the Nazis for the help he was giving Jews and other targeted people. His daughter, Jean, was nine at the time of his arrest and remembers it clearly:

'There was a great deal of tension at the time, with people coming and going to our house, and our Nazi neighbours had got suspicious. From early on my father had started helping people who were suffering because of their beliefs and were in distress... We had Nazi police standing outside our gate, and the policeman had a big coat, which my brother and I hid beneath. My parents were undergoing a most dreadful time. They were separated into different rooms and my father was tormented because documents he held for safe-keeping from journalists, from Jewish people, from political opponents, were taken. He was taken to Alexanderplatz prison, but was released after 24 hours due to the intervention of a Nazi woman who told them, 'You've got this all wrong. This man is a friend of Germany...'

It was in April 1933 that Bertha faced perhaps the greatest challenge of her life when she became the secretary of the Germany Emergency Committee based in London. She started her work with one part-time assistant, dealing with 18 cases in 1933. But very soon the persecutions increased and the numbers hoping for sanctuary grew rapidly. By 1938 she had responsibility for 59 staff. As she explained:

'The flood was getting greater and greater and greater, so that we in Friends House had become Public Nuisance Number One! We'd taken on what was a quiet room, for quiet retirement and meditation, and we'd put up shelves in the corridors for people to fill out their papers and we really were a nuisance...'

Under Bertha's guidance, Friends from Britain and Germany helped those persecuted by the Nazi regime, including inmates of concentration camps, to deal with the increasing bureaucratic obstacles to obtain emigration documents. As the desperation of Jews increased throughout the 1930s, she became the central figure in a large network of people who helped the refugees settle in Britain, providing hostels, language training, and employment projects as well as obtaining guarantors in Britain who would undertake financial responsibility for the refugees and their families. Bertha made frequent visits to Germany, staying with Mary and Leonhard Friedrich in Nuremberg, whose lives became increasingly difficult and dangerous as they continued their humanitarian work at a Quaker Relief Centre. Such trips greatly increased her first-hand knowledge of the deteriorating situation of German Jews. She was quick to note how 'the cream of the population' – the most talented and able – were among those forced out, feeling, 'it was extraordinary that the Nazis didn't realise that'. Bertha was one of the few British Friends who were able to bring pressure on the Nazis through her network of contacts, which included some eminent people in both Britain and Germany; she often managed to secure the release of Jews who had been imprisoned.

Bertha even gained the cooperation of certain Nazi leaders because, as she explained, 'They remembered the *Quaker-speisung*, the Quaker feeding programme between the wars – they had been the children receiving things.' At one point she received a letter from Reinhard Heydrich, head of the *Sicherheitsdienst*, or SD, the intelligence branch of the security service, regarding an enquiry she had made about two men who had disappeared. One of her letters about a German social worker in need of help was even sent direct to Hitler by one of the committee members, as Bertha recalled:

'We didn't know whether he got the letter, but the social worker was released and became one of our most valuable social workers in Paris… Yes, we had small concessions, my correspondence had letters not only to Heydrich but to Goering's and Hitler's offices too. At one time I thought this might look suspicious and went to the Foreign Office to explain it.'

Information that Bertha gathered on Hitler's regime was passed to her contacts in the British Foreign Office. She mentioned how it was only when war broke out in 1939, that the Foreign Office realised the importance of the material she and other Friends had sent in. A lasting regret of hers was that in the early days of the Nazi Party, she had not released material to newspaper men who came to her for information they knew would be reliable, fearing it would be used as part of war propaganda. The material, she explained, '…was about what was happening to our friends and people trying to help them in Germany and who were dismissed from their posts'.

Much later, in 1945, when the first members of the Friends Relief Service entered Bergen-Belsen concentration camp, witnessing the full horror of what was later to be called the Holocaust, she wondered, 'Did we make the wrong decision not to speak out, when so many appalling details had lain in the files of Friends House?' She was not alone in this dilemma. Other Friends such as Corder Catchpool and Leonhard and Mary Friedrich, who were visiting prisons and concentration camps in Germany, also felt uneasy about what they witnessed there, but decided to maintain the Quaker neutral stance in order to be able to continue helping people for as long as possible. Their neutrality was not always noted: Leonhard Friedrich spent the last three years of the war as a prisoner in Buchenwald concentration camp.

Bertha always had a special interest in children and young people which stretched way back to her early work in Vienna and Germany in the 1920s. In 1934 she worked hard with Dutch friends to establish The Quaker School at Ommen in Holland for 100 German Jewish children. But her greatest challenge came after the *pogroms* in Germany and Austria on *Kristallnacht*, 9–10 November 1938, when Jewish parents were desperate to get their children to safety. Wilfred Israel, a prominent member of the assistance organisation, the *Hilfsverein*, and who had worked closely with Frank Foley, was also a friend of Bertha from her Nuremberg days. Soon after *Kristallnacht*, on 15 November, he sent a strong appeal to the Council of German Jewry in London to save German

Jewish children up to the age of 17. A small team of Quakers set off to report on the situation in Germany and discuss what could be done – by then it was safer for Quakers than Jews of any nationality to travel to Germany. Bertha also went on a fact-finding visit to Berlin and returned with Ben Green, one of the Quaker team. On 21 November, a small delegation which included Bertha met the Home Secretary, Sir Samuel Hoare. That same day, emergency permits were granted permitting 10,000 children admission to Britain temporarily; these were mainly Jewish, with the exception of a very small group of non-Aryan Christians.

A plethora of voluntary bodies rallied to the task of getting the children out of Germany on *Kindertransports*, and providing accommodation for them once they arrived, including Jewish organisations such as the Central British Fund, the German Jewish Aid Committee, the Austrian Self Aid Committee and the Women's International Zionist Organisation. Non-Jewish organisations who helped consisted primarily of the Society of Friends, the Christian Council for Refugees, and the Catholic Committee for Refugees. The umbrella Refugee Children's Movement (RCM) was set up to manage the exodus and coordinate the work of the voluntary bodies. So as not to be a burden on the British state, £50 per child was required by the Government to cover expenses; given the numbers involved, this proved impossible for the RCM to finance.

The non-sectarian Lord Baldwin Fund came to the rescue following attempts by Bertha and George Bell, the Bishop of Chichester, to initiate fund-raising appeals for refugees. Stanley Baldwin, the former Prime Minister, was asked to help their efforts by making a Christian appeal. But he said, 'No, I will make a *national* appeal,' and succeeded in raising £500,000. Launching the 'Earl Baldwin Fund' on the radio in December 1938, he said, ' I ask you to come to the aid of victims, not of any catastrophe in the natural world, not of any earthquake, not of famine, but of an explosion of Man's inhumanity to Man.' Of the £500,000 raised for refugees, £220,000 was designated for refugee children The first *Kindertransport* of 200 children arrived from Germany on 2 December. In all more than 9,000 children were saved.

John Silberman, who came to Britain on a *Kindertransport*, said it was only when the watershed of *Kristallnacht* occurred that his parents, in common with many other Germans, realised 'they're going to kill us' and they had to get out. He explained:

'Survival in the life-threatening sense was the only thing that mattered. Even then nobody understood what the Germans had in mind for the Jews – the mass genocide – it was only perceived to be the mass takeover of Jewish assets and driving the Jews out...

I remember in my carriage there was a baby of two or three years old, and this child was given to a teenage girl who was told, "Look after her until you get to England". What courage it took for those parents! We travelled from Berlin for several hours until we came to the Dutch border. It made a huge impression on me: here I'd been in an ever-deepening situation of bad treatment, bullying, vulnerability, victimisation and here comes the Dutch border. Trains used to stop on one side of the border while the German officials did their stuff, then the train shunted over to the Dutch side and the same thing happened there all over again. But, with one difference: accompanying the Dutch officials came a load of ladies in grey uniforms and I think it was the first time for years that non-Jewish people said something kind to us. They brought chocolate, soft drinks; they gave us postcards to mail home to our parents that we had crossed the border. Somebody had gone to a lot of trouble there to understand what kids would need. We hadn't expected it and to this day I have great fondness for the Dutch.'

Hedy Epstein's parents painted a wonderful picture of England to encourage her on her *Kindertransport* from Berlin:

'"You'll be learning a new language, you'll make new friends, and we'll all be together again soon, if not in England then in the

United States. This is just temporary..." As they put me on the train they were still smiling about this wonderful thing I was going to. The window was open and we chit-chatted, last minute admonitions: always be polite, always say please and thank you – two words of my very limited vocabulary. Then someone called, "*Alles einsteigen!*" – all aboard. Then the tug and groan of the train, then a whistle and it started to move very slowly. And my parents who had this very artificial smile on their faces started to move with the train as it moved out of the station, and as it moved faster and faster, they ran faster and faster, tears running down their faces, waving goodbye with their handkerchiefs... I watched them getting smaller and smaller until they were two dots and then they were gone. I didn't know at that point that I would never see them again...'

Kristallnacht was a wake-up call for the British Government, as it had a huge impact on British public opinion, alerting Britons to the true nature of Hitler's regime and causing a wave of public sympathy towards European Jewry, especially the children. Margareta Burkill, a Cambridge don's wife, involved in the placement of refugee children in the town recalled:

'When *Kristallnacht* happened in November 1938, it went through Great Britain like an electric current: in every little town, every village in England they said, "We must save the children". It was quite a fantastic thing. People who'd never thought about the Nazis, when they heard about this murder and burning, that was the reaction. We were very early on the scene in Cambridge; I started it and got Sybil Hutton to join me. We were responsible for quite lot of children in other places, in the small villages around Cambridge.'

The actor Warren Mitchell, then a schoolboy, remembers the impact it had on him and his Jewish family:

'My father showed me the pictures of *Kristallnacht*, of the smashing of Jewish shops, and there was a picture of a Jew being beaten by passers-by outside his shop; my father had sheer blind hatred that such crimes could be committed. I suppose *Kristallnacht* was the beginning of the realisation of what a monster was being spawned on the Continent.

My main involvement with it came when Jewish families in Britain were asked to take Jewish children. Jewish organisations were collecting and giving money and getting boatloads out. My father responded to an article in the *Jewish Chronicle* and I went with him one Sunday morning in 1939, to Liverpool Street Station to meet this train. Something like five or six hundred children came off that train. They were so frightened, so traumatised by what had happened to them. It was bad enough for kids in this country who were evacuated, but some of these children had been persecuted for months, like the case of Ilse, the girl who came to us. She hadn't been out of her house for six months, frightened to go out.

Ilse came to live with us, she didn't speak for about a week, she was so traumatised by what had happened to her. Her father had been in a concentration camp. She began to speak English very quickly. She began to tell us what had happened and the appalling thing was that it wasn't the Nazis – the Gestapo or the SS (*Schutzstaffel*) – it was the neighbours, the ordinary people who behaved so abominably towards the Jews in their community. Ilse and her sister Lotte got out. She was very tearful, she didn't think she'd see her parents again... Ilse was my second sister, we played Monopoly together and we argued and fought just like brother and sister.'

Many non-Jewish families opened their doors and their hearts to the *Kinder*, as they came to be known. The parents of David and Richard Attenborough, for instance, took in two Jewish girls of nine and twelve.

Margaret Thatcher's father, through his Rotarian group in Grantham, arranged for a young Austrian Jewish woman to stay with each of the Rotarian families in turn, including his own, until arrangements could be made for her to live with relatives in America. Janet Shipton, the daughter of Clement Attlee, then leader of the Labour Opposition, recalls:

'We had two children in our village. One was Hans Paul who was eleven… He was sent to the local boys' private school and Mother was horrified because all he came back with were swear words. He stayed with us in our home for six or seven months and then went to somewhere safer in the country…this was the beginning of my understanding of the troubles in Berlin. To me it's very important that we had a German Jewish refugee who came over with the *Kindertransports*. That's how Hans Paul came.'

Margareta Burkill knew at first hand the devastating effect the experience had on the Jewish children, and the challenges they faced when they first arrived:

'They had left their homeland, where their life had been abused, where they could no more go to their schools, where their parents, from being honest, hard-working citizens, had to use any subterfuge to keep alive and to eke out enough to support themselves and their children, never knowing when the fatal knock on the door would come. From this experience and this insecurity they were transplanted to a country with a different language, completely different mores, and frequently placed with people who did not share their religion, who did not light candles on Friday nights, and for whom Saturday was a working day.'

Set against the mainly positive story of the *Kindertransport*, there are many recorded cases of Jewish children being less than welcomed with open arms, and treated with lack of understanding by Jewish as well as

The first group of German-Jewish children, complete with identity tags, arrive in England on an early *Kindertransport* in December 1938. They are met at Harwich by representatives who will help care for them during their stay.

Three Jewish children from Germany and Austria, waiting to be collected by their relatives or sponsors at Liverpool Street Station, London, after arriving on a later *Kindertransport*, July 1939.

non-Jewish families. One grateful *Kindertransport* survivor, Bertha Leverton, also makes the point:

'…everybody in the whole world closed their doors… If they had opened their doors they could have saved European Jewry… That is a guilt that the whole world has to bear as well as Germany. And if Britain had done what it could have done: opened the gates of what was then Palestine, they could have saved European Jewry. But they did more than any other country in the world in saving Jews, and that record stands.'

On 30 September 1938 at Munich, when the British, French and Italian leaders gave in to Hitler's demands for the Sudetenland, which, together with its 22,000 Jews, became part of Greater Germany from 10 October of that year, it caused, in Bertha's words, 'A difficult situation…then it was a problem to keep any kind of balanced judgement…' Bertha, like all Quakers, was a pacifist, but she was not a supporter of the British appeasement policy:

'My [German] friends used to say, "We had some decent chancellors who were prepared to cooperate but had no reciprocal gesture of understanding or support [from the British government]. Hitler comes and bangs on the table, and within three months, you've got both Eden [then Foreign Secretary] and Sir John Simon coming to Berlin!'

She recalled the very strong appeasement group who 'weren't very discriminating. There were far too many of them; little groups of outstanding people who entertained Ribbentrop, not realising how poisonous it was.'

With the vast increase in the stream of refugees after the annexation of Austria and the Sudetenland in 1938, it was decided that all the refugee organisations, Jewish and non-Jewish, could operate more effectively together in Bloomsbury House. This was the former Palace Hotel in Bloomsbury, which had enough room to accommodate them all. In February 1939, Bertha's staff of 80 case workers with 14,000 case files moved from Friends House, which by then had reached bursting point, into their new home. This is when the coordinating body, the Inter-Church Council for German Refugees, was set up, with Bertha as its secretary. 'We all worked together in Bloomsbury House, on various committees: student work, organisations for women coming over and going into domestic work, with Roman Catholics looking after Catholic children… There were good relations between different groups.'

Interviews with Jewish refugees seeking help in Bloomsbury House have often indicated their dismay with the confusion they experienced there. Margareta Burkill, who had regular contact with the place, explained, 'Bloomsbury House was chaotic, there were no trained secretaries, most of the work was voluntary, and done each day by a different person, with little continuity, but everything from the regions had to go through Bloomsbury House.' When asked about this Bertha was '…not surprised that Bloomsbury House had a bad name with *some* refugees'. But she added that she was cheered by a comment from the man on the door, who said one day:

> '"Miss Bracey, we have some very unpleasant incidents at times but we have noticed that when people have come to the third floor, the Quaker floor, they are always quiet and usually satisfied." That was rather nice to hear. The staff of the Jewish Committee weren't always very tender… We took a toll one day, as a matter of interest, to see how many visitors were in the various offices of Bloomsbury House at one moment; and we found, not counting staff, fifteen hundred visitors. It was pretty crowded.'

One of the difficulties Bertha and others faced as war was drawing near, was trying to find countries that would accept refugees who were stuck in transit camps set up with the intention of moving refugees on to other states. But undaunted she pressed on, as she explained:

'Then a rather delightful thing happened. We'd been sending young men to get preliminary training, but experts said, "Don't train them too much, give them a facility, ploughing or harnessing a horse, but don't take it much further than that because any situation they go to outside this country will be totally different, just do the basic things." Well, we prepared these lads and sent some to New Zealand and Australia. We had a cheering note from Australia, "If you've got any more lads like that, let's have them, we'll be glad to take them". It was lovely because on the whole countries were not too willing… One of the difficulties with America was that in the Jewish community, for an authentic synagogue service they need ten men [a *minion*]. To get ten adult men in a group, as the Jews wanted in order to have their service, meant that they did form overlarge pockets, not readily absorbed in out-of-the-way places where the jobs were.'

More pressing challenges came when war was declared and some 60,000 Jewish refugees in transit were then denied permission to proceed to countries overseas where they had hoped to settle. Many were destitute, all were in need of practical and psychological support. Bloomsbury House continued the training schemes, helping them to obtain work in Britain or in any country willing to accept them. The fact that the work on offer was mainly menial caused distress to those who came from the middle, professional classes, requiring great powers of adaptation which proved difficult as Margareta Burkill, working in Cambridge, also found:

'We had of course endless letters and one of the difficult moral problems for us was to decide when we should help and who was not so urgent in need. We were of course all voluntary workers. We could get women out on domestic permits. The only way women could be brought to England was either as domestics or as ward helpers. Men could only come out, if they had no guarantors of course, as agricultural workers or working in the mines. As you can realise none of these occupations were exactly Jewish occupations. But I think the Cambridge Refugee Committee brought out 500 women on the domestic ticket… It was a great shock to find that people, whom you respected and known well, treated these women when they became their servants in a shocking manner, though the background of the "servant" had been like theirs before the Hitler regime.'

Arieh Handler, director of the *Youth Aliyah*, who was facing the demanding task of finding training places for young Jews, paid tribute to the Friends: 'The Quakers were very helpful. They let us have a training centre at Avoncroft Farm, Bromsgrove. It was known as the "Bachad Settlement"…they helped tremendously. Some of the church people were very strong and ordinary British people, a great help.' Despite the huge challenge of finding work for refugees, by the end of the war 95 per cent of refugees were self-supporting.

Another challenge came after the Fall of France in May 1940, when Britain faced the real prospect of invasion. Fears of a German fifth column prompted Churchill's government to intern 'enemy aliens', thousands of whom were German Jewish refugees who had come to Britain to escape Nazi persecution, some having been rescued from concentration camps. There were also 4,000 resident Italians, like the German refugees mostly anti-Fascist. Several makeshift camps were set up; the main, permanent camp was on the Isle of Man, in Douglas and other places on the island, where men and women were interned in separate quarters, mainly in small hotels or former boarding houses, which were wired off from the local community. A substantial proportion of the men were deported to Canada and Australia. A great tragedy occurred when the deportation ship the *Arandora Star*, on its way to Canada, was torpedoed and sunk with 1,500 German and Italian internees on board, over 600 of whom were drowned.

The refugee organisations reacted vigorously to this new challenge and combined to form a Central Department for Interned Refugees.

Bertha acted as its chairman, bringing her wisdom and experience into play when dealing with different government departments to overcome the many problems experienced by the internees, not least the splitting up of families, the provision of married quarters, and the situation of the children of those interned.

In the summer of 1945, although immigration policies were still in force in Britain, the United States and other western European countries, the British government declared its willingness to take in 1,000 young orphaned camp survivors. The 'Boys' as they are known, 732 young survivors – girls as well as boys – were flown to different parts of Britain in 1945 and 1946 from Prague and Munich. Bertha played a large part in bringing 300 of the orphans from Theresienstadt concentration camp in Czechoslovakia to a reception camp near Lake Windermere, where they were brought back to health, educated, and trained for life in Britain, the United States or the newly created state of Israel from 1948. In a note she wrote, 'When concentration camps were being opened up at the end of the European War, I went with Mr Leonard Montefiore to the War Office and persuaded them to put at our disposal ten large bomber planes which, with the bomb racks removed, enabled us to bring 300 children from Theresienstadt, Prague to England.' Roman Halter, a young Polish Jew who had survived the Lodz ghetto, Auschwitz and Stutthof camps, and slave labour in Dresden, and who had lost all of his large family in the Holocaust, recalled the flight and their arrival in Britain:

'We were loaded up and I saw this very tall officer who was talking from the side of his mouth, emitting these very quick sounds and I thought, "I will *never* learn that language…" He had a pipe in the side of his mouth and this moustache and spoke terribly fast, but he was very nice and asked his crew to take off their caps and put them on all our heads, and we all felt like pilots. There was a tea reception, not a single slice of black bread, all beautifully white. We hadn't seen that before. I thought: we have come to a country of bread and honey…'

Bertha's work did not end when hostilities ceased. Like Foley's, her life turned full circle as once more she returned to Germany, again the devastated, demoralised country that she had worked in following the First World War. In 1946 she was appointed by the Allied Control Commission (ACC) in Germany to take charge of refugee affairs. Later, Bertha undertook the task of providing leadership training for women's groups in the British and American zones, in true Quaker style, always seeking to reconcile those who had recently been enemies. She remained there until her retirement in 1953 at the age of 60.

The Society of Friends was one of the most active groups of rescuers in saving Jews from the Holocaust and many tributes have been paid to its members for the courageous way they saved countless lives. Brenda Bailey, the daughter of Mary and Leonhard Friedrich, described a very brave Quaker woman who married a Jew: 'Before the war, when Jewish children were stopped from going to the public school, she ran a little home school for about a dozen children. Eventually the whole school was taken off to a concentration camp to be destroyed and she voluntarily went with them.' Friends' work with refugees has been compared by some Quakers as equal to the struggle for penal reform, or the fight against slavery in earlier times. Bertha Bracey's role, from the start of the persecution in the 1920s right through to the aftermath of the Second World War, is exemplary and inspirational. She was awarded an OBE in 1942 in recognition for her work with refugees.

There were, of course, many Friends whose individual actions saved Jewish lives and at risk to themselves and their families – Corder and Gwen Catchpool, and Mary and Leonhard Friedrich, for example. Recognition for the entire Quaker humanitarian contribution was given in 1949 by the award of the Nobel Prize to both the British Friends Service Committee and its American counterpart.

Bertha Bracey ended her days in a Quaker retirement home. Brenda Bailey, who visited her often, tells of how, although suffering Parkinson's Disease towards the end of her life, she remained very lively, '…in a way quite formidable, her intellect fantastic and she knew all about philosophy, geology and outer space. But refugees were always her main concern'. Ever modest, little was known of the details of her refugee work by her family, friends and many Quakers. It was only when she died at the age of 95 and obituaries were published, that her outstanding humanitarian achievements became more widely known. In July 2001, a sculpture was placed outside Friends House in London where she had spent so many exhausting but satisfying hours helping anguished and often destitute Jews crowding every inch of space, desperate for refuge. The statement on the plaque has a simplicity of which she would have approved: 'To honour Bertha Bracey (1893–89) who gave practical leadership of Quakers in quietly rescuing and re-settling thousands of Nazi victims and lone children between 1933–1948.'

NICHOLAS WINTON
1909–2015

'Nicky gave us, our children and our grandchildren the chance of life.'

It was Esther Rantzen's television programme *That's Life*, in 1988, that first brought worldwide attention to the vital role Nicholas Winton played in rescuing 669 Czechoslovakian Jewish children from the Nazi threat in what later became known as the Czech *Kindertransport*. Over the intervening fifty years memories of this important humanitarian task that he undertook in 1939, at the age of only 29, had faded. It was only with the discovery of an old suitcase in the loft containing documents and photographs of the children he had saved, that they came flooding back. This led to the television programme which brought many of 'his' children back into his life, changing it forever. For those Winton had saved who were too young to remember any of their life in Czechoslovakia, it was the start of an understanding of their own history. It brought a new awareness of how and why they had been saved and also of the many others who had shared their experience, as well as the sad realisation that, with time running out, all but a tiny minority of the 15,000 Czech Jewish children left behind had perished in concentration camps.

Winton first arrived in Prague in late December 1938, some months after the Munich Agreement. This settlement had delayed war for a time, but it immediately impacted upon the refugee situation in Czechoslovakia, causing thousands of people to flee into Bohemia, Moravia and Slovakia, particularly after 1 October when the Sudetenland was ceded to Germany. By the end of 1938, an estimated 40,000 refugees, 22,000 of them Jews, were in need of resettlement. There were a further 300,000 resident Jews spread throughout the Czech provinces of Bohemia, Moravia and Slovakia. Although far from willing to accept Czech refugees within its borders, the British government, unlike its reaction to the situation in Germany and Austria, decided to offer the Czechs financial help with the refugee problem. This was intended to ease the Czech authorities' difficulties as well as assuaging British guilt after the way the Czechs had been sacrificed by the British and French in the Munich agreement. Thus in October 1938 a total of £10 million was allocated, £4 million of this for the relief and resettlement of refugees within Czechoslovakia and overseas, but not to Britain. In late October 1938, the British Committee for Refugees from Czechoslovakia (BCRC) was formed. This was a non-sectarian organisation whose priority was, and remained, the rescue of political refugees, many of whom were Sudeten Germans, and political opponents of Hitler from Germany and Austria – the 'old Reich refugees'.

The BCRC's Prague office was set up in October 1938 under the leadership of a young English academic from University College, London, Doreen Warriner, assisted by her secretary Bill Barazetti and a handful of others, including several Quakers. Warriner has written how she had no real grasp of the complexity of the refugee problem in Czechoslovakia when she arrived, but that she was 'desperate to do something'. The main aim of the BCRC was getting out those adults perceived to be in the greatest danger. Often this meant married couples leaving singly or as a pair, having to leave their children behind. Danger was the main criterion of selection which meant that political refugees were seen as being under the greatest threat and were given priority over Jews, unless they happened to be political activists. The first 350 visas, which had been granted for admission to Britain under great pressure, were temporary only and guarantees for maintenance were demanded. These were followed by several further batches and by mid March 1939, permission to come to Britain for re-settlement elsewhere had been granted for a further 2,900 people.

At the time of Winton's arrival in December 1938, great concern was being felt about the large number of children left behind and living in squalid, ever-deteriorating conditions. Warriner has given vivid descriptions of the appalling state of the refugee camps, as well as the shortage

Nicholas Winton with a Czech *Kinder*, 1945.

German troops march through the famous ornate gates into the first courtyard of Prague Castle (Hradschin) after the invasion of March 1939.

of funds. She had flown to London a few days before Christmas 1938 to check on the situation at that end. She returned to Prague on Christmas Eve, explaining:

'I had stupidly believed I could bring back some hope for the camps, but there was none. On Christmas morning I went round to see the children in the Y.W.C.A. and the home, with presents, and there heard of the diphtheria epidemic in *Dolni Krup*, in which four children had died. The Czech authorities forbade anyone to visit the camps. Douglas Reed had a fine article in the [*News*] *Chronicle*, 'Manger Child 1938', about a child born in one of the camps... Immediately after Christmas Martin Blake and his friend Nicky Winton came out and relieved my mind by taking over the emigration of the children. Large transports of 200 Jewish children at a time were being despatched from Vienna, but nothing of the kind had been organised in Prague...'

Although a few children had been taken out to safety, until Winton arrived in late December 1938, no one had the specific task of organising the rescue of larger groups. Some of these children were orphans, others were the offspring of adults who had managed to get out either singly, or who had found work, hoping for later reunions. Some were the children of parents unable to leave, but increasingly desperate to get them to safety.

One of the three children of Rudolph and Barbara Wertheim, Nicholas Winton was born in 1909, into an affluent home in West Hampstead. Although his mother was from a Jewish family from Nürnberg, Germany, and the family were well integrated in West Hampstead society which contained a large and vibrant Jewish community, Winton had little awareness of a Jewish identity and, like his siblings, had been baptised and later confirmed. In 1938 the family changed its name to Winton. His educational background was typical for a boy of his class: private schooling at University College School, then, at the age of fourteen, to the public school, Stowe.

On leaving school, following in the footsteps of his banker father, he started a career in the city of London before leaving for Germany, first Hamburg and then Berlin, to gain a wider, European banking experience. In Germany, although not personally affected, Winton became aware of the upheavals caused by Hitler and his Nazi Party and had witnessed some early thuggish behaviour by Nazi stormtroopers against Jews. Later, this experience proved significant when he was confronted with the brutal manifestation of Nazism in Czechoslovakia. Back in England, after two formative years in Europe, he settled down to a city career and was admitted to the London Stock Exchange in 1937. It was then that he became increasingly aware of the deteriorating situation for German Jews through the refugees who arrived at the family home in West Hampstead seeking temporary refuge. He recalled various anti-Semitic incidents he had witnessed during his time in Germany, and these began to take on a new importance for him.

There were also other influences. One was Martin Blake, a left-wing schoolmaster from Stowe who had become a good friend. Blake was well informed about the persecution of Jews in Germany and anticipated a similar threat to the rest of European Jewry. Through Blake, Winton met other left-wingers such as Aneurin Bevan and Jennie Lee. These influences, together with his first-hand experience of the dispirited, fearful refugees he met in West Hampstead, led to the urge do something. It was his friend, Martin Blake, who presented the opportunity which Winton reacted to with such alacrity and determination.

He was due to accompany Blake on a skiing trip to Switzerland in late December 1938. But responding to Blake's urgent request for help, Winton cancelled his bookings to Switzerland and diverted to Prague for the two weeks' leave he had been granted by his city firm, Crews and Company. He arrived just before Christmas 1938 where he met Blake, then a representative of the BCRC, who briefed him on the refugees' increasingly desperate situation, particularly the dire situation of the Czech children, the majority of whom were Jewish, and for whom no one person had responsibility. Winton immediately accepted that responsibility, reacting with total commitment to what was to prove a challenging, life-saving task requiring all his skills of quick-thinking, urgent independent action and hard graft.

The situation was complex. There were five different committees in Prague, each dealing with its own group of refugees: Austrian and German, Catholic, Communist, Jewish and other politically endangered people. Winton's first task was to compile a single list of the most urgent cases. Given the chaos of the situation, he found it almost impossible to get anywhere with the five different communities. Exasperated with the delay, he telephoned them all to say that one list had been received and with the ultimatum that unless theirs was received within 24 hours, that would be the only list. It did the trick, and he was able to compile a master list which was updated as the situation changed and from which the children were eventually selected. As he later explained:

'The task of assessing the problem was enormous. There were thousands of children needing help... My day usually started with interviews in my bedroom whilst I was shaving (sometimes at six am). Some parents said they would willingly take the risk of staying in the country if we could only find ways of getting the children to safety. A few had plenty of money, others not the price of a meal...some relief could be given with money, but our resources were very limited... Some of their questions were unanswerable... If Doreen told the parents that she could get them to safety, but not the children, there was weeping and there was also weeping when we had to say that, at the moment, we could help neither parents nor children. And there was more weeping when we told the parents that if their children were found places in England we could not guarantee if, or when, they would be reunited. It was all quite overwhelming...I felt quite dazed. What suffering there is when armies start to march!'

Prague at this time, just prior to the German occupation of the whole of Czechoslovakia in March 1939, was a dangerous place, teeming with Gestapo and SS, and Winton was conscious on more than one occasion of being followed. Doreen Warriner confirmed this was the norm. But there were occasions when Winton's lack of official status was an advantage, allowing him to take chances and get away with it. Once, for instance, a young woman representative of the Swedish Red Cross offered to transport 20 children to Sweden. Despite suspecting that she was working with the Germans, he decided to take the risk, successfully getting the first transport of 20 children to Sweden by air.

Winton worked 18-hour days throughout his stay, with numerous meetings, interviews and visits to the squalid refugee camps. He managed, with some difficulty, to extend his leave to three weeks, the last week ever more hectic. By this time he'd had the good fortune to meet up with Trevor Chadwick, a young English teacher who had heard about the desperate refugee situation and offered to help. Chadwick had given up his teaching job and worked alongside Winton all hours of the day and night. When Winton and Chadwick returned to London in January 1939, Barazetti took responsibility for the children until Chadwick flew back to Prague in March 1939 to continue the work of trying to get the children out to safety.

Having returned to his old job in the City after three weeks of incessant work in Prague, Winton now had the task of finding foster homes and guarantors for the hundreds of children on his priority list. He desperately needed the support of an established organisation to ease his way; Doreen Warriner in Prague had realised the importance of this. Before he left Prague, she had appealed to Margaret Layton, the honorary secretary of BCRC in London, requesting that the organisation of the Czech children refugees be delegated to Winton and to grant him the status of secretary of the children's section. Layton's refusal was a blow; nor did Winton have better luck with his appeal to the Refugee Children's Movement, with whom Bertha Bracey had worked to organise the Kindertransports from Germany and Austria; although funded by the Baldwin Fund, insufficient resources was given as the reason. The fact that Czech children were a lower priority puzzled Winton, especially as so many of his children were in fact Austrian and German refugee children from the Czech camps. After the German takeover of the whole of Czechoslovakia in March 1939, the RCM did agree to take and place 40 of his children, which was of some help.

Disappointed with the lack of support but undaunted, Winton pressed on knowing full well that without official status he wouldn't get far. But ever resourceful, he had notepaper printed with the invented name of the British Committee for Refugees from Czechoslovakia, under which he had printed in bold type, The Children's Section, and his private address. As he explained, 'This looked official and impressive.' He first approached the Home Office before the German invasion of March 1939 and was dismayed at officials' complacency regarding Hitler's intentions. Doreen Warriner in Prague was also frustrated with the dilatory attitude of the British authorities. As she wrote, 'In Prague we lived on tenter-hooks, but London was detached and calm: it was impossible to get through the cotton wool which prevented them from hearing.'

There was certainly no easing of Winton's rescue task, in fact it had intensified: not only did he lack the valuable first-hand assistance of Chadwick and the team available in Prague, but he had returned to his work in the City which took up his day until 3pm. Only then could he deal with the rescue work and, from then until the early hours of the morning, the tasks facing him were unremitting. The Home Office's demands were far more stringent than they had been for the German and Austrian *Kindertransport* children. A separate application was required for each child, plus a medical certificate, details of a guarantor, and a nominated foster home ready to keep the child until the age of 17 years. Added to this a £50 deposit was required to cover the expected eventual return to the homeland, or to cover re-emigration to another state. This was a hefty sum in those times, way beyond the means of working-class families and a struggle for lower middle-class people to afford. In her book, co-authored with Muriel Emanuel, *Nicholas Winton and the Rescued Generation*, Vera Gissing poses a challenging question, 'How many of us today would be prepared to take in a child, a foreigner whose background and family were unknown to us and whom we had never met and take on the responsibility for that child for an unlimited period without outside financial or social help?'

Winton has explained how he spent endless, exhausting hours writing appeals for help. A stroke of luck occurred when he was approached by Barbara Willis, a friend of Martin Blake, who offered her services and, unofficially, gave him the list of BCRC's contacts throughout the country. Not one to refuse such an offer, and with no hesitation about the 'unofficial' aspect, a paper outlining the crisis situation in Czechoslovakia was sent to all, and offers began to arrive. At this time his group of helpers expanded to four people. Winton's mother also began to play an active role and would often meet transports once they started to arrive in Britain.

Details of Winton's plan were carefully laid out: a photograph of six children was presented on a single card from which people could choose. Lists of selected children with their guarantors were then submitted to the Home Office. Delays were frequent and exasperating – everyone knew that time was getting short. This led to the situation when Chadwick and Barazetti in Prague forged documents which, amazingly, got through the Czechs and later, after 15 March, even more surprisingly, got past the occupying Germans. The fakes were quietly swapped with the official ones, which had meanwhile arrived at the British end, before the more-vigilant British immigration authorities spotted them. A great moment came when the first group of 20 Czech children successfully left Prague on 14 March, just one day before Czechoslovakia was invaded and occupied.

Doreen Warriner was on her way across Prague, delivering a batch of passports, when she witnessed the German entry into the city:

> 'When the taxi reached the Charles Bridge, the army was marching over, and we had to stop. I got out, not wishing to sit there and watch, and went into the Krizovnicka church by the bridgehead.

It was completely full, and absolutely silent... The Czechs stood watching the soldiers, stunned with despair, tears streaming down the women's faces. At every minute there was a fresh shock: the great guns at the bridgeheads, the swastika flying from the Castle. For the Czechs nationalism is bound up with concrete things, and most of all it is Prague they love, their ancient city, every corner of which carries a memory of a national hero, or a national tragedy.'

Tessa Rowntree, a young Quaker woman who had hastened to Prague to help Warriner, recalled the panic when the Germans arrived:

'...a lot of the consulates had been holding the passports of would-be refugees and the first thing the Germans did was to seize these [and thereby identify who were Jewish], and many were rounded up and put into concentration camps... I was only there about three weeks after the invasion and one of the things I remember was that Doreen managed to get hold of a batch of these passports and papers and we spent a day tearing them up and stuffing them down the loos of the grandest hotel in Prague – the only thing we could do. Then I went out with a convoy of children, at that stage we were interested in getting the children out – one didn't have papers and somehow we managed to bluff our way without the papers for one of them... As Jews were forbidden to take valuable possessions out of the country, quite a few Jewish people were trying to get us to take things out for them, most of the time we refused but very occasionally we helped with this. I ended up going out in a convoy with my rucksack in which I had one or two rings hidden in boxes of raisins, and a roll of drawings from a famous artist who was going to educate his family with these for the rest of their lives. The drawings looked just like squiggles, all done up in a roll...'

After the incorporation of Czechoslovakia into the Greater Reich, Winton's rescue work intensified; his list now included Slovakian refugee children who had been living in even worse conditions in Bratislava than their counterparts in Prague. But the shock and horror at Hitler's betrayal of the terms of the Munich Agreement led to a dramatic rise of support for Winton's task at home and an expansion of his network as appeals were made on every conceivable outlet; this resulted in a steady stream of offers of homes and sponsors from a wide variety of homes, Christian as well as Jewish.

Of course there were problems, not least the objections that were made when siblings had to be split up. But Winton's arguments were unrelenting; he realised that it was a 'phenomenal undertaking' for a poorer family who offered to take just one child into their home, explaining, 'Had I waited for families willing to take two or more, most of those children would not have got away.' Guarantors and potential foster homes also mainly asked for young girls of seven to ten and, if possible, fair. Boys of twelve and upwards were hard to place – all this was in line with the later evacuation experience of British children from 1 September 1939. There were also complaints, as with other *Kindertransport* children from Austria and Germany, that many children found themselves in Christian families and institutions. Any hint of potential religious conversion led to angry protests, particularly among orthodox rabbis. When they confronted him about their suspicions, Winton stood firm telling them, rather as Foley had with the Shanghai affair, 'I've got my work to do, you've got yours. If you prefer a dead Jew to a proselytised one, that's your business.'

Support from the Anglo–Jewish community ranged from generous and warm-hearted to reluctant or even to turning a blind eye to the desperate need. But Jewish institutions such as schools, training places and hostels did their utmost to accommodate the children, enabling them to maintain their Jewish identity. Agricultural training centres were set up in different parts of Britain by the *Youth Aliyah*. As its director, Arieh Handler, explained, 'We ran 30 such places, including Whittinghame Farm (given by the Balfour family) and Grwych Castle in north Wales... We didn't have the ear of the so-called Anglo–Jewry. They all paid lip-service, but the leadership did not understand the concept [of Zionism] or responsibility of the Jewish nations.' These centres were a godsend for the older children who were far more difficult to place in foster homes. Handler explained the value of these in combining agricultural training with educational and Zionist values: 'They kept alive the Jewish flame throughout the war and were instrumental in helping to build *kibbutzim* in Israel [after 1948], giving new Jewish spirit to our youngsters and the community.'

By the end of March 1939 the grip of the Gestapo in Prague had started to tighten and there are many descriptions of the terror created by them as transports left the stations. Doreen Warriner witnessed many departures:

'They came to terrorise, to reduce everyone to a state of helplessness and fear. There is no system, only a boiling cauldron into which every now and again a certain quantity of bones and blood must be thrown; it doesn't matter whose, but it does matter that those who are still free should see and tremble… It gets on one's nerves, as it is meant to do, because behind all the theatricality there is the reality: the concentration camps are filling, people do not return.'

Kathe Fischel was a 16-year-old art student living in Prague who left on one of Winton's transports in the spring of 1939:

'My brother was seven years younger and my mother couldn't bring herself to add him to the Winton list… It was a terrible wrench, but I remember that I very much wanted to go. I had heard of Nicholas Winton and we had a postcard to say that I was going to be included in this transport. I remember I had to go to the Gestapo. I needed some exit papers. There was a long queue. The actual scene at the station I have completely pushed out of my mind. Only [later] when Nicholas Winton showed me this film with the same station and the same vista, I felt this is what it was like. I was the oldest by far in this compartment. There were four or five very little ones which I was supposed to look after. I wasn't very good at it because they were sick, and they cried and dirtied themselves and I had no idea how to handle this. At some stage in

Germany we were all told to get out of the compartment and we were all lined up on the platform. I don't remember any more of that either. Then we crossed the frontier and came to England from the Hook of Holland… I was scared for my mother, father and brother because there wasn't any way of getting them out.'

Doreen Warriner wrote of the relief when the big transports of Jewish children organised by Winton in London, and Chadwick in Prague, left successfully – it was 'a great mercy'. By April 1939, with evidence that the Gestapo were on her trail, she was advised to leave Prague and crossed the Polish frontier on the morning of 23 April, just in time – four days later the Gestapo arrived at the BCRC office to arrest her. Chadwick left Prague after Warriner, in the summer of 1939, where he continued his good work in London.

Throughout the summer of 1939, as the tension mounted, Winton wrote to every conceivable agency he could think of, pleading for help to get out as many as possible of the 5,000 children still left on his list. By early August only one more transport was set to leave, with 68 children. This last group left Prague on 3 September 1939 but was stopped in Germany, just as the Second World War started. It was heartbreaking for Winton, Chadwick and everyone who had worked so hard that so many were left behind, most of them to perish. Winton and his team had done everything in their power to get them to safety, but he was fighting all the time against lack of funds, red tape, the failure of other states – particularly the United States – to offer more generous refuge as well as the complacency and apathy within the British institutions which had continued even after the shock of the Nazi invasion of 15 March. But it was thanks to Winton's unremitting efforts in finding the funds and homes that 669 Czech children were saved. Working behind the scenes in London, from January 1939, few children were aware of his role in their survival. If they remembered anyone, it was Chadwick who had been on the spot to organise the transports from Prague, comfort the children distressed at leaving their parents, and see them on their way to safety.

Winton resigned from his banking job at the start of the war. Since his schooldays at Stowe he had held pacifist beliefs which had been reinforced with all he had seen of Nazi militarism. As his rescue work reveals, he was also a great humanitarian and it was a combination of these tendencies that led to his volunteering first for Air Raid Precaution duties, and later for ambulance work for the British Red Cross. It was the latter that took him to France with the British Expeditionary Force, only to arrive as the retreat had started, having to witness, once more, a pitiful refugee crisis with the hordes of fleeing, desperate civilians. He was evacuated from Calais to Britain in the desperate months of 1940. This is when, working with the ambulance service of the Red Cross helping victims of the Blitz of 1940–1941, he began to question his pacifist stance and decided to volunteer for the RAF. He served in the administrative and special duties branch of the RAF, initially as an airman, eventually achieving the rank of Flight Lieutenant.

After D-Day, Winton's duties with the RAF took him through the devastated landscape of Germany to the liberation of the beautiful and undamaged city of Prague where, in perfect symmetry, he met up with his old friend, Martin Blake.

One of the Second World War's most tragic legacies was a large-scale refugee crisis. Between 1940 and 1951, more than a million people left their homelands in Europe and spent years in displaced persons (DPs) camps waiting for resettlement elsewhere. The end of the war did not end Winton's humanitarian impulses; witnessing the misery of post-war Europe, he was anxious to help. Instead of returning to banking on his demobilisation in 1946, he took up an appointment in the International Refugee Organization, the successor to the United Nations Relief and Rehabilitation Administration which had overseen the repatriation and resettlement of the huge displacements of populations in the aftermath of war.

Winton then embarked on what must have been one of the most surreal experiences imaginable: the task of organising the sale of the mountains of valuable goods looted from Jews. Profits from the sales were used for the benefit of displaced persons with 90 per cent going to Jewish survivors of the Holocaust. Winton was responsible for supervising the gruesome task of valuing, packing and eventually overseeing the smelting of the precious metals – a job that took him into the very depths of the bestial horror of the Holocaust: he was dealing with gold rings and gold fillings wrenched from corpses that had been removed from the gas chamber before being shoved into the crematoria. The end product was made into gold bars, ready for sale, his past experience in banking proving useful when dealing with merchant banks. Profits from the sales reached the figure of $728,000.

Winton went back to work in international banking after 1948, settling in Maidenhead with his Danish wife Greta. The couple spent much of their married life involved in charity work, including a housing society and Mencap (The Royal Society for Mentally Handicapped Children), for which Winton was awarded the MBE in 1983. Over the years he received many more honours; in the 2003 New Year Honours, he was knighted by Queen Elizabeth II in recognition of his work on the Czech *Kindertransport*. Due to his family's Jewish roots, he is not considered eligible for the recognition of 'Righteous Among the Nations' by Yad Vashem in Jerusalem, but Winton did receive a warm letter of appreciation from Ezer Weizman, the then president of Israel, which said, 'In the darkness enveloping Europe in 1939 your selfless dedication to the salvation of children in Prague shines out… Your name is written large on that page of history.'

Since his first reunion in 1988 with a group of the children he had saved, Winton's contacts with the rescued has grown. Vera Gissing explained his importance to those *Kindertransport* children:

'With pitifully few exceptions, all of us Winton children had lost our parents and most of our extended family; some had lost siblings who were left behind. The Holocaust had deprived not only us, but our children, of grandparents, cousins, aunts and uncles and old family friends. Is it any wonder that this kind, compassionate man to whom we owe so much has become a much loved father-figure, even a grandfather-figure of a very large family? ...Nicky gave us, our children and our grandchildren, the chance of life.'

At the first *Kindertransport* reunion of 1989 more turned up, starting a close relationship which has lasted to this day. Prior to this there had been no group for the *Kinder* to bond with and learn more of their history. Sadly, Bertha Bracey had died a few weeks earlier. By the time of the second reunion, held in June 1999 in London to mark the 60th anniversary of the *Kindertransport*, 250 Czech children had been discovered. Not all could make it to the reunion but the 75 'Wintons' who did attend, many with their families, made the occasion particularly emotional. It was at this reunion that Nicholas Winton, told the audience:

'I should like to issue a word of warning: we must remember, but remembering is not enough. I don't think the world can go on living like that. I feel very strongly that people have to live more ethical, honest lives. We've got to take the reasons for remembering and the lessons we have learnt through remembering and see what good we can do, especially the people who have been saved.'

Vera Schaufeld who left Prague as a nine-year-old child has explained the importance of meeting other *Kinder* at the reunions:

'...all sorts of people I had come across and until that reunion I never realised they'd ever come on a *Kindertransport* and that we had anything in common. It was extraordinary, a really fantastic experience for me and it was after this that I really had the courage to get my parents' letters translated and to read them... Then I met Nicholas Winton. I hadn't realised he'd been responsible for organising the *Kindertransport* from Czechoslovakia until that reunion... I've also found out through the reunions what a complex story the *Kindertransport* is: some people had much more unfortunate experiences than I did, suffering harassment, brutality or discrimination. I experienced a lot of kindness. I was fortunate in what happened to me.'

The next decade's anniversary was marked by a very special event. On 1 September 2009, a 'Winton train' of original 1930s locomotive and carriages steamed out of Prague's railway station heading for London via the original *Kindertransport* route. On board the train were 22 of the surviving 'Winton children' and their descendants, who were welcomed by Sir Nicholas in London. The occasion, joyful though it was, marked a particularly painful event for Winton – the 70th anniversary of the intended last *Kindertransport* which was due to set off on 3 September 1939 but never did, because of the outbreak of the Second World War. Of all the people honoured by the British Government in March 2010, Sir Nicholas Winton, at the age of 100 years, was the one most well known to the British public. Since Esther Rantzen's initial television programme, many other events have been held to mark his achievement, and his rescue work has been the subject of several films in the Czech Republic and Slovakia as well as Britain. On 20 January 2011, *Nicky's Family*, the latest film on Winton by the Slovak filmmaker Matej Mináč, was premiered in Prague. Winton, then 101 years of age, and 20 of those he had saved, attended the gala event at the Prague Congress Centre.

Sir Nicholas Winton's work is particularly inspiring because the eight Prague transports were not officially part of the *Kindertransport* movement. Winton had to work independently in very difficult circumstances where many of the foster homes had already been taken by the German and Austrian *Kindertransports* which had started earlier and under a much more emotional atmosphere and with relatively relaxed rules and regulations, and more generous funding. It was the energy, vision and, above all, the humanitarianism of this modest man that drove him. Without the actions of Nicholas Winton those who he saved would have perished in the concentration camps, alongside the rest of their generation. To these survivors, they and their descendants are living proof of his outstanding achievement.

New York, here we come! Ida (left) and Louise in their homemade finery, complete with opera cloaks.

LOUISE AND IDA COOK
LOUISE 1901–1991 IDA 1904–1986

*'The same naive technique by which we had got ourselves
to the States for our pleasure was used when we
stumbled into Europe and began to save lives.'*

It would be difficult to imagine two less likely rescuers of Jews from Nazi persecution than Louise and Ida Cook. These sisters, both spinsters and civil servants, were living comfortable but uneventful lives in their London suburban family home during the 1930s when they heard a recording of 'Un bel di, vedremo' from Puccini's *Madame Butterfly*, sung by the famous soprano Amelita Galli-Curci. In a moment, their lives changed. The opera's most famous aria immediately sparked a passion for the art form, and a turning point in the sisters' lives that was to take them to the United States and then to Europe to listen to, meet, and befriend, the famous stars of this 'golden age of opera'. And it was this love of opera that would eventually lead them to many daring undercover visits into the very heart of Nazi Germany and Austria in the late 1930s, to rescue at least 29 Jews and their families who were under the threat of death.

Born at the start of the twentieth century – Louise in 1901 and Ida in 1904 – they grew up during the years of the First World War and its aftermath. They remained single, like so many young women of the time, due to the 'lost generation' of young men who had been slaughtered in that conflict. But marriage did not seem a particular concern of theirs; they were devoted to each other and were part of a close-knit, happy family living contentedly at home with their parents and two younger brothers, Bill and Jim, neither sister apparently craving the excitement the post-war city had to offer. Until they discovered opera.

It was Louise who, after attending a lecture on music by Sir Walford Davies which included a gramophone recording, invested £23 in a hand-cranked model of the day and a set of ten classical records, an innovation in a home which, prior to this, had lacked all forms of music. It was also Louise who, with Ida away on a visit to the north, climbed up to the gallery at the Royal Opera House, Covent Garden, to hear her first opera, *Madame Butterfly*. With Ida back home, both sisters returned to hear *Tosca*, *La Traviata* and *Rigoletto* after which they became regulars in the queue for gallery seats. It was the soprano prima donnas who initially became their heroines and the sisters would hover for hours outside the stage doors hoping for a word, an autograph or, after they had purchased a small camera, a photograph of their adored stars. They were particularly devoted to Galli-Curci and after hearing her sing at the Albert Hall, and, learning that she only performed opera in New York, they decided, however long it took, to save up and travel there to hear her. Fired up with their plan, they wrote to her outlining their intentions and to their delight she replied, not only promising them tickets for all her appearances during their stay in America, but also inviting them to the Albert Hall to say goodbye.

With such encouragement and with great excitement they worked out the logistics and the likely cost, which they estimated at £100 for the whole trip, including travel by ship – no regular passenger air-flights then – a hotel in New York, and new outfits for the occasion. One hundred pounds was a large sum then and with wages of £2.6.0 [£2.30] a week for Ida, a little more for Louise, some hard saving was in order.

It took two years of scrimping and saving, substituting snacks for proper lunches, walking instead of taking buses, and making other economies wherever possible to save enough money. They had to make do with home-sewn outfits for the trip. Ida, relying on the periodical *Mabs Fashions* to keep them up to date, set to work on these, taking special delight in their new opera attire – scarlet for Louise, pink and silver for Ida, with the finishing touches of opera cloaks.

At the end of the second year of saving, they managed to get six weeks' leave from their jobs, half of it unpaid, and at the end of 1926 they set off for their big adventure in New York, travelling third-class on the liner *Berengaria*. On their arrival in New York, the sisters were treated as minor celebrities by the newspapers keen to interview and photograph 'the two girls who saved their money to cross the Atlantic…'. Galli-Curci kept her promise, received the sisters like dear friends and treated them to tickets for all her performances at the Metropolitan Opera House on Broadway during their stay. To the sisters' delight, at the end of her performance as Violetta in *La Traviata* with Beniamino Gigli and Giuseppe De Luca, the prima donna picked them out from the audience in the stalls, waving to them when taking her applause, making Ida feel 'the nearest thing to royalty I shall ever be'. Galli-Curci, with her husband, Homer Samuels, entertained the sisters on more than one occasion in their Fifth Avenue apartment on what was then called Millionaires' Row, sending their Cadillac to pick up the pair from their modest hotel in Washington Square West.

This highly successful first visit to New York was life-changing for the sisters, revealing not only that there was life outside the narrow confines of suburban London, but that their confidence and tenacity of purpose was justified, and that the opera stars were theirs to befriend. Although Galli-Curci was always to have a very special place in their hearts, once they returned home they became infatuated with the American soprano Rosa Ponselle who also became a good friend. The singers, on their part, were touched by the sisters' zest for life, their simplicity and innocence as well as their genuine love of opera. Over the years Ida and Louise became good friends with Gigli, Ezio Pinza, Elisabeth Rethberg and Maria Callas among many others, maintaining their friendship with Galli-Curci and Rosa Ponselle. But it was their affection for the Austrian conductor Clemens Krauss, director of the Vienna *Staatsoper*, whom they first saw in 1934 conducting his wife Viorica Ursuleac in Richard Strauss's new opera *Arabella* at Covent Garden, that led to their first contact with Jewish refugees.

The sisters made contact with Krauss and Ursuleac in London and, with their permission, photographed them outside Covent Garden. Learning that the Salzburg programme for 1934 was to include the first performance of a new production of *Don Giovanni*, under Bruno Walter and that Strauss's *Die Ägyptische Helena* was to be performed, Ida and Louise decided to spend their summer holiday there. They arrived in Salzburg just after 24 July when Dollfuss, the Austrian Chancellor, was murdered. Innocently oblivious of the significance of this as the first European event that was to have such repercussions on their lives, their main concern was, 'would it put a stop to our holiday in Salzburg?' But soon they heard that the frontier between Austria and Germany, which had been closed, had been re-opened for tourists and they breathed a sigh of relief that their 'glorious feast of music' was safe for their enjoyment. This trip was followed by one to Amsterdam for the Strauss Festival Week in early December. For the first time the sisters heard Strauss conducting with Ursuleac singing the part of Arabella.

It was during their visit to Amsterdam that the sisters were introduced to Mitia Mayer-Lismann, a Jewish musicologist, described by Ida as a 'distinguished white-haired lady' they had noticed earlier in Salzburg. When the sisters arrived at the station to see Ursuleac depart from Amsterdam, Mitia Mayer-Lismann was also present. This is when Ida and Louise had their first intimation that events were more complex than they appeared because Ursuleac, with a seriousness that baffled them, asked them to look after Mitia on a forthcoming short trip to London. Assured of their promise to do so, Ursuleac then turned to Mitia, telling her 'Now you will be all right'. Ida and Louise had no idea at this point that this would lead to their first contact with a refugee, or of the seriousness of Mitia's situation. It was only later, when taking Mitia sightseeing in London on this visit, that they discovered that she was Jewish. At the time this meant little to them; although they had seen signs of anti-Semitism and unrest, they were unaware of the full import of this, nor the tragedy that European Jewry was to face. But during the short time Mitia stayed in London, she explained the dire consequences of Hitler's rule for the Jews of Europe. As Ida explained, 'We began to see things more clearly... But our understanding of the problem grew quite naturally... To us the case of the Mayer-Lismanns was curious and shocking, but not incredible. We were shocked, but we did what I suppose most people would have done. We asked, "Where did they hope to go? What had they to offer in the work markets of the world? And, finally, what could we do to help?"'

In order to fulfil their wish to help, the Cook sisters needed money. By this time, fortunately, Ida's financial situation had improved. After their return from their first visit to the United States, Ida had contacted Mrs Taft, the editor of *Mags Fashions*, and submitted several articles which were accepted including 'An Evening with Galli-Curci'. On the basis of these, Mrs Taft asked Ida to write 'a really strong' serial for the magazine. Ida accepted with alacrity, bought a penny notebook from Woolworths and quickly produced the first three episodes, each with its 'cliffhanger' which, although somewhat on the torrid side for the homely magazine, were nevertheless accepted with the go-ahead to finish the story. Entitled *Wife to Christopher*, this was serialised in the magazine during the winter of 1935–1936 under Ida's new nom de plume Mary Burchell. It was then suggested that Ida contact a publisher of romantic fiction. Mills & Boon was Ida's choice; the publisher accepted the book eagerly, with the proviso that Ida signed a contract promising the next two stories to them. Immediately she got to work, bashing out *Call and I'll Come* on her typewriter in the little attic room of the family home. This was to earn the accolade 'The best romantic book of the month', giving her not only further requests for articles and interviews, but a huge increase in earning capacity.

Over the next fifty years Ida became one of Mills & Boon's most prolific and celebrated writers, producing 120 romantic novels. By the late 1930s she was earning £1,500 a year with her writing, a vast increase on her salary as a civil service typist. Initially, the Cook sisters started day-dreaming of what the new-found wealth could mean to them on a personal level. 'Cars and fur coats came under rapid review...we even discussed Louise's possible retirement from the office. Indeed we spent thousands in our imagination...' Ida said. But by now their awareness of the true nature of Nazi Germany, and the 'terrible need' of European Jewry, led to the overriding thought 'I could save a life'.

Their first refugee was not Mitia Mayer-Lismann, but her daughter Else, a 17-year-old music student. By now it was 1937, and things were becoming really desperate for Jews. The sisters were fully aware of the British policy for immigration: children under eighteen were allowed into the country provided a British citizen stood as their guardian. The pair obtained the necessary papers, took responsibility for the financial guarantee and brought Else to London under their care. Else's parents and brothers were brought out later, with their help.

The sisters now began to view their opera trips to Europe with renewed purpose. The horrors of Nazism had been made clear to them by Mitia Mayer-Lismann and, being compassionate women, they then began to see the misery and fear of the European Jews as something for which they felt a responsibility and an urge to do more. Throughout the years 1937–1939 Ida and Louise visited Frankfurt, Munich, Cologne, Berlin and Vienna, with stops en route to their destination, to meet the people they hoped to help. Actually meeting those they intended to rescue was an important aspect of their mission, as they saw the problem not in terms of lists of anonymous names, but as real, desperate human beings. The two Englishwomen quickly realised that they were the only hope for those in such obvious danger. Their regular, short trips to Nazi Germany and Austria were under the guise of obsessive opera aficionados prepared to travel anywhere to pursue their beloved art form. Clemens Krauss who, with his wife, Ursuleac, had been instrumental in setting them on the rescue path, was at this time director of the Munich Opera House and was of crucial importance. The sisters would inform him of their next visit, he would then provide them with details of operas to be performed on those dates, the list of the singers and, very often, letting them choose the performance – with their genuine love of opera, this was an ideal arrangement, an excellent cover. If awkward questions were asked at the borders, as increasingly they were, the sisters were thus well armed.

They would leave London on Friday evening, returning in time to start work on Monday morning. Sometimes they would take a small party of opera lovers with them – 'Cook's Tours' as they were known.

John Cook, the sisters' nephew, mentioned how his father, Jim, some-times accompanied his sisters on these tours, and how, because there were restrictions on the amount of money that could be taken out of Britain at this time, this was a great help financially as part of the group's allowances would be used for the sisters' rescue work. He also explained how once Jim had 'an encounter with a brown-shirt in Cologne'. In this way, other Britons were getting a taste of the reality of National Socialism. Arriving at their destination in Germany, or sometimes Austria, the sisters would immediately get to work interviewing their refugee cases, often up to fifteen people one after the other. Louise took German language lessons to help the interviews along and the sisters made it a rule never to refuse to hear a story. As a part of a close, happy family themselves, they decided that wherever possible, they would concentrate on rescuing whole families. Listening to the harrowing tales of humiliation, brutality and separation was a very emotional, upsetting experience which often reduced the soft-hearted sisters to tears.

Although Ida and Louise spent their own money helping Jews escape, even with Ida's increased income they did not have enough to cover the demand. An essential part of the rescue plan was to secure the financial resources of those emigrating to England so that they would have the means to support themselves when they arrived. They did this in several ways which Ida called the 'sidelines' of their work. Jews were forbidden to take money or possessions out of Germany. They were, however, able to buy exportable goods which the sisters took back to England where they were sold and the proceeds deposited in British banks under the refugees' names to await their arrival. This meant that the refugees would be financially independent and, therefore, acceptable to the immigration authorities.

The sisters also became adept at smuggling out precious jewels and furs, again to be sold to provide financial support when their refugees arrived. Often these were very expensive, ostentatious diamonds and pearls which the sisters always wore with great panache, never concealing the items on themselves, or in their luggage. As the tension increased in the late 1930s, border checks became far more rigorous. The sisters solved this problem by going in by one route, sometimes by air from Croydon airport, wearing no jewellery, then they would return by another frontier with their cheap sweaters, blouses and coats spangled with glittering gems, dazzling the border guards who took them to be fakes on these overdressed women. A great challenge arose when, to their horror, they were asked to take a brooch, 'a great oblong of blazing diamonds'. But undeterred, Ida fixed it on her 'six-and-eleven penny [35p] Marks and Spencer's jumper', in an eye-catching spot, opened her coat and successfully brazened it out, thinking it wouldn't possibly be seen as 'anything but Woolworths'. The sisters were as cunning as they were bold and took great pains with details, for instance, as neither of them had pierced ears they always made sure that they carried no earrings for these.

The smuggling of furs presented a real challenge. Before leaving for Germany, they would appeal to London furriers, or to friends who possessed good fur coats, for British labels to switch with German labels before leaving Germany. They also made sure to go out wearing the coats in public places while in Germany. The sisters never acted in a furtive manner: part of their deception was to go about openly and be seen. They would stay at the most expensive hotels, such as the Adlon in Berlin, where they often glimpsed well-known Nazis including Goering, Goebbels, Himmler, Streicher and Ribbentrop who, according to Ida, once gave Louise 'the glad eye'. They even saw Hitler, from the back. 'If you stood and gazed at them admiringly...no one thought you were anything but another couple of admiring fools,' Ida later explained. Such 'sidelines' and calculated behaviour illustrates the ingenuity, determination and courage of both sisters.

Their names were soon known to the refugee committees in Bloomsbury House as well, through the grapevine of desperate Jewish people hoping to escape from the Continent. With the existing censorship of mail in Germany, and Austria after the *Anschluss* of March 1938, the sisters were often asked to take verbal messages, having to learn by

The famous Adlon Hotel on Unter den Linden, Berlin, was frequented by top Nazis such as the Nazi Minister of Propaganda, Joseph Goebbels, who, in this picture [below], collects money for the Winter Charity Fund at the hotel, 5 December 1936.

heart the content of a letter or document. Very often these proved vital in expediting escape plans.

Back in London, the rescue work did not stop. As well as financing guarantees with their own money, they persuaded friends to subscribe for one as a group. The sisters were also active in speaking to church groups and other likely sponsors, travelling throughout the country to raise money and support. They made touching appeals in church newspapers under headings such as 'Will Somebody Save Me?' In a chauvinistic age, no doubt they were considered bossy women by many of the officials they approached. Like Foley and Winton, they were not shy of bending the rules, organising forged documents where necessary and persuading civil servants to backdate letters. Sometimes they resorted to bullying tactics. When a 'hidebound' Home Office official's laid-back attitude towards an urgent case incensed Ida she stayed rooted in his office until, worn out by the persistent woman and desperate to get home, he agreed to search for the missing file in question. Eventually, the rescue was accomplished. As Ida put it, 'You never know what you can do until you refuse to take "No" for an answer.'

The sisters were eventually bringing out so many Jews that they bought a flat in the then newly built Dolphin Square apartment complex on the Thames in London with their own money in order to provide a safe haven for the refugees once they arrived. Their first guest was Else Mayer-Lismann. The flat seems to have been their one extravagance; they otherwise never departed from the values of thrift, hard work, decency and modesty instilled by their parents, who had also instilled a bedrock of morality. They continued to make their own clothes, still travelled third class during their European opera trips, and continued sitting in the gallery at Covent Garden during the season, directing all their resources to saving as many Jews as they could from Hitler's concentration camps. 'Why not?' Ida exclaimed. 'It was no hardship to arrange our lives as we had always known and enjoyed them.'

As well as making huge demands on their funds and stamina, there were dangers and risks to their rescue work, especially with the surge of refugees after the events of *Kristallnacht*, November 1938. By this time, the women faced ever more restrictions and rigorous inspections at the borders, and tensions within Germany and Austria had increased to fever pitch. But their incredible faith in the protective power of their British passports never waned and the risks were played down; as Ida explained, 'In a way, of course, it was not really very dangerous for us, except for the smuggling.'

In fact, they were often not aware of the extent of the danger until well after the event. One such risky case was that of Walter Stiefel and his wife, whom the women rescued at the very last minute, a seemingly straightforward case for them at the time. With hindsight though, they recalled the special precautions he insisted they took when meeting him in Germany, which at the time they thought were rather paranoid. Later, when the Stiefels were safe in Britain, to their amazement he informed them of the full dangers inherent in his rescue as, unknown to them, he had been in the anti-Nazi underground for six years, and if arrested and made to talk, it would most certainly have led to their arrest. Ida's response on hearing this was '…All these years we'd been heroines, without the pain of knowing it.' John Cook also mentioned how the family regarded the sisters' adventures at the time in a 'matter-of-fact' manner. But how, 'After the war we all realised the dangerous game they were playing and the children were very much aware of the risks they ran, though they [the aunts] played them down.'

As war drew nearer, their rescue mission became an anxious race against time. Ida writes of how they dreaded going into 'the hateful, diseased German atmosphere' and how it took 'that extra bit of courage and determination which took us back time and time again'. Their final rescue mission was made as late as August 1939, and they reached home less than two weeks before the outbreak of war. Their last successful rescue, a young Polish boy, arrived as war started; he had left Gydnia as the last person to board the last boat leaving the port. His escape was thanks to a backdated paper that Ida had pressured a Bloomsbury House official to grant. To the sisters' great distress, many of the people they had interviewed for rescue on their last visit were then trapped; some were ill. On a visit to a hospital in Heinrich-von-Gagernstrasse to check on one of their contacts, they were shocked to find it full of emaciated concentration camp victims who, as part of the cat-and-mouse tactic the Nazis used at that time, had been released to recover sufficiently only to be re-arrested for more work. As Ida explained, 'It was a strange and terrible experience – unshared, I think, by any other, or by very few British people…every patient had been made ill deliberately. Only two surgeons had been allowed to remain to look after the unfortunates.' By this time Ida and Louise had a realistic idea of what awaited the Jews of Europe, although the 'Final Solution' extermination policy was yet to come.

During the war, like most British families, the Cook family was split up, with the boys going off into the armed services, the parents eventually evacuated, and Louise and Ida for the first time had to live separate lives for a year when Louise's office was moved to Wales – a terrible wrench for the devoted sisters. Ida, with her usual zest and determination, cheerfully worked as a shelter warden in the Thames riverside area of Bermondsey throughout the Blitz of 1940–1941, regaining something of the contact with people that she had missed when the refugee work ended. The former opera arias were replaced with jolly, and sometimes poignant, sing-songs with Ida fully entering the spirit of it all. She worked in the shelter there during the two largest Blitz raids, on 16 and 19 April, as well as the last raid of the Blitz on 10 May 1941.

The refugee work had taken its toll on the sisters' funds. Ida, in particular, had gone into the war deep in debt. During the last stages of their rescue mission, she had borrowed heavily and mortgaged future writing to support the refugees they had managed to save. She had also undertaken to pay half her income for maintenance of those unable to support themselves. Her problems were compounded by the fact that, denied of the stimulation of opera and the adventure that had gone with it in the years 1937–1939, the wellspring of her inspiration had evaporated and she found writing hard labour rather than a pleasure. It took her nearly three years into the war to regain financial stability.

But the sisters never gave up on their humanitarian efforts and did whatever they could to help refugees, continuing their fund-raising activities to help those in need, and making the Dolphin Square flat available for those in want of accommodation. Throughout the trials and tribulations of wartime living, they kept their spirits up with the thought of returning to America to meet up again with Galli-Curci and her husband and to trace Rosa Ponselle – their 'star gazing', although put on hold during the war, evidently undimmed. When hostilities ended, not only did the sisters return to the States to renew their friendship with the opera stars, but they also met many of the refugees they had helped, including the Mayer-Lismanns, all now proud American citizens, who welcomed them with gratitude and open arms making the visit, as Ida put it, full of 'joy and wonder'. In London, to their great delight, they met again with Krauss and Ursuleac.

Krauss's relationship with Nazi Germany had proved controversial. In 1935 he had transferred from Vienna *Staatsoper* to succeed Furtwängler in Berlin's *Staatsoper* for a while, which had opened him to the charge of having Nazi sympathies and the requirement of facing a de-Nazification committee after the war. But to the sisters, he was the one who had provided cover for their rescue missions, and they knew that he also had close relations with Jewish people, including the Mayer-Lismanns whom he had asked them to help. The couple were given a warm welcome to the Dolphin Square flat, being told to regard it as their London home. Krauss and Usuleac, who had started the women on their rescue missions, now had the key to the London refuge which had sheltered so many of the Jews they had helped to save.

Apart from the resumption of their passion for opera, there was another, more serious, side to post-war life for the sisters. Their humanitarian instincts had not abated and, like Bertha Bracey and Nicholas Winton, they too became involved with the huge European problem of displaced persons, in their case joining the Adoption Committee for Aid to Displaced Persons (later, Lifeline) with special interest in camps housing non-German refugees in Germany. These were mainly Poles, but also some Russians, Balts, Hungarians and Ukrainians, many of whom had been used as slave labour by the Nazis and were reluctant to return home to live under Communist regimes. By now experienced fundraisers, Ida and Louise raised money to provide milk for young children and medicine and treatment for the many post-war tuberculosis sufferers in the camps. True to style, they came to know the displaced people and the staff caring for them, not just as cases, or lists of names, but on a personal level – the leitmotif of their refugee work.

Ida's muse had reappeared after war had ended and she continued writing novels for Mills & Boon, albeit with a reduced readership as her style was becoming increasingly outdated. She did, however, become president of the Romantic Novelists' Association after it was formed in 1960, acting as mentor to a new generation of romantic fiction writers. Louise continued in her civil service work. They both gained great publicity when Ida published her book *We Followed Our Stars* in 1950 (re-edited as *Safe Passage*), fascinating readers with their tales of gala opera evenings and intimacy with the opera stars along with their daring undercover rescues into the heart of Nazi Germany and Austria. BBC broadcasts followed as well as a great deal of press coverage. Then, in 1956, Ida was chosen as a subject for the television series *This is Your Life*, presented by the popular Eamonn Andrews. The show aimed to reconstruct the lives of unsuspecting subjects who had been lured into the studio – in Ida's case, Louise was given this responsibility. The appearance of participants in the story was central to the programme and an impressive group of people appeared for Ida including former refugees, significant people from the Displaced Persons camp in Bavaria and the Bermondsey shelter. Also, to Ida's great surprise and delight, Ursuleac, by then retired, appeared in person and a transatlantic telephone call was received from Rosa Ponselle. All paid tribute to the sisters' incredible, often bizarre, story.

But there is little doubt that their greatest reward was the love and gratitude of the refugees they had saved and with whom the sisters kept in touch throughout their lives. Laura Sarti, a well-known opera singer and recitalist, who later gained an international reputation as a teacher of singing, had heard of the Cook sisters and what they had done through the group of refugee music-lovers and performers she met frequently in London. She told me of the high esteem in which Ida and Louise were held by the refugees, many of whom had been brought over by them. Also how, when being introduced to the sisters, 'I was very surprised how ordinary and rather dowdy they were, given the incredible things they had done.' Else Mayer-Lismann, the first refugee Ida and Louise had saved, went on to become a renowned musicologist, writing and lecturing for Glyndebourne Opera among other institutions. In a tribute to them, she recalled their special qualities: '...the entrance of the Cook girls into our lives was revolutionary, because we never ever even realised or knew that anybody like Ida and Louise existed. They were so unique...they were never depressed...[their] attitude to life has been something which is an enrichment...'

In the story of Ida and Louise, the impression is often given that Ida was the dominant personality. John Cook agrees with this, but with a qualification, '...but not in a domineering way. Louise was content to be "under command"...Ida was the "doer" and "fixer", though you shouldn't construe that to mean that Louise was a shrinking violet; their temperaments and characters were just different'. Doreen Montgomery, who was part of the agency team looking after Ida's romantic fiction and subsequently her memoirs supports John Cook's impression, describing Ida as being 'the face of the sisters'. She went on to explain:

'Via this association, I came to know the sisters personally and to feel the warmth and generosity of their friendship. Their passion for opera was life-long and, after the war, they were always ready and willing to sponsor financially up-and-coming singers, who they regarded as having the right potential, more often than not disregarding their own needs... Two wonderful, selfless women.'

Throughout their remaining years, the sisters continued living in the family home in south London, devoted as ever to each other. It was only when Ida died of cancer in 1986 that Louise moved into the Dolphin Square flat, ending her days in 1991, just prior to her 90th birthday. To the end they remained, as Ida put it, 'Once a star gazer, always a star gazer.'

The sisters had never been involved in any overt political activity, but during their opera trips to Germany and Austria found themselves confronted with the unfolding tragedy of the Jews. Refusing to be bystanders to the events they witnessed, and working against the prevailing mood of apathy, they responded energetically and with great commitment and courage, doing their utmost, in both material and physical terms, to help Jews and others persecuted by the Nazis to escape; and they continued to support them once they had gained safe refuge. Their story is an inspiring testimony of the power of compassion, generosity and goodness of, seemingly, ordinary people in this depressing period of European interwar history.

*

Frank Foley, Bertha Bracey, Nicholas Winton and Ida and Louise Cook were a handful of witnesses of Hitler's rise and the dire impact it had on European Jewry at a time when the world was turning aside, appeasing Hitler and his Nazi Party. Not only did they do their utmost to alert the British authorities and public to what was going on, but they courageously intervened to save tens of thousands of European Jews who otherwise would have perished in the Holocaust.

THE SECOND
WORLD WAR
1939–1945

THE HOLOCAUST

A scene from inside the Warsaw Ghetto, showing trams for Jews that travelled through the ghetto.

Jews who have been rounded up for deportation 'eastwards' endure the long wait at an assembly point in the Krakow Ghetto, 1942.

After the Nazi invasion of Poland and the outbreak of war on 3 September 1939, there was a period of stalemate on the land front – the so-called 'Phoney War'. But it was not long before Hitler turned his attention to the west. In April 1940, Nazi forces invaded Denmark and Norway, and a month later Luxembourg, Holland, Belgium and France; on 1 July it was the turn of Britain's Channel Islands. The next year Yugoslavia and Greece were conquered. By May 1941, Germany dominated the continent of Europe, trapping many foreign nationals within its new borders, including a number of Britons. It also meant that the Nazis were confronted with the problem of dealing with vastly increased numbers of Jews. This is when the medieval practice of separating Jews into ghettos was revived.

The first ghetto had been set up in Piotrkow, Poland, as early as October 1939, following a directive by the Reich Security Police Chief, Reinhard Heydrich. Such segregation gave the Nazis much greater control over the Jewish population, as well as making it easier to exploit Jewish labour for the war effort. By mid 1941 nearly all Jews in Poland had been forced into ghettos. These were to form a model for the network which later spread across the map of eastern Europe. Ghettos in larger towns and cities were usually sealed and guarded, with the population completely cut off from the outside world, apart from a few exit permits granted for those working for the Germans. Jews from surrounding areas and, later, other countries, were forced into these ghettos, which soon became overcrowded and conditions rapidly became increasingly squalid.

In 1940–1941, instead of murdering Jews outright, the Nazis waited for conditions in the ghettos to take their toll.

On 22 June 1941, with 'Operation Barbarossa', the *Wehrmacht* turned eastwards to invade their former ally, the Soviet Union, conquering large tracts of the western part of the country very quickly. In contrast with the less draconian policies initially adopted in western-occupied countries such as Norway, Denmark and Holland, the Poles and Russians were considered, along with Jews and gypsies, *Untermensch* – sub-human; they were to be reduced to a state of abject slavery through erasure of their cultural identity and political autonomy, along with seizure or destruction of their property. Their lands would, in turn, provide the Reich with *Lebensraum* – living space – for the expanding German population. Among all these perceived enemies, Jews were considered a special category, the foremost racial enemy. Now millions more were caught in the Nazi net. As the *Wehrmacht* advanced into Soviet territory, four *Einsatzgruppen* (extermination task forces) followed in its wake, searching out and destroying Jewish communities along the way, often with the help of local volunteers from the traditional anti-Semitic places they swept through, such us the Ukraine, Latvia, Lithuania and Estonia. The form of execution was crude and brutal: initially the victims were forced to strip and line the edges of a prepared pit or ravine into which they would be shot. One million Jews were killed in this way from 22 June until December 1941. But this was not fast or secret enough, and some of the murderers were psychologically affected by killing women and children face-to-face. This is when experimental gas vans were used. The vans and gassing system often broke down and the same psychological problems remained for the troops. Something far more drastic was needed.

At the outbreak of war, the concentration camp system consisted of seven main camps: Dachau, Buchenwald, Sachsenhausen (originally Oranienberg), Flossenburg, Mauthausen, Neuengamme and Ravensbrück, a camp for women and children. With the subsequent occupation of most of Europe these camps were expanded into a network of thousands of camps organised into 23 major categories that criss-crossed the Continent, holding about two million prisoners. The main categories were: *Konzentrazionslager* (KZ or KL), concentration camps; *Arbeitslager*, labour camps; *Durchgangslager*, transit camps. On 20 January 1942, in order to deal with the vast increase of demand, a new, monstrous series of camps, *Vernichtungslager* (extermination camps), was agreed at a meeting of top Nazis held in a villa on the shores of the Wannsee, a lake outside Berlin. All were to be situated in occupied Poland.

The 'Wannsee Conference' was called by Reinhard Heydrich, under the authorisation of Hermann Goering, its aim being to discuss the Jewish question and pursue *Endlösung der Judenfrage* – the 'Final Solution' – the annihilation of Jews. At this meeting, the Jews of all European countries were listed – over 11 million, including 330,000 British Jews, all destined for extermination after 'evacuation to the east'. Fit Jews would be selected for hard labour under conditions likely to cause their eventual death; those not fit for such work would be immediately killed. Four camps, Belzec, Chelmo, Sobibor and Treblinka, were set up strictly for extermination; Auschwitz and Majdanek had dual functions as both concentration camps and extermination camps. The 'Final Solution' was the culmination of a conversation between Hitler and Himmler in December 1941, but the concept had been evolving from the initial intimidation of German Jewry that occurred even before Hitler became Chancellor in 1933.

The decision was made to deal with Polish Jewry first and spread the Final Solution from there. Between 1942 and 1944, Jews in every occupied country would ultimately take their turn at the *Umschlagplatz* (assembly place), for *Aussiedlung* (deportation) to the east. Starting in the spring of 1942, the majority of Polish Jews were transported in locked, overcrowded cattle wagons, mostly without food or water, ventilation or sanitary facilities, to the newly established death camps. After Poland, it was the turn of the *Grossreich* to be rendered *Judenrein*. The period from March 1942 to February 1943 saw the intensification of deportations which then included the Jews of Holland, Belgium, France and Norway. The Nazi attempt to impose the Final Solution on Denmark failed; anti-Semitism there, unlike most other European countries, was not widespread and only 485 were deported to Theresienstadt due to a large-scale Danish effort which conveyed nearly 8,000 Jews to neutral Sweden. From 1943 to early 1944, south European Jewry was dealt with and the Jews of North Africa and Slovakia were next on the list. Finally, in 1944, the Jews of the Axis Allied states – Italy, Romania and Hungary – were targeted.

From the initial round-ups for deportation, the whole system of the 'Final Solution' was based on deception, with the deportees being told that they were bound 'eastwards' for a labour camp and better conditions. On exiting the trains at their destined camp, they were told that they had reached a transit camp en route to the labour camp and had to shower and have their clothes disinfected before moving on, and turn over any cash or valuables they had for safe keeping. They were then hustled toward the 'showers' – gas chambers disguised as such. Once locked in, depending on the location and method used, it took victims from between ten to thirty minutes to die from the poison gas injected into the chamber. Members of the *Sonderkommando* (special detachments of Jewish prisoners) took the bodies from the chamber, examining them closely for any hidden jewels and wrenching out any gold from their teeth. They were then hauled to the crematoria where the bodies were burned, or were buried in huge pits. What happened in the extermination camps between 1942 and 1944 was murder on an industrial scale.

From April 1940, as Hitler's *Blitzkrieg* swept westwards, a number of Britons living in the British Channel Islands, and others trapped in France, Holland, Greece and Hungary, came under German occupation. Despite the severe restrictions and the draconian laws they were forced to live under, there were many who refused to turn aside from what was happening to Jews and other victims of the Nazis, but courageously intervened to do what they could to help, often saving lives at great risk to themselves, and sometimes, their families. The stories of the ten

British men and women that follow are set within this wartime period when the Final Solution was implemented in the countries in which they were trapped. They were to learn a great deal first hand about its terrible reality, three of them enduring its very fulcrum when interned in concentration camps, two paying the ultimate price: death in Ravensbrück and Auschwitz-Birkenau.

German troops marching along Cheapside, St Helier, Jersey after the invasion of July 1940.

A German sentry guards the entrance to a Napoleonic-era fort entrance in the Channel Islands.

THE CHANNEL ISLANDS: JERSEY
1940–1945

With the capitulation of France on 22 June 1940 following the rapid German advance through the Low Countries, Britain faced 'Operation Sealion', the German plan for invasion. The Channel Islands – the main islands of Jersey, Guernsey, Sark, Alderney and Herm, and their three smaller islets – were particularly vulnerable, lying just twenty miles off the Cherbourg peninsula. From the outbreak of war until the spring of 1940, the islands' tourist industry was still advertising with slogans such as 'Jersey – Ideal Winter Resort', and the islanders believed that their homes would be defended. But their confidence was shattered with the news of the German *Blitzkrieg* through the Low Countries and France and they were confronted with a choice: to stay, or evacuate. On 28 June, just before the Germans landed on 1 July, the Channel Islands were bombed in a daylight raid, killing nine civilians and injuring many others.

The Channel Islanders spent four years under German occupation – an experience they shared with France and the rest of occupied Europe. It was the only part of the United Kingdom to be occupied and the invasion was seen by the Germans to be a dress-rehearsal for the invasion of the mainland. It became a 'model Protectorate', treated less harshly than other occupied territories. Just as in France, the Germans preferred to run their occupation of the Channel Islands as far as possible through the existing government authorities which came under the German military authorities, not the SS. The islanders, like others living under occupation, found the experience deeply humiliating and destructive, but, in the main, also wanted to continue as normal a life as possible, concentrating on surviving. But it proved an uneasy and very complex relationship and, like the situation in occupied Europe, many compromised, collaborated and fraternised with their new masters.

Until Paul Sanders published his books on the occupation of the Channel Islands in 2004 and 2005, the issue of collaboration had been to the fore, but his detailed and scholarly analyses present a far more complex picture of the islanders' interaction with their new masters. In many ways the experience of the islanders under occupation was unique: they existed under both the British Crown and the Nazis with their titular government at war with Germany. Also, given the small size of the islands and the vast coastal fortifications as well as hordes of German troops crowding the islands, there developed a particular 'suffocating intensity' compared with other occupied countries. For instance, in Jersey there were more Germans per square mile than in Germany itself; in Guernsey, in an area of approximately twenty-five square miles, there were 20,000 troops and the same number of local people.

All this meant that large-scale organised resistance movements like those in most European occupied countries – France and Greece, for example – were not possible and many islanders were inhibited against resistance in any form by concerns of reprisals that would affect the whole community. Leslie Sinel, a journalist living in Jersey throughout the occupation, explained:

'You couldn't do anything. The place was too small… There was no sabotage comparable with what happened on the mainland because after all, Jersey's only 48 square miles and where could you run to? You could blow up a train in France and be 200 miles away in a couple of hours. And over here the repercussions would have been bad. That's not to say that there were not a lot of irksome things done such as changing round signposts and a lot of pinpricks. The Germans would ask the superior council of the island, the Estates, for something and they'd go along and the Jerseyman would shrug his shoulders and they weren't even sure if he said 'yes' or 'no', he was stalling on a lot of things. So there were a lot of little things, but in the aggregate it gave you a bit of a lift to put one over them. But compared with the sabotage in France it was a different story.'

Despite these unique restrictions, there was an impressive range of resistance on the islands and there were many examples of outstanding individual courage and daring from a diverse range of islanders. At least 170 men and women from Jersey were deported to the mainland of Europe for imprisonment or incarceration in concentration camps, and twenty of these died for their defiance of the Nazis. It is also estimated that 144 people were deported from Guernsey and 47 from Sark.

Jews on the Channel Islands were well aware of the danger the Nazis posed to them, and anticipating the imminent arrival of the Germans, most of those who were able to do so escaped to the British mainland in 1940. Fifty were left after the initial evacuation, mostly elderly or foreign nationals. Only eight of these were deported, five of whom survived. The remainder lived in fear of their lives.

There had been a Jewish community in Jersey since the 19th century when a synagogue was built in 1842, in St Helier. Although this had ceased to be used by the end of the century, Jewish families on the island continued to hold their services in private homes. Most of what we know about the twenty Jews who remained on Jersey comes from the historian Frederick Cohen. His research shows that anti-Jewish policies on the islands followed that of France and all German Orders were registered into the laws of the islands. These covered a number of familiar discriminatory measures such as the registration of persons and of property. The few Jewish businesses initially were ordered to display the sign 'Jewish undertaking' on their premises, but before long they were Aryanised, depriving their owners of any means of support. Jews were prevented from obtaining employment, were prohibited from entering public places or attending places of entertainment, and their hours of shopping were restricted. Jews were also subjected to attack and ridicule by anti-Semitic articles in the German-controlled local press and by anti-Semitic films such as the 1940 film *Jew Süss* which were shown in cinemas; these were specially adapted with English sub-titles.

The first Order came in October 1940 when all islanders with more than two grandparents 'deemed as Jews' were ordered to register as Jews. Just twelve Jews registered on Jersey and four on Guernsey. On 31 May 1941, this Order was redefined as having at least three grandparents of pure Jewish blood. Although the Jersey Bailiff, Alexander Coutanche, and his administration complied with the majority of Orders that followed, the one branding Jews with the wearing of the Yellow Star was considered a step too far and was not implemented – this Yellow Star would have been the only one to bear the word 'Jew' in English. As the occupation went on, gradually the small Jewish community on Jersey became increasingly fearful as they found every aspect of their lives severely curtailed. They had been lured into a sense of false security by the island authorities who complied efficiently with all but one of the Nazi Orders, giving them the appearance of normality. As Esther Lloyd, a Jewish woman who had registered and was subsequently deported, wrote in her diary in transit to the camps, 'Never shall I be honest again. If I had not declared myself, this wouldn't have happened...' In June 1941, Clifford Orange, the chief aliens officer in Jersey, reported that, 'There are no Jews, registered as such, in the island who are carrying on businesses.' This meant that Jewish businessmen, like Nathan Davidson, deprived of their livelihoods, fell into poverty. In Davidson's case this led to his premature death in a mental institution.

There was controversy at the time, and has been since, about the role which the Jersey authorities played on the island throughout the war. The island authorities at first denied that there were any Jews on the islands, but then carried out a thorough investigation, including interviews with those suspected of being Jewish. Robert Le Sueur was very critical at the time but, with hindsight, now thinks they did the right thing:

'They had to make a very difficult decision. They could have simply wrapped up and gone home and said, "That's that," and left the whole responsibility of running the islands to the Germans when things for the civilian population could have been much worse. So they collaborated with the Germans so far, under the terms of the Hague Convention on occupied territories... One knows now that they dug their heels in on issues that seemed important and sometimes got away with it... At the time of course nobody knew. I remember feeling very disgusted that when the Jews had to register and when this notice appeared by command of the occupying forces, it was under a notice from the States of Jersey. And I felt very disgusted on principle that they had been involved in that. Their argument would have been that there were only a handful of Jews on the island and there was much more at stake for the island as a whole. It was absolutely true. I still think on that one they were wrong. But by and large I think they were right... It must have been agonising at times. They were not pro-German. They were trying to do the best for the people who had elected them.'

It is also accepted that although the authorities in the Channel Islands cooperated readily with the German anti-Jewish measures, unlike many other occupied areas, this was not done within the context of traditional anti-Semitism.

During the research for his book, Frederick Cohen was dismayed to find that though much of the documentary material relating to anti-Jewish measures on the islands had been lost or destroyed, it nonetheless revealed the enormous amount of administration needed for such a small number of people. With such a gap in evidence, it is difficult to ascertain the full details of what the Jews of Jersey experienced, but a number were deported in February 1943, and sent to internment camps in France and Germany, and one man, John Finkelstein, survived Buchenwald and Theresienstadt camps. Unlike Guernsey, not all Jews on Jersey were deported: two Jewish half-sisters, Connie le Marquand and Stella Harvey, lived openly as Methodists throughout the war; others survived by going into hiding. Several were taken ill – no doubt the threat of deportation a factor – and died in hospitals on the island and one man, Victor Emanuel, committed suicide in April 1944. A beekeeper, Hyam Goldman, it is rumoured, was retained on the islands by the Germans, because of his much-needed expertise at a time of great sugar shortage. On Guernsey a well-documented case tells how three Jewish women, all foreign nationals – Auguste Spitz, Marianne Grunfeld and Therese Steiner – were transported from the island on 21 April 1942 to mainland France. In July of the same year they became part of the first mass deportation of Jews from Western Europe to Auschwitz-Birkenau. None of them survived the war.

A pitiful and shocking sight that the Channel Islanders could not avoid was that of the lines of starving, bedraggled and weary slave labourers who were forced to build the islands' massive fortifications as well as a large underground hospital in Jersey. These were mainly from Eastern Europe and the Soviet Union, but there were also a number of prisoners from Republican Spain and at least 1,000 Jews. Most were housed in camps on Alderney, but it was those working in Jersey that Leslie Sinel remembered so vividly:

'That was pathetic... Some of them only had rags around their feet and I used to see them down on the south coast there when they were building walls. They would dish them out a drop of goulash in the middle of the day and one felt very, very sorry for them... They came from all over the place, there were some from Spain and there were many Russians. I know a friend of mine tried to help a Russian and it wasn't a very happy experience... It was a great risk. Even going through the town, somebody I know threw a cigarette to one of them and of course the Germans chased this bloke all over the town but he knew the town better than they did and he got away.'

Nearly 400 graves of slave labourers were found on Alderney after liberation. Many more bodies had been dumped at sea.

After the war had ended, twenty Jersey people were recognised by the Soviet Union for risking their lives and their families' safety by giving refuge or support to Soviet escapees from slave labour camps. Among these were three siblings, Ivy Forster, Harold Le Druillenec and Louisa Gould (posthumously). Gould was also among 'The Twenty' murdered by the Nazis, in her case in the Nazi concentration camp, Ravensbrück. Albert Bedane, a physiotherapist from St Helier, was also honoured by the Soviets. Not only had Bedane sheltered several escaped slave labourers, he also took the enormous risk of sheltering a Jewish woman, Mary Richardson.

ALBERT GUSTAVE BEDANE
1893–1980

*'I had a few nightmares occasionally, but I thought that if I was going
to be killed, I'd rather be killed for a sheep than a lamb anyway.'*

Born in Angers, France in 1893, Albert Bedane's family moved to Jersey
in 1894. He served during the First World War as a soldier in the 1/9th
Hampshire Regiment, in India and Siberia. After the war he married, set
up a home and established a clinic in Roseville Street, St Helier with his
wife, Clara, where his daughter Valerie was born. Bedane was Clara's
second husband; she had five children by her first husband, and by the
time Bedane married her, was a wealthy, property-owning widow.
Bedane had been naturalised as a British subject in 1921 and became
established as a masseur and physiotherapist. Before the Nazi invasion,
Clara and Valerie were evacuated to Devon where they spent the war.

When Jews on the island were ordered to register by the end of 1940
most of them, like Esther Lloyd, trusted the island authorities to protect
them, and did so. Others decided to hide their Jewish identity, living as
Christians. Some, including Mary Richardson, went into hiding. Mary was
a Dutch-born Jewish woman, married to a local man, a British sea captain.
She did not register in 1940, but was forced to do so in February 1941 in
order to obtain an identity card necessary for obtaining rations. Her real
name was Erica Olvenich, but she tried to hide her identity by saying that
she was born in British Guiana and her maiden name was Algernon.

Mary became known to the Nazi authorities in June 1943 when she
was interviewed by the *Feldkommandantur* (German civil affairs unit) at
Victoria College. There are different versions of her escape, but it has
been confirmed that she went into hiding on 25 June 1943, under the
protection of Albert Bedane in Roseville Street, after fleeing from a
mandatory visit to a photographers, for official photographs for her identity and registration cards. For over two years Mary was given refuge by

Bedane. His clinic was attached to the family home and was only a few hundred yards from the Richardsons' home where her husband, Captain Edmund Richardson, was still living, feigning senility when the Germans frequently came to question him.

Beneath Bedane's clinic there was a secret three-roomed cellar, less than five foot in height, which was used not only to shelter Mary, but also for several slave labourers who had sought refuge with him. After the first few months, Bedane decided that it was safe for her to move to a room on the upper floor of his home; whenever the clinic was searched, she descended to the secret cellar. With rationing increasingly severe as the war went on, Bedane would ask for payment in kind rather than money from his farmer clients, and in this way he managed to feed everyone in his household without arousing suspicion.

When Nazi soldiers came to his clinic for treatment, as they often did, little did they realise that hiding quietly below them were several Russian slave labourers and one French escapee as well as a Dutch Jewish woman. While in hiding, Mary changed her hair style and, wearing dark glasses, would sometimes sit out in the garden, darting back to the secret cellar whenever danger appeared. She lived in Bedane's cellar until the final weeks of the war when she left to care for her husband, by then a genuine invalid, hoping that with the replacement of German troops over time, she would have been forgotten. It worked: Mary survived the occupation without detection, as did the others given refuge by Bedane.

Bedane was taking huge risks in hiding Mary and other fugitives from the Nazis; notices were regularly published warning islanders of the severe penalties if they aided escapees, and a number of islanders were deported to concentration camps for this. Francis Le Sueur, a non-Jew, who was also hidden by Bedane, testified in 1944, 'Mr Bedane not only helped me for two weeks but sheltered a Dutch Jewess for two-and-a-half years, and he must have known that during all that time he could be caught.' Speaking to the *Jersey Evening Post* in 1970, Bedane told the reporter, 'I had a few nightmares occasionally, but I thought that if I was going to be killed, I'd rather be killed for a sheep than a lamb anyway.'

Like so many of the people honoured by the British Government in 2010, Bedane's courage went unrecognised for most of his lifetime. It was the Soviet government that first showed their gratitude for the risks he had taken, when, in March 1966, Bedane and nineteen other Jersey men and women were presented with gold watches for saving Soviet citizens. The Jersey authorities by that time were less reticent about occupation events than they had been hitherto, and when the representative of the Soviet Embassy arrived on the island for the presentation, he was greeted by Bailiff Robert Le Masurier. In his speech, the Russian chargé d'affaires paid tribute to all the Channel Islanders who had helped his persecuted countrymen at great risk to their own safely, not just those on Jersey.

Bedane died in Jersey in 1980; he had been a widower since 1944, when Clara had died in Britain, unaware of his courageous and compassionate actions. An application was made to Yad Vashem in May 1999 after the discovery of a letter from Mary Richardson thanking him for saving her life; this was sent to the museum by Frederick Cohen, president of the Jersey Jewish congregation. It was this which helped place Bedane among the 'Righteous Among the Nations' in January 2000. His medal and certificate are now on display in the Maritime Museum on New North Quay. In 2005 a banner with his portrait on it was displayed in St Helier to mark the 60th anniversary of the liberation of the Channel Islands. At the ceremony, Frederick Cohen said, 'There is a Talmudic expression that says, "He who saves one man it is as though he has saved the world." Albert Bedane is the epitome of that…'

LOUISA GOULD,
HAROLD LE DRUILLENEC,
IVY FORSTER
1891–1945 1911–1985 1907–1997

*'Then you are coming with me. I have lost one of my boys in the war
and the other is away and I'll try to make up by looking after you.'*

Louisa Gould, Harold Le Druillenec and Ivy Forster were three siblings among the nine children of Vincent Le Druillenec who had arrived in Jersey from Brittany towards the end of the 19th century. Louisa, born in 1891, was the eldest of the three. Their stories of humanity, subsequent imprisonment, torment and, in Louisa's case, murder, by the Nazis, are inextricably linked in a unique family story.

When the Germans arrived in Jersey, Louisa Gould was running the general store at La Fontaine, Millais at St Ouen. She was living alone: her husband had died before the outbreak of war and both of her sons were serving in the British armed forces. Edward, the eldest, an officer in the Royal Navy Volunteer Reserve, was killed in action in 1941. When the Order came for the islanders to hand in their radios, Louisa concealed hers and continued to listen to the BBC, relaying items of news to her customers, friends and neighbours, some of whom would visit her home to listen in.

Like most islanders, Louisa was well aware of the slave labourers working on the fortifications and was horrified by their pitiful state and brutal treatment by the Nazis. But it wasn't until 1943 that she became actively involved in sheltering a Russian escapee from one of the grim labour camps – an act that was eventually to cost her life.

Feodor Buryiv, or 'Bill' as he became known, had been on the run for some months and had been given refuge, along with another couple of escapees, by a local farmer, René le Mottée. They were all forced to flee when the Germans started searching homes in the vicinity of the farm. This is when, in desperation, Bill appealed to Louisa for help. Without hesitation she told him, 'Then you are coming with me. I have lost one of my boys in the war and the other is away and I'll try to make up by looking after you.' This she did and in no time at all this young Russian had become her surrogate son.

Bill, an airman in the Soviet air force, had been taken prisoner by the *Wehrmacht* when his plane was shot down in October 1941 on the eastern front. He had escaped to join a partisan group in the area, but was recaptured at the beginning of the German advance in the spring of 1942. The Nazis categorised Slavs as *Untermenschen*, along with Jews; this meant, as Bill quickly learned, that Soviet prisoners were seen as unworthy of coming under the terms of the Geneva Convention, the usual treatment being starvation to the point of death in the freezing open-air camps until their value as slave labour was recognised. This was performed under the most arduous conditions, with every ounce of hard work being squeezed out of the emaciated, poorly clad men until they expired.

In June 1942 Bill was transported in a large group of prisoners on a long, horrendous journey to St Malo, then by ship to the labour camp Immelman at St Peter, Jersey. A few weeks after his arrival he made another unsuccessful escape attempt for which he received a terrible punishment which ended in the ordeal of having to stand naked in the open all night. Feeling that he had nothing to lose, he was determined to have another attempt at escape and this time did so successfully, in September 1942. As he later explained, 'Better to die on your feet as a man, than on your knees as a dog.'

Harold Le Druillenec, Louisa's brother, was a regular visitor, helping her to hide Bill and teaching him English; he also took the opportunity to listen to her radio. At first Louisa and Bill were both very careful, but over time, Louisa's trusting personality got the better of her, and she started to take only the most basic of precautions, allowing Bill to do odd jobs around the place, even allowing him to serve in the shop occasionally. Louisa sheltered him for 20 months before they were betrayed by a neighbour's anonymous letter to the German authorities – such denouncements were by no means unusual on Jersey, as many islanders resented those who were 'rocking the boat', antagonising the Germans by disobeying Orders and making life difficult. The reward of £100, a great deal of money in those days, was also an inducement. By a stroke of good luck, the letter of denunciation was incorrectly addressed and instead of going to Victoria College House, which housed the German administration, it landed in the hands of the vice-principal at Victoria College who steamed it open, read and readdressed it, creating a day's delay. Meanwhile, Louisa had been tipped off with enough time to hide evidence of Bill's stay as well as her radio.

Unfortunately she wasn't thorough enough and signs of his presence were found, along with her illegal radio. Bill, in the meantime, set off for the Forster home where he was given refuge for a short while until, once more, he was on the run. Ivy Forster had been far more security-conscious than her sister. Her son, Rex, has told how all the family were sworn to silence and lived up to this. Nonetheless she had been denounced by the same letter to the authorities. Like her sister, she had also taken in an escaped Russian prisoner, Grigori Koslov, 'George', and had secreted him in the attic of the family home. When the German Field Police raided her home they also found a concealed radio and a rifle which she had failed to hand in when requested to do so.

The trial of the three siblings took place soon after D-Day, so was accompanied by the sounds of the fierce battles raging in nearby Normandy, adding drama to the event. It ended on 22 June 1944. Louisa was given a harsh two-year prison sentence for her failure to submit her radio and 'prohibited reception of wireless transmissions', as well as 'aiding and abetting breach of the working peace and unauthorised removal', in other words, assisting an escapee. The court failed to prove Le Druillenec guilty of sheltering a prisoner, but he was sentenced to five months' imprisonment on the grounds that he listened to his wireless radio which he had failed to surrender, and to his sister's radio too. Ivy Forster also received a sentence of five months' imprisonment.

The Germans, concerned about the possibility of Allied landings on the islands, were moving people to the mainland very quickly. Soon after the trial, on 29 June 1944, 20 Jersey men and women, sentenced for political crimes, set off as part of a convoy for France, among them Louisa and Harold Le Druillenec. Complications en route meant that they did not disembark in France until the morning of 1 July. They were taken first to Rennes in Brittany from where Le Druillenec was quickly moved to Belfort in eastern France. Louisa was still in Rennes when the railway station was bombed by the Allies and the prison was badly damaged. She was then transported by train to Ravensbrück, the women's concentration camp north of Berlin. The camp at that time contained nearly 27,000 inmates.

Harold Le Druillenec saw his sister for the last time when his carriage stopped next to hers at Belfort station as they were en route to their different destinations and they were able to exchange a few words. It had never occurred to him that he and Louisa might end up in concentration camps, instead of ordinary French prisons. It was only in September 1944 that the Wehrmacht High Command rubber-stamped a new system whereby all prisoners from the western occupied countries could be sent directly to a concentration camp without serving their prison sentence first. This was virtually a handover of power to the Gestapo and SS. It was the fate of this little group of Jersey prisoners that they became victims to the new policy at this final stage of the war.

Le Druillenec's first experience of concentration camp life was at Neuengamme, just outside of Hamburg. Like most concentration camps, Neuengamme was surrounded by a number of subsidiary camps, the labour being drawn from the main camp. The population of the main camp in early 1944 was 12,000; further transports from Poland and Hungary during the summer brought in another 13,000. Most of these were sent to satellite labour camps. Le Druillenec was among them, his destination Wilhelmshaven, a principal naval base, where he was put on forced labour as a welder – demanding physical work for a former headmaster. It was here that he was briefed on the principles of survival in camps: the importance of keeping on good terms with the *Blockalteste* (the block leader), and to avoid judging the 'mad' behaviour of camp life against the standard of normal behaviour. Soon he witnessed many of his fellow prisoners succumbing to illness and dying, all part of the policy of *Vernichtung durch Arbeit* (destructive labour), aided by a starvation diet.

With the Allied offensives gaining momentum, on Good Friday 1945 the camp was evacuated for what proved to be the most terrible part of Le Druillenec's ordeal. Suffering an injured foot, he was loaded on a crowded cattle truck with others – 450 men in four wagons – where he existed for five days and nights without food, water or sanitation. Terrible as this was, it was infinitely better than the plight of those who were able to walk and were forced on one of the notorious death marches. The train was caught up in one of the many raids that interrupted their journey outside Lüneberg, where one of the wagons containing 100 prisoners received a direct hit. Later, when this part of their nightmare journey ended, the 250 survivors were split into two groups; Harold was put with those loaded into lorries and driven to Bergen-Belsen. Although his ordeal there was to prove the most horrific part of his whole internment experience, the alternative would have been fatal: he later heard that the 100 prisoners left behind were executed.

The location of Bergen-Belsen was used as a training establishment for the German army from 1935–1938 and became a prison camp only after this. In 1940 it was used to accommodate 600 Belgian and French prisoners of war. During the years 1941–1942, Russian POWs were interned there, in terrible conditions: in Stalag XIC/311 (one part of the camp), for instance, 11,000 to 14,000 prisoners perished, a record number for any POW camp in Germany. From 1943 it was used as a place to house Jews for possible exchange with Germans interned in Allied countries. Later, another camp was added into which survivors of the death marches were crammed. Conditions deteriorated so badly that by the time the British troops liberated the camp on 15 April 1945, there were 10,000 bodies scattered around and a further 60,985 starving people packed together in filthy, cold barracks without food or water. Norna Alexander, a British Red Cross nurse, spent a period nursing in the camp just after the liberation:

'They were nearly all skeletons, they hadn't eaten for months, they were really gaunt, all their bones were sticking out, they were all in a terrible state. Just at that time there was a doctor who thought he'd like to do a post-mortem and I sort of helped, just fetched and carried as he did the operation, but I remember seeing it. You know that flower 'Honesty', that's sort of silvery? Well their bowel was just like that, almost transparent. He took it out and it was almost falling apart, it had dehydrated because they hadn't had food or drink or anything.'

Although not an extermination camp as such, the prevailing ghastly conditions served this purpose. During the first ten days, the British buried thousands of dead which had been piling up long before their arrival. Frederick Riches, a British ambulance driver, witnessed the mass burials:

'The chap I felt sorry for most was the little chap in the Engineers who was driving the bulldozer which used to dig the holes out.

He used to go right to the end to clear it all out and he was the only one allowed to smoke while he was working because the stench he was creating was terrible. His main job then was to push those who were at the side into the holes.'

Despite heroic efforts by army medical personnel and a group of volunteer medical students from London teaching hospitals, a mass outbreak of typhus occurred between 19 April and 5 May, and nearly 11,000 of the 60,985 inmates alive at liberation died of typhus. At liberation, Le Druillenec was in a terrible state, barely alive. He later described the camp as 'the foulest and vilest spot that ever soiled the surface of the earth'. He was the only British survivor from Belsen.

Ivy Forster had not been deported. After the trial she spent a short time in prison; but she was saved from deportation by Dr Noel McKinstry, the medical officer of the Jersey Public Health Department and the doctor at the General Hospital, who told the Germans that she had tuberculosis and was too ill to be sent to a camp, signing an illegal document to that effect. By the time she had 'recovered' enough to travel, the transports had stopped, and she remained under surveillance in Jersey until the liberation. By all accounts she was a formidable woman, and went on to be the first woman ever to be elected as Deputy in the States of Jersey Government in 1948.

On 8 May, as VE Day was being celebrated on the mainland and in liberated Europe, the Channel Islands were still awaiting liberation. Cut off from supplies after the Normandy landings, many islanders were on the point of starvation. The Germans did not surrender the islands until 9 May, when the arrival of the first British troops in Jersey and Guernsey was greeted with immense joy and relief. Sark was liberated on 10 May, Alderney on 16 May. With the war in Europe over, the relatives of Harold Le Druillenec and Louisa Gould were anxiously waiting to hear what had happened to them. Eventually the first news

Belsen, after liberation: a British Army bulldozer pushing bodies into a mass grave.

came that Le Druillenec had survived and was in hospital in England, but there was a total blank regarding Louisa's fate. It was the arrival of Mrs Tanguy, a survivor of Ravensbrück, who ended hopes of Louisa's return. Mrs Tanguy told the family how she and Louisa had become friends in the camp and teamed up to share the burden of work. Also, how, on 14 February 1945, worn out and ill, Louisa Gould was selected for the gas chamber.

Gassing had only been used as an extermination method in Ravensbrück since the beginning of 1945, shooting being the usual method before this. With the speed of the Russian advance this was deemed too slow, so those selected for death during a daily roll call were squeezed 150 at a time into a small, improvised gas chamber, 29 by 15 feet, and murdered. 2,400 women in all were killed in this way. Mrs Tanguy lived up to the promise that she had made to Louisa before she died: that she would go to Jersey and break the news to Louisa's family.

But the family had more news of Louisa's fate. A letter arrived from a Madame Ballard, who had met Louisa during the journey across France in crowded cattle trucks; it told of her earlier ordeal when travelling from Rennes to Belfort. How, during the 15-day journey, they had received food and water only intermittently when stopping in one of the stations en route. And how, on arrival at Ravensbrück they were put in a barrack with hostile Polish and German criminals from whom they suffered much abuse. The two women, by then firm friends, were separated a month after their arrival. Madame Ballard told the family how Louisa had set an example of courage and endurance in the way that she coped with her suffering.

Harold Le Druillenec's wife, Phyllis, left Jersey for England, to give the support her husband desperately needed. He had survived the war weighing barely five stone and was in a very bad way, mentally as well as physically. He was treated in Epsom Hospital. Like many survivors he was obsessed by food, always ravenous, feeling the need to hoard scraps of food in his locker 'just in case'. Yet despite his debilitating weakness, he returned to Germany four months later to give evidence at the Belsen trial held by a military court in Lüneberg in September 1945. This was an extremely courageous thing to do as he was forced to relive many painful, distressing Belsen-Bergen episodes, often before the very perpetrators of such gross inhumanity. Moreover, on 12 April 1946, three days before the first anniversary of the liberation, Le Druillenec narrated the script for a radio play *The Man From Belsen*, based on interviews of his concentration camp experience that he had given Leonard Cottrell, who wrote the play for the BBC. It received high acclaim. Soon after this Le Druillenec was sufficiently recovered to return to his job as headmaster of St John's School, Jersey. He died in 1985.

Both the Russian fugitives connected to the family survived: they had lived on false papers until the end of occupation thanks to Dr McKinstry. Eventually Bill went back to the Soviet Union. Like all prisoners of war returning after the war, he was treated with suspicion and remained under surveillance for almost twenty years; he was fortunate not to have been sent to a Gulag labour camp, as so many were. Grigori Koslov, on the other hand, was far more wised-up. Although it wasn't easy to escape the clutches of the NKVD, the Soviet secret police, he succeeded after several unsuccessful attempts and, after going into hiding for a time, ended up living in West Germany.

Recognition for the humanitarian service that Louisa Gould, Ivy Forster and Harold Le Druillenec had performed was slow in coming. The relationship between the relatively small number of those who had assisted fugitives on the islands and the majority who had been bystanders, or merely indifferent, was not an easy one and took years to resolve. Among those honoured by the Soviet Union, along with Albert Bedane, were the siblings Louisa Gould (posthumously), Ivy Forster and Harold Le Druillenec and Dr McKinstry. As for the twenty Jersey men and women who had defied the Germans during the occupation, suffering deportation, imprisonment and death for their humanitarian actions, it was not until 1996 that their brave deeds were recognised by their country. On 9 November of that year, a memorial was unveiled by Sir Philip Bailhache, the Bailiff of Jersey, on the New Quay in St Helier.

Vel d'Hiv deportation of thousands of Jews, including 4,051 children, 16 and 17 July 1942. They were all taken to Drancy camp, Pithiviers or Beaune-la-Rolande before being deported to their final destination, Auschwitz.

A view of Drancy camp during the war. The camp was guarded by French gendarmes and came under the Gestapo's section of Jewish affairs. Most of the initial victims, including those from the Vel d'Hiv, died on the long, slow train journey to Auschwitz, due to lack of ventilation, food or water. Those who survived were gassed.

FRANCE
1940–1945

With the defeat of the Allied forces in France on 21 June 1940, the French ministerial delegation was ushered into the same railway carriage that had been used for the signing of the 1918 Armistice, where Hitler and the top leaders of the Third Reich were waiting. The treaty was signed at 6.42pm on the following day for the French by General Charles Huntziger on orders telephoned through by General Maxime Weygand. This Armistice came into force on 25 June and the French military leader, Marshal Pétain, announced to the demoralised French nation over the radio, 'Honour is saved! We must now turn our efforts to the future. A new order is beginning!'

The new order divided France into an occupied zone controlled by the Germans in northern France and the Atlantic coastline, and an unoccupied zone administered by the newly formed collaborationist Vichy regime, led by Marshal Pétain, in central and southern France. German rule in France depended to a large extent on the cooperation of French administrative systems; this meant that fewer than 1,500 German officers and officials were based in France spread over both zones – a great contrast to the situation on the British Channel Islands. In November 1942, the Nazi takeover of the former unoccupied zone formalised what had been the reality for some time: the complete domination of France by the Third Reich, although Pétain nominally continued to run the French state in both occupied and unoccupied zones.

There were about 350,000 Jews in France in 1940, almost half of whom did not have French citizenship. Early in the occupation, the

Vichy government was allowed considerable independence from its German masters. As early as October 1940, without any request from the German authorities, the Vichy authority enacted its first comprehensive legislation on the Jewish question, the *Statut des Juifs* (Statute on Jews). This defined Jews in more radical racial terms than those applied by the German authorities in the occupied zone: Jews were excluded from public service, from the officer corps of the army and many professions; access to many public places was also limited. These anti-Semitic policies were extended to Algerian Jews a few weeks later.

It was the foreign Jews who bore the brunt of the early persecutions and this was to continue throughout the war. Many had arrived in the 1920s and 1930s from Eastern Europe; others had fled south to the unoccupied zone in the wake of the Nazi onslaught on Belgium, Holland and northern France to seek protection from Vichy in the south, only to find that they were subject to the same fierce discrimination practised by the Germans in the north. They were ordered to live under police surveillance in southern villages, or placed in labour detachments in France or North Africa. More than 40,000 were held in internment camps under French control; some of these, previously used for refugees fleeing Franco's Spain, such as Gurs and Rivesaltes, were now used for housing Jews. Three thousand are known to have died of poor treatment during the harsh winter of 1940–1941. In the first two years of war, German treatment of Jews in the occupied zone lagged behind the more enthusiastic efforts of Vichy officials.

The creation of a *Commissariat Général aux Questions Juives* (General Commission on the Jewish Question) in February 1941 was the first serious effort to coordinate Jewish policy in the two zones and for a while the Nazis allowed Vichy officials to take the main responsibility for Jewish policy. But it was not long before the German officials implemented their far-reaching plans for dealing with the Jewish Question throughout France. In May and June 1941 the first round-ups of foreign Jews in Paris began. On German orders, and without demur, the Vichy regime started its round-ups of foreign Jews. In December of the same year the first round-ups of French Jews began.

Within a few weeks of the convening of the Wannsee Conference of January 1942, the programme for the 'Final Solution' in France was started. The first deportations of foreign Jews in France to Auschwitz began on 27 March 1942. The deportation of a convoy of French Jews from the unoccupied zone followed. Deportation of all Jews in France was accelerated from June 1942. On 16 and 17 July a massive *rafle* (round-up) of Jews occurred in which 13,152 were held in the *Rafle du Velodrome d'Hiver* – subsequently known as the *Vel' d'Hiv* – an indoor cycle track in Paris. Of these, 5,802 were women and 4,051 children. Families were split up, never to be reunited. Conditions in the *Vel' d'Hiv* were appalling: there was only one water tap, and there were no working lavatories: of the ten available, five were locked and the other five were blocked. Quaker and Red Cross visits attempted to offer some assistance, but given the numbers this was totally inadequate. Those who tried to escape were shot; others committed suicide.

At an earlier planning session on 2 July, René Bousquet, secretary-general of the national police, had raised no objections to the arrests, his only concern being the 'embarrassing' fact that French police would have to carry them out. A compromise was reached when the promise was made that only foreign Jews would be rounded up. The agreement was ratified by Vichy the following day. This meant that the operation was aimed mainly at Jews from Germany, Austria, Poland, Czechoslovakia and the Soviet Union. The Roman Catholic Church and other religious groups were among those protesting against the *Rafle Vel' d'Hiv* and in September 1942, Pierre Laval, Vichy's head of government, felt obliged to ask the Germans to ease up on their demands for more Jews. He also managed to limit the deportations that continued to being that of only foreign Jews, and was later to argue at his trial in October 1945 that allowing the French police to conduct the round-ups had been a trade-off to protect the lives of Jews of French nationality. The *Rafle Vel' d'Hiv* proved a turning point in French public opinion and by 1943 escape routes had been set up to Spain and Switzerland, and many French individuals and families risked death to shelter Jews. *Vel' d'Hiv* remains today a symbol of national guilt, mainly through the zeal with which sections of the French police cooperated with the Germans.

Although there were many internment camps throughout France, Natzweiler-Struthof in Alsace was the only concentration camp set up by the Nazis on French territory. This included a gas chamber which was used to murder at least 86 detainees, mainly Jews. After gassing them and stripping their bones of flesh, a number of the skeletons were used by a Nazi professor, August Hirt, as a collection of Jewish types and characteristics for the study of race theory.

In August 1944, the last deportation for extermination left France as the Allies entered Paris. Between March 1942 and that date, 100 convoys containing between 80,000 and 90,000 Jews were sent for extermination, mainly from Drancy transit camp, north of Paris, the majority of them non-French Jews. Included in this figure were 8,000 under the age of 13 years; 2,000 of these were less than six years old. It is estimated that only 2,500 of those deported from France survived. Three-quarters of native-born French Jews were not deported, due to the policy of the Vichy regime to 'barter' them for foreign Jews.

For British and Commonwealth passport holders trapped in France in 1940 by the rapid German advance, it was a question of trying to get out by whatever means possible, or going into hiding if they were lucky enough to have the right contacts. If these options failed, it meant detention in one of the internment camps set up for British passport holders. Sofka Skipwith was actually planning her escape when she was arrested on 9 December 1940. She was to spend four years in internment during which she had direct contact with Jewish survivors of the Warsaw Uprising of May 1943, which spurred her into action on their behalf.

SOFKA SKIPWITH
1907–1994

*'This was the heaviest aftermath of the war… One owes it to them
[the murdered Jews] never to let oneself forget.'*

In April 1940 Sofka Skipwith left Britain for what she intended to be a
quick visit to Paris to visit her mother and stepfather, White Russian
refugees, Princess Sophy and Prince Pierre Volkonsky. Little did she
realise that she was about to face what she later described as the 'greatest
catalyst of my life'.

Sofka had already lived through one of the most turbulent events of
the twentieth century, the Russian Revolution, escaping from the
Bolsheviks just in time. But the Nazi occupation of Paris, just weeks after
her arrival, saw her facing arrest and deportation to an internment camp
where she was cut off from her country and family for four years. It was
during this time that she was confronted with the full extent of Hitler's
persecution of the Jews and made the decision to do whatever was in her
power to help them.

Sofka was born on 23 October 1907 into an aristocratic St Petersburg
family. A pampered only child, she was very close to her grandmother,
Olga Dolgorouky. Both her maternal and paternal grandparents were
closely involved with the Tsarist Imperial family; the Tsar's daughters
were known to Sofka and she often played with the young Tsarevich,
Alexei. She was seven years old at the outbreak of the First World War
and although her grandparents and parents were greatly affected, Sofka's
privileged and protected life went on much as before until the Bolshevik
seizure of power in November 1917 drove her, under the protection of
her grandmother Olga, to Yalta for safety. When events became really
desperate she boarded HMS *Marlborough* and left Russia on 19 April
1919 for Britain with her grandmother, her English governess, and
19 members of the Imperial family – 1,170 evacuees in all. It was a

dramatic, historic departure. 'God Save The Tsar' was played as they left the shore; and, as she later wrote, 'that was the end of childhood'; she was then thirteen. Arriving in Portsmouth, via Constantinople and Malta, they embarked on a royal train for Victoria Station in London where they were met by King George V and Queen Mary.

Although life in Britain was relatively austere for the émigré family, they still had the means to live comfortably by British standards, and were able to afford a small retinue of servants in their rented London home in Gloucester Place. Sofka adapted well, especially when she started her formal education at Queen's College in Harley Street. She made friends with young people of her own class and background, from both Russian émigré and English families, and became fully integrated into British socialite life but never losing touch with her Russian hinterland. Her first marriage was to the Russian émigré, Leo Zinovieff, with whom she had two sons, Peter and Ian. The marriage did not last. Soon after her divorce in 1937, she married Grey Skipwith, the eldest son of a baronet, with whom she had one son, Patrick. By that time Sofka had gained the reputation as a beautiful, bewitching woman, highly sexed with many affairs behind her – much later in life, she told Patrick, that she'd had over 100 lovers. She was a woman who never missed a chance for excitement, adventure, travel and romance, even if this meant leaving her children, shocking many of the more traditional people in her circle.

When Sofka arrived in Paris in April 1940, she was 32 and at the peak of her beauty. She had managed to travel there on a British troop-ship, helped by a well-placed male friend who worked for the British Foreign Office. At that time her mother and stepfather were living in penury. Her intention was to stay a couple of months, supporting them by finding whatever work she could, hoping to leave them in a better position. But soon after her arrival, the *Wehrmacht*'s *Blitzkrieg* swept through Europe, into France.

Sofka, like other British civilians, was caught by the speed of events, and she was still in Paris when the Germans arrived, hoisting the

Sofka Skipwith – the 'Red Princess' – on a visit to Oxford in the mid 1950s, to see her son Peter. A copy of this photograph was found by her granddaughter, Sofka Zinovieff, in the files of MI5.

swastika flag over the Eiffel Tower and other iconic places. She soon became despondent: on 9 August she noted in a diary that English civilian men were being interned, and on 23 August that English women had been ordered to report daily to the *Commissionariat* to sign in. It was at this time that she was horrified to witness anti-Semitic actions including attacks on Jewish shops. She became increasingly depressed and panic-stricken, dreading a prolonged separation from her husband and sons. But she was not inactive and was actually in the throes of planning her escape back to Britain via Spain, aided by one of her many Russian émigré admirers, when she was arrested on 9 December 1940.

From the local police station, Sofka and several hundred other British passport holders were driven in open trucks to the Gare d'Este, then locked in a long train which moved slowly eastwards towards Besançon, to *Frontstalager* 142, an ancient seventeenth century internment camp which housed 2,400 women. There she lived in a bug and rat-infested barrack, enduring ghastly living conditions and fed with disgusting food. Despite her robust nature, she soon became despondent.

May 1941 saw the release of many of the inmates; the rest, including Sofka, were transferred to Vittel, or *Frontslager* 121 in north-east France, near Nancy. This was, relatively, one of the more comfortable and hospitable internment camps. It was located in various hotels which had been requisitioned in the pleasant spa town, near Epinol, Vosges. The camp was a paradise compared with Besançon, with spacious grounds, tennis courts, and was adequately furnished with beds instead of straw palliasses, clean sheets and modern sanitation. Although the internees were surrounded with wire fences and were under guard, compared with other internment situations, they enjoyed a certain amount of freedom of movement. Sofka soon sorted out a small attic room for herself which became her treasured retreat. It was in Vittel that she met Madeleine Steinberg, a young woman whom she called 'Rabbit', forming a lifelong friendship with her. To keep themselves sane during the four long years of internment, the pair spent hours in Sofka's little eyrie studying, and having long discussions on the English and Russian authors they read.

The camp's population was very diverse consisting of 48 different nationalities, with ages ranging from small babies to some very old men. It also changed over time: in 1942 a group of Americans arrived; later, 60 Soviet passport holders joined the internees and some French Colonial prisoners arrived as workers. Escapes were rare, but did occur: a young New Zealander and two British women successfully broke out, making their way back to Britain. Mabel Bayliss, a British internee, recalled an unsuccessful case:

'It was always sad to see any internee who had escaped brought back to the camp. We knew she had been imprisoned and punished. Silence enveloped the mystery; we never knew if she had been denounced, or caught at the demarcation line between occupied and unoccupied France. Naturally, when the Germans took possession of the whole country, escape seemed useless.'

Very soon social strata developed, and with so many people herded closely together, relations between the internees were often strained to the limit, the atmosphere charged with rumour, rows and collusion and, with women vastly outnumbering men, lesbian relationships flourished. But there were also obvious advantages of having such a diverse range of people, as it meant the range of skills proved a godsend in combating boredom. As one hears in so many other internment situations, classes were soon started: the nuns took responsibility for teaching the children within the camp; others set up classes for bridge, art, music, dancing, gardening, languages and many other subjects. A library, which started out with about forty books, ended up with 13,500 volumes in all. Mabel Bayliss explained its importance:

'How many monotonous hours were changed into interesting study or reading owing to these books! Receiving about 150 books from an American friend enabled me to carry on a small circulating library of my own... These books were sent to us in parcels of about ten at a time. Of these the German censor would frequently retain one or two; maybe the author was a Jew, or had written an article or book they did not approve of...'

Sofka did her bit by starting a dramatic society and putting on plays by playwrights such as Shakespeare and Chekhov; she also lectured on Russian poetry.

It was in Vittel that Sofka was introduced to Marxism for the first time; and it was through her membership of a small politically motivated group, *la Petite Famille*, that she joined the underground Communist Party. Given her aristocratic background and earlier socialite lifestyle, this seems surprising, but in fact she had started to question the established order of things much earlier. During the Depression she had accompanied her friend 'Douglo' Douglas-Hamilton, the Marquess of Clydesdale, on his election campaign when he was running in Glasgow for the Conservative Unionists. When campaigning for him in Govan, a poor, slum district of Glasgow, Sofka was appalled at the extreme poverty and misery she saw, a striking and disturbing contrast with the affluent lifestyle of her friends, the Douglas-Hamilton family, and the circle to which she belonged. She had also experienced poverty and deprivation first-hand when her first husband, Leo Zinovieff, lost his job in the early 1930s. But it was through the stimulating discussions she had as a member of *la Petite Famille* that she began to find answers to the questions that had worried her since Govan about the injustice she had seen there and the wide gap between rich and poor; and no doubt her thoughts would have returned to the revolutionary events in Russia that she had experienced as a child. As she explained, she had found an ideology that could '...eventually provide mankind with an equitable basis for existence that no theory ever had'.

La Petite Famille had also established links with the local French Resistance. Workmen entering the camp would give the inmates up-to-date news and provide useful items such as wire cutters, essential for escapes. At one time Sofka slept with a pair tucked under her mattress;

and during a search, she put them on a chair, sitting on them as she watched the guards searching her bed. High-ranking German visitors occasionally came to the camp, among them Ribbentrop, the former ambassador to Britain, and Otto Abetz, the German Ambassador to Vichy, France.

Sofka's second husband, Grey, was serving as a rear-gunner in the Royal Air Force at the time of her internment. This was a highly dangerous job, and in early June 1942 her worst fears were realised when she was told that he was 'missing in action'; his death was confirmed in September of that year. This was a severe blow for Sofka: she described Grey as 'the love of my life'. She retreated to her attic, suffering a severe breakdown; her subsequent illness led to her meeting Dr Levy, a Jewish doctor interned in Vittel, and eventually to her support and rescue of Jews.

Dr Levy was also connected to the French Resistance. In their many talks during her medical treatment, Sofka began to learn of the humiliation and degradation he had suffered as a French Jew, and his fear for his wife and child in hiding, as well as the threat of deportation hanging over him. Then, in the spring of 1943, a group of 280 Jewish prisoners – men, women and children – suddenly arrived. They were interned well away from the Grand Hotel, in the Hotel Providence – an irony not lost on the new arrivals. These were Polish survivors of the Warsaw Ghetto which had been totally destroyed after the Jewish uprising there in April and May of that year. They were emaciated, weak and terrorised. Pictures drawn by the children gave some idea of what they had been through: horrendous scenes of shooting and sadism including people being thrown out of tall buildings in the ghetto. Many of them had been issued with papers for emigration to Latin American countries, or were expecting documents from Zionist organisations for Palestine. Itzhak Katzenelson, the poet, and his son Ivi were among the group. Itzhak was bewildered by the seeming normality of the camp in stark contrast with the sordid, brutal and hopeless situation they had lived through in Warsaw. Before he was deported in 1944, he buried his epic poem, *The Song of the Murdered Jewish People*, placed in bottles, in the grounds of Vittel; later it was taken to Israel. Katzenelson was murdered in Auschwitz.

Sofka was regaining her health and former energy when the Jewish prisoners arrived; she was deeply shocked at their pitiful state, and spent more and more of her time with them, desperately trying to help. She struck up a close friendship with one of the Poles, Izidor 'Izio' Skossowski, whose wife had perished and who was accompanied by his mother and daughter, Visia. Rabbit joined Sofka in giving English and French lessons to many of the Jews hoping this might aid their survival if a chance to escape occurred. All the while the two women were learning about the torment the Jews had endured, as well as their continuing fears. As Sofka wrote, 'For the first time we heard of the deaths by torture, by starvation, the floggings, the humiliations.' One baby who arrived with the Poles had been rescued alive from the notorious extermination camp, Treblinka. The child had been thrown into the burial pit with its dead mother, but someone with a spark of life left had pushed its little body to the surface. The child's cries were heard by a Polish peasant and miraculously it had ended up in Vittel. Sofka was spurred into action by what she heard and decided to get news of the Poles to the outside world. In order to do this, and make their situation credible, she copied lists of their names in minute writing on to flimsy cigarette papers, concealing these into a capsule that could be easily swallowed if necessary, and passing it to the Resistance for safe passage to a trusted authority.

In April 1944 a train with boarded-up windows arrived at Vittel. This caused great anguish among the Jewish inmates: they knew it as a clear signal for deportation and death. Panic spread and there were many suicide attempts, three successful. Mabel Bayliss witnessed the pitiful state of the survivors:

'One night and early morning stretcher after stretcher was carried to the hospital. Some had poisoned themselves, others had cut arteries, one woman threw herself from the fifth floor window…

these events caused a general depression in the camp and from bad to worse news leaked out. All the Poles, dying and dead, were quickly hurried from the camp and none of us knew the exact number of suicides. How thankful we were to be British.'

Many of Vittel's inmates seem to have treated this as an unavoidable tragedy, or with indifference; others were keen to help. The Resistance rallied, offering to take a number of the children. Sofka immediately wrote several letters to her mother's old friend, Jock Balfour, at the British Foreign Office, and other likely places, appealing for help for the desperate Poles. She also tried, without success, to get the camp's inmates to sign a petition to save the remaining Jews. The arrival of a second boarded-up train a month later added to the despair and panic among the Jews – the sight of the SS on the scene removed any doubts about their likely fate. The Jewish section of the camp was sealed off. Sofka begged Izio to hide but he refused to leave his mother and Visia, who was ill in hospital. They were all deported with the rest, Visia being seized – with other sick people – from the hospital, some still bleeding, into a waiting van to join the deportation. All these terrible events were witnessed by a heart-broken Sofka who felt that all her efforts to help had been in vain.

During the months that followed, Sofka and Rabbit sheltered frightened Jews who had escaped deportation in their rooms, and took food and other necessities to those hiding within the Casino complex. One of their most satisfactory rescues was smuggling a baby out. The child had been born just before the second deportation. His mother was seized, but somehow the baby was missed. The rescue was a small team exercise: Dr Levy sedated the child, wrapping him up within a Red Cross box; Sofka and Rabbit took the box to the wire fence. They had cut the wire in advance and when the time came, it was Rabbit, the smaller of the two, who made it through the fence to hand the baby to a woman from a nearby village. The child survived the war and eventually went to Israel where he ended up on a *kibbutz*.

As a war widow and mother, Sofka had been offered repatriation to Britain in 1943. But she had heeded the Communist Party's advice to remain and continue to help the Polish Jews. Once the Jews had departed, a depressed and miserable Sofka applied to go. She was in the first group of 900 British passport holders repatriated in July 1944, a month after the Allied invasion of Normandy. Again she had written lists, this time the names and addresses of relatives of the deported Jews; these were concealed within the clothing of other, more law-abiding, returning internees – by this time Sofka was regarded with great suspicion by the German authorities due to her championing of the Jewish internees. Even during the long journey to Lisbon, she found the chance to ingratiate herself to the SS guards, gaining their trust and picking up valuable information which, together with messages from the French Resistance, she passed on to Jock Balfour who was waiting for her in Lisbon.

London was experiencing flying bomb raids when she returned. She was disoriented, homeless and still grieving for Grey. But ever resilient, she recovered sufficiently to start work again. After reunions with her sons and friends, she returned to the job she had taken after her divorce in 1937, as private secretary to Laurence Olivier at the Old Vic theatre company. When the war ended, the company travelled, under ENSA's (Entertainments National Service Association) auspices, to Hamburg. It was during her time in Germany in the immediate aftermath of war that she visited Belsen. At the time information on the dreadful emaciated, near-death state of the inmates, and piles of dead bodies, on liberation was foremost in the news, and although barred from entering the camp because of the typhus which had broken out, she was able to see for herself, just looking through the wire, the skeletal figures and grim huts and learn something of the ordeal her Polish Jewish friends had suffered.

It was at this time, back in London working with the Oliviers, that Sofka started up her famous 'Saturday soup parties', in her Chelsea home, which attracted all manner of artistic bohemian people who brought colour and stimulation back into her life; members of the British Communist Party would also appear. Sofka had joined the Party on her return to England and helped run the Chelsea branch. She soon attracted the attention of MI5, which held files on her activities. These were later searched out by her granddaughter Sofka Zinovieff after her grandmother's death. Some of the comments were spot on: 'This woman is outstandingly intelligent, courageous and active. She is a brilliant linguist with vast contacts in all spheres... She is an invaluable recruit for the Communist Party and should be watched.' Another reported, '...she is over sexed and this has led her to having many affairs.'

MI5's interest in Sofka grew apace from the 1960s, when group visits were permitted behind the Iron Curtain and she had joined the newly formed Communist travel agency, Progressive Tours. As a very well informed and stimulating guide, she escorted groups to many of the previously inaccessible Eastern European countries as well as her country of origin, then the Soviet Union, where she was warmly, even royally, received, re-establishing old family links and visiting many of her old haunts. It was during one of her tours that she met the Communist and trade unionist, Jack King, who became her partner until she died in 1994 at the age of 86. They spent the last decades of their lives together, retreating from city life to a small cottage on Bodmin Moor, delighting in the isolation and peace, tending their garden and animals, with Sofka at last gaining the stability that had eluded her since her exile from Russia in 1919. Rabbit, with whom Sofka had kept in touch, was a frequent visitor. They would often mull over their Vittel experiences, especially the times spent with the Polish Jews, agonising over their likely fate. With new information on the horrors of the Holocaust gushing forth since the Eichmann trial of 1961, both Sofka and Rabbit became interested to the point of obsession with the horror of the 'Final Solution' of which they had seen a small part, discussing it endlessly.

Eventually, via their old Resistance contacts, they heard details of what had happened to the Jews from Vittel; how 35 had avoided the deportations of 1944, two men had escaped safely to Switzerland, some remained undetected in hospital, and the rest went into hiding until liberated by the Americans at the end of 1944. As for the fate of the

Poles who had not escaped deportation, Rabbit spotted their names on a transport from Drancy transit camp, near Paris, to Auschwitz. They had evidently all been shot on arrival, after one of the women bit the hand of a Nazi officer. Among them was Izio and his family. Sofka wrote, 'Surely a death more merciful than the march to the gas chambers, the suffocation by Cyklon B.'

It was only towards the end of her life that Sofka heard that some of the desperate measures she had taken to save the Jews had been successful. Research carried out by Dr Abraham Oppenheimer, from the London School of Economics, revealed that her efforts had borne fruit and 50 of the deportees from Vittel had made it to Palestine; confirming the names she had so meticulously written down was an important factor. He explained how her letters to the Foreign Office and Red Cross via the Resistance meant that those with Palestinian papers had survived, due to the pressure exerted on the Nazis.

In her autobiography, published in 1967, Sofka wrote: 'Now we are the ones who read all the books about the camps, about the ghettos… This was the heaviest aftermath of the war… One owes it to them never to let oneself forget.' Sofka never forgot, nor did she let others forget, remaining to the end a powerful witness against the Holocaust deniers.

SISTER AGNES (CLARE) WALSH
1896–1993

'Sister Agnes and Sister Granier remain for me
symbols of sweetness, candour, calm and good will,
unusually associated with courage and determination.'

No two characters could be more different than the colourful, bohemian Sofka Skipwith, and the Carmelite nun Sister Agnes Walsh, who had lived her life in the seclusion of a Catholic convent, devoting her life to God and to the welfare of others. Yet these two women had something very precious in common: their service to humanity. It is probably due to the retiring nature of convent life and work that far less is known about Sister Agnes than many other 'Heroes', and she remains something of an enigma.

It is known that Ada Valinda Walsh was born in Hull in 1896 and joined the Daughters of Charity of St Vincent de Paul in 1916 when she was given the name of Sister Agnes. She had been placed in Ireland with her order, serving from 1917–1924 first in Dunmanway, then Pelletstown until 1932, when she moved to Jerusalem. She had been mistakenly issued with an Irish passport when leaving for Palestine, which later turned out to be a fortuitous mistake. While showing a visiting nun around Bethlehem in 1934 Sister Agnes fell down some stone steps and was injured seriously enough to be hospitalised for a while.

When well enough to travel, she went to France for further treatment and convalescence. She was in France when the Second World War started and rather than declare her British nationality, which would have meant internment along with other nationals like Sofka Skipwith, she continued her work in Paris and Andernos-les-Bains in Bordeaux, confident that as Ireland was a neutral state, her Irish passport would get her through. In 1940 she travelled to a small St Vincent de Paul community, in the beautiful Dordogne village of Cadouin, in the unoccupied zone, where it was felt that she would be less conspicuous and could live and work in relatively safety.

Sister Agnes settled happily in Cadouin as '*Soeur Assistante*' – deputy to the Mother Superior, Sister Louise Granier, helping Sister Louise and twelve other Sisters run a school for between thirty and fifty country girls aged from ten to thirteen, where they were taught the basic skills considered necessary for being a good farmer's wife. Sister Agnes, as well as teaching some of the practical classes, also ran an art class, teaching the girls to draw and paint. As the war went on and food became scarce, the Sisters were encouraged to raise chickens, rabbits and pigs, and the convent could boast of rearing the only boar in the village. The parents of the students were asked to pay at least part of the fees in meat, vegetables and fruit.

After the Germans occupied the whole of France in November 1942, Sister Agnes's situation became more vulnerable. Sister Louise feared that someone in the area might denounce her to the Germans. It was at this point that Sister Louise arranged with a communist member of the Resistance, known as 'The greatest bandit in Cadouin', to whisk Sister Agnes away on the back of his motorbike should the Germans come looking for her. Sister Louise later said, 'He was very proud that I had chosen him and I knew I could count on him.' This plan was never put to the test, but it does leave a lovely image of a Sister in a nun's full habit, astride a motorbike speeding down a country road.

About fifteen months after the unification of France, in the spring of 1944, Sister Agnes answered a telephone call to the convent. The call came from Pierre Cremieux, a Jewish man who was desperately appealing to the convent for refuge for himself, his wife and small children who were in imminent danger of arrest and deportation. Without hesitation he was told to bring his family to the convent immediately, which he did.

As the law demanded, the Cremieux family had declared themselves as Jews in 1940, but they rapidly realised the danger of remaining in occupied France and had illegally crossed the line which divided occupied and unoccupied France, moving to Villeneuve-sur-Lot, north of Toulouse, in 1941. In spite of the German occupation of the entire country in November 1942, they had lived there in relative safety until 1944 when Jews and Communists were being openly hunted and arrested by the French police. This forced the remaining Jews to look for safer places of refuge. Alain Cremieux, in a letter to the St Vincent de Paul Community in 1993, explained why his father had decided to seek refuge for his family in the convent:

'My father had met Sister Granier fifteen months earlier while both were waiting for a train on the platform of a railway station. Trains were irregular and I suppose people used to talk to each other more easily than today. This was in fact the very day of the invasion of southern France by the Germans. The threat had caught up with us.'

Sister Louise had apparently expressed her hopes that now the country was unified, things might improve. Cremieux disagreed, informing her of the reality of the anti-Semitism going on around the country and moves against the Jews. Alain continued the story, 'When my father asked whether we could come to Cadouin, the answer was immediate: "*Et bien, venez!*" (just come). To appreciate this at its just value one should not forget that, at the time, helping a Jew was a crime.'

Madame Cremieux arrived at the convent with their twins of nine months, Jean-Pierre and Colette, and, Alain, then six. The family's true identity was not revealed to the other nuns: Madame Cremieux was introduced as a distant relative of Sister Louise, who needed a good rest after the birth of the twins. She was given a room above the laundry with the babies. The family had to pass as Christians and attend Mass on Sundays. Alain, being male, was given refuge in the local presbytery with a priest. Sister Agnes would visit, giving him English lessons.

A huge advantage was that the family were French Jews, totally assimilated with French culture and language, as Alain explained:

'Many Jews living in France at the time would have been betrayed by a foreign accent or just their ignorance of the French culture and the Catholic religion which was familiar to us and part of our daily environment. My father remained in Villeneuve-sur-Lot. He used to come for weekends and tried to help the Sisters in all the minute things which are difficult to do or get during war and restrictions.'

Sister Agnes and Sister Louise did their utmost to shelter the family from the terrors of both the Germans and the French police who, until the very end of hostilities, were still rounding up Jews for deportation and the death camps.

The Sisters were certainly taking great risks – if caught, the Jewish family would have been deported to certain death, and their protectors would be severely punished. If Sister Agnes's true identity had been revealed, she would probably have joined the deportation to a death camp. Her British identity had always been a real risk to the convent community, as she was in effect an enemy alien. Her real identity was suspected by many in the region – she only had to open her mouth to reveal this. It is known that one day Sister Agnes was accosted sternly by a local man who knew her and said, 'Sister, you are not Irish. You are English, aren't you?'

Alain describes how the Resistance was active in the area and how there were numerous skirmishes between them and the Germans who, on one occasion, threatened to burn the village. A wave of arrests happened towards the end of the family's refuge in the convent including those of two prominent locals who were members of the Resistance. The convent then received a phone call from Colonel Delluc, the adjutant to the mayor and a friend of Sister Agnes, warning that their 'friends from Paris' had better get out before the Germans came for an inspection. The family left immediately, although the threat never materialised. The Cremieux family returned to Villeneuve-sur-Lot, joining their father, Pierre, and went into hiding there. The whole family survived the war and finally managed to get to the United States.

Alain Cremieux recounts how Sister Agnès met some British soldiers towards the end of the war who appeared in the town: 'They were surprised and delighted to find an interpreter.' No doubt she was equally delighted to meet some of her countrymen. He also explained how shocked the Sister was by some of the arbitrary acts of violence towards 'collaborators' she saw and heard of, including the case of Maurice Chevalier, the famous French singer whom she admired.

After the war Sister Agnes remained in the convent for a while before leaving for Epinay-sous-Sénart, a village near Paris where she continued her humanitarian work in an old people's home. In 1967 she returned to the British Province of the Community of St Vincent de Paul. As there was another Sister Agnes in the house, and to avoid confusion, her name was changed to Sister Clare. She served in London, first in Ladbroke Grove between 1967–1970 and then in Ealing in 1980, greatly beloved by the young children she taught at various times. She died in 1993 in the Mill Hill community.

The Cremieux children never forgot the kindness of the Sisters who certainly had lived up to the name of their community – The Daughters of Charity – and the risks they took in sheltering them. They corresponded with Sister Agnes (now Clare) for the rest of her life. Alain, who was attached to the French Embassy in London, visited her regularly when she lived in Ealing, giving her the chance to meet and know his children. As Alain has written, 'Sister Agnes and Sister Granier remain for me symbols of sweetness, candour, calm and good will, unusually associated with courage and determination.'

German parachutists dropping on The Hague during the invasion of Holland, May 1940.

HOLLAND
1940–1945

At dawn on 10 May 1940, German airborne troops were dropped behind the Allied lines in Holland, in order to secure vital installations. The ensuing battle lasted for three days, during which Rotterdam was flattened by repeated bombing raids – a taste of what was to come in Western Europe. With Utrecht about to fall, the Dutch surrendered on 14 May.

Although the Nazis claimed that they were not planning any anti-Jewish measures when they occupied the country in May 1940, a series of discriminatory decrees began to appear as early as October of that year. By April 1942, these had led to Jews being deprived of their livelihoods and property, required to wear the Yellow Star of David when in public places, and virtually isolated as outcasts from the rest of the population. By the end of July 1942 over 6,000 Jews were in German hands, many of these arrested in mass raids for deportation. The last mass raid, on 23 September 1943, captured a total of 10,000 Jews. From 1943 until the end of the occupation German police continued to arrest individual Jews wherever they could be found.

There were four main concentration camps within Holland. Barneveld was the camp where about 700 prominent Dutch Jews were interned: musicians, professors, artists and other eminent people with by far the best conditions. Amersfoort, a transit camp for political prisoners, was a dreaded place in which thousands of Dutch Jews were imprisoned and tortured. Westerbork, which had been founded before the Nazi occupation to house refugees fleeing westwards, served from 1942–1944 as a transit camp for Dutch Jews before they were deported to the camps in

German-occupied Poland. Trains, in which Jews were packed liked cattle, left regularly for the east every Tuesday from July 1942–1944. Vught, a concentration camp in the south, was also used for the deportations.

The German deportations utterly devastated the Dutch Jewish community. The Nazis' efforts to ethnically cleanse Holland of Jews were even more effective here than in the other occupied countries. Of the approximate 140,000 people registered in 1940–41 as *Volljuden*, 'full Jews', 107,000 were deported to the east. Of this number, only a pitiful 5,450 returned after the war. Eighty per cent of the Jews targeted for extermination were liquidated. This was the largest percentage in any western territory (with the exception of Norway which contained a very small group of Jews). A major factor in this high death rate was that Holland, like Norway, was administered by a party functionary, the fanatically anti-Semitic Austrian, Arthur Seyss-Inquart, who whole-heartedly supported the Nazi extermination policies and executed them with ruthless efficiency. The large numbers of Dutch collaborationist organisations such as the *Groene Politie* (Green Police), which was heavily involved in the round-up of Dutch Jewry, and the significant number of Dutch sympathisers to Nazi ideology also gave the SS a free hand compared with other occupied western states which came under the authority of military administrations, and whose priorities usually lay in matters other than the persecution of the Jews.

The general Dutch population accepted the persecution of Jews as an inescapable and inevitable aspect of the regime, distasteful though it seemed to many; most Dutch people were concerned with the business of survival, often dealing with severe food shortages. In striking contrast, thousands of Dutch citizens did risk their freedom, and their lives, in attempting to help their persecuted fellow human beings. In 2010, 5,009 Dutch men and women formed the second largest group of holders of the title 'Righteous Among the Nations', outnumbered only by the Poles. This is a significant figure given the submissiveness of such a large proportion of the population. Queen Beatrix, when speaking to the Israeli Knesset in 1995, paid tribute to the Dutch men and women who had risked everything to save Jews, noting not only their brave resistance, but admitting, 'They were the exceptional ones.' Among these 'exceptionals' were Henk Huffener, a Dutch youth who had joined the Resistance, and June Ravenhall, a British woman, living in Holland with her family.

Henk Huffener

HENRICUS 'HENK' HUFFENER
1923–2006

'You are a shining light amidst the darkness of the Holocaust,
your stunning bravery is a testament to all humanity.'

Henk Huffener was a Dutchman, born in Utrecht, who moved to England in 1950 and lived there for the rest of his life. He was originally part of a family of nine children, living with his father Hendrik and stepmother Tien. His father worked as the site manager of a large, ultramodern tuberculosis sanatorium on the outskirts of Bilthoven; the substantial family home was situated within its large grounds, in an isolated spot. It was an ideal place for hiding Jews and other fugitives from the Nazis, with the added deterrent of being within the vicinity of the sanatorium – tuberculosis was at that time a much-dreaded, contagious disease. Theirs was a close, happy and cultured family and Huffener was particularly attached to his elder sister Ann, and younger siblings, Joep and Francisca.

At dawn on 10 May, the family was rudely awoken by the sound of Junkers transport planes dropping German troops in the opening stages of the invasion. The Nazi occupation which followed had an immediate impact on the young Huffener's life. To begin with, he had to leave school where he was already excelling in art and, more dramatically, he became actively involved in the burgeoning Dutch Resistance. His father had been anti-Fascist from the mid 1930s; as an active member of the Resistance when it started, Hendrik encouraged his older children to join and before the war ended, all the Huffener family were involved in supporting and rescuing Jews. The isolated situation of their home proved ideal for meetings which were held regularly from 1941, often under the guise of musical evenings.

Huffener, by his own admission, was a precocious youth; from his early years he was gregarious, with an avid interest in ideas, and by the time war started was already showing signs of being an accomplished artist. He also had a large and diverse circle of friends which included many artists, poets and painters as well as Quakers, Protestants, atheists and Jews. He had made friends with Betty Cadbury, a Quaker from Birmingham. She had married Kees Boeke who ran a progressive board-ing school – the Werkplaats School. The couple introduced Huffener to an interesting group of people including the British MP Fenner Brockway, the Quaker Corder Catchpool and the publisher Victor Gollancz. Brockway and Catchpool, two well-known pacifists, had been imprisoned as conscientious objectors in the First World War. It was Huffener's contacts with this group that proved such a formative influ-ence on his left-wing politics and intellectual life, especially Betty Cadbury whom he said made him 'an ardent pacifist'. Although his family was staunchly Catholic – one daughter became a Trappist nun – Huffener was not religious.

On the staff of the Boekes' school were two German Jewish teachers, refugees who had joined them in 1940. In 1941, when the Nuremberg Laws were introduced in Holland, it became forbidden to employ them. Betty, being English, was known to the Nazis and she soon became concerned about the amount of incriminating material she had pertain-ing to Jews. Huffener came to her assistance with his handcart, removing the papers and books and concealing them in safe places.

During the early months of the occupation, Ann Huffener was installed in a country 'safe' house near the Huffener home, to set up and run, together with her husband Jeff Le Jeune and brother Joep, then only 15, a daring escape route to Switzerland, Spain and Portugal. This became a covert reception centre and hostel where Dutch politicians, diplomats and others wanted by the Dutch government in exile in London, were hidden until their travel arrangements were made. Later, Allied airmen shot down over Holland, and other escapees from the Nazis, also became part of the escape route which had grown increas-ingly risky; if caught, all of those involved would have been interrogated under torture and executed. Secret documents concerned with military installations, troop movements and the like, were also smuggled out in micro-photographed form, by the same routes.

During the war the scheme expanded to involve 50 couriers working in relays; Ann gathered the material and packed it for despatch. Huffener was involved with gathering intelligence for this for a while and proved adept at learning of German troops' movements and installations: 'Although I was then 19 and looking 15 and going around with a big Belgian Shepherd dog called Max, I chatted up the army officers with a mobile communications outfit, a high-tech part of a signals corps, using radio telephones and transmitters. They fed the dog with scraps while I looked around...' In other situations, he would often behave like the village idiot, amusing the Germans who would drop their guard before this seemingly funny and stupid boy. Initially, the rescue of Jews was not involved in Ann's operation, but in 1942 Huffener persuaded his sister and Jeff to include them in the scheme. As he explained:

'By this time we had the first signs of serious persecution. They had begun to round Jews up from their own homes and they had established two camps, one in the south at a place called Vught, and one in the north, near the German border, called Westerbork. And they started to intern Jews waiting for the camps in Germany to be ready for them. Eventually most of them went to Auschwitz, but also to other camps.'

Ann's successful escape route functioned until the southern part of Holland was liberated in 1944. As Huffener explained in a letter to his daughter, Clare, 'At the last count it was established that Ann harboured at least 60 people, Dutch and Allied aircrew plus a smattering of spies who had originally arrived on their native land by parachute.'

Another very important aspect of Huffener's rescue work concerned a Zionist *kibbutz*, known as the Molenwaard. It had been established in Loosdrecht in 1938 after *Kristallnacht*; the members were young Jewish refugees from Germany hoping eventually to reach Palestine. They had enjoyed two years of peace before their former persecutors appeared creating 'a nightmare re-lived'. Knowing full well their fate if taken by the Nazis, they contacted all non-Jews known to them as trustworthy for help when the time came to flee the *kibbutz*. As Jews in urban areas were given top priority by the Nazis, they were safe for a time; but it wasn't long before they were tipped off by a member of the Jewish Council in Amsterdam to get away within a month, or they would be sent to Auschwitz. Huffener was connected with the group and when the decision was made to vacate the *kibbutz*, he and other members of the Resistance organised their rescue. He had the task of escorting them singly, or in small groups, to places of refuge which had been found. The escapees and their rescuers were dressed for a healthy hike or cycle ride in the country – activities that would win the approval of the exercise-obsessed Germans.

Huffener was just congratulating himself that things were going according to plan when he was asked to accompany Mira Weinberg, a somewhat difficult young woman, to her new home. Mira was reluctant to leave the *kibbutz* where she had felt safe and happy, and Huffener became increasingly anxious, impatient with the delay she was causing, ever conscious of the curfew then in place. When they eventually set off on their bicycles, it was 'in icy silence'. En route, as they rode along, they spotted a group of soldiers ahead. Seeing that they were about to be waved down by two SS, the ever quick-witted Huffener hastily dismounted, urged Mira to do the same, grasped her in his arms and, to her astonishment and obvious dismay, kissed her, watched by the two SS. As one of them approached, Huffener continued to brazen it out, and in answer to the SS's questions, told him that they had forgotten the time as they were enjoying themselves so much, and that being so late returning home, her family would be furious. The German, having used his imagination as to what they had been up to, roughly told them to '*Geh los!*', 'Get away'. As Mira had no identity card, it would have been very serious for both of them had they been apprehended.

Soon after this, he was asked to deliver a letter to Mira's parents who were then living in the *Judenviertel* (Jewish district, a euphemism for 'ghetto') in Amsterdam and who were greatly relieved to hear that she was in safe hands. The conditions they lived in appalled him, and spurred him on to great efforts:

'I looked around the dreary room. An old steel watch hung on a nail above the fireplace instead of a clock. The only light bulb in the room was shielded by a crooked black paper shade. Packed and labelled cardboard boxes stood incongruously around the room. Bright areas of the faded wallpaper surrounded by dark, dusty lines were evidence of earlier pictures. Even the chair I sat on was unsteady. Ill at ease, I wandered to the window and looked out over the quiet, almost deserted bleak street. An old bearded Jew stepped out of the house opposite but did not venture far. Four doors away, he tapped on the window and was swiftly let in... Two men in a sinister black car with German name plates drove slowly past. The menace was never far away...

Leaving the poor couple, I made up my mind to help any Jews while it was still possible. The miserable place would come back to haunt me; three times unforeseen events had drawn me within its enforced boundaries... It bothered me that [apart from the member who tipped off the *kibbutz*] the rest of the Jewish Council did not seem to appreciate what disastrous fate awaited the people they were leading. Complacency, apathy and denial that it could ever happen to them, made them obey and cooperate with orders which had been devised to destroy their flock.'

Huffener found it impossible to understand why the Jews cooperated with the Jewish Council, '...which made the Jews register, they were responsible for supplying identity cards with a great 'J' stamped on them, they made Jews wear yellow stars that had to be sewn on their clothes. And in the end they saw to it that they were gathered in ghettos'.

He approached Professor Polak of the Jewish Council, confronting him with his fears regarding the compliance of the council with Nazi orders, only to be told that these were unfounded. But Huffener thought otherwise: 'All the Nazis really intended, however, was to deceive the Jews, who lived in hope, but were to die in despair. My pleading was to no effect.' But undeterred, 'I went around warning Jews not to play along with the council any more and to get away from the ghettos as far as possible, and that there were still opportunities to hide... [But] they tended to trust the Jewish Council, apart from the German Jews who said, "they're crazy – don't take any notice of them at all".'

It was a rescue connected with the Da Costa family that stretched Huffener's resourcefulness to the full. During preparations to move them from one refuge to somewhere safer, a home had to be found for Elly, their young Down's syndrome daughter. Ann came to the rescue through a trustworthy psychiatrist she knew, who was in charge of a home for disabled children and who agreed to take Elly. It was Huffener's job to take Elly there on the pillion of his bike; she arrived shrieking with laughter from the excitement of the ride.

A far more difficult task for Huffener was when he was called on to help Bep and Mani Aalsvel, the Da Costas' daughter and son-in-law. The couple had escaped from Amsterdam to Arnhem with their baby daughter, but Mani was recognised by a neighbour who betrayed them to the German authorities. They escaped out of the back door of their home just before the Germans arrived, and were in desperate need of safer accommodation. Huffener had found them a temporary refuge with some trusted friends in the Bilthoven area, but the problem was the child, whose cries would inevitably endanger them all. Finding safe places for babies was always very difficult, but he managed to find a foster home and, with his girlfriend Katja, took the baby there by train. Hans, the Aalsvels' little toddler son, being fair and blue-eyed, proved easier to hide.

Many of those in hiding were completely dependent on the Resistance; as Huffener explained, 'I used to go around and see to it that they had adequate food, and also that they had the means of getting food, somebody to get their ration cards for them and to go out and do their shopping.'

A Jewish family have just been arrested and leave their house in Amsterdam for deportation to a concentration camp in Poland.

Money was also needed for the rescue work. Huffener would call on eminent and wealthy Jews in hiding who, as well as helping with funds, enriched his ever culture-hungry life with their stimulating conversation. Eddy Salm, a former publisher from Amsterdam, was one of these. Another was the delightful character, Kurt Leipziger, a man after Huffener's own heart, who had gained a reputation in the film industry for his part in producing the first films with a soundtrack. He was forced to leave Berlin in 1935 and after a few years of relative success in Holland, he ended up hiding in a converted hayloft, living a solitary existence. Yet Huffener found that even this humble abode was made into a 'cosy pad' with a 'touch of class', with its easy chairs and velvet-covered divan. When he visited him one snowy winter night with some supplies to celebrate Leipziger's birthday, to his surprise, Leipziger said:

"'We go downstairs, down the ladder, we go do a bit of digging." And we went out in the deep of night and he said, "You have a spade and I have spade," and we cut some turf and he said, "This is the place, watch out because we will hit glass." And he had hidden, of all things, his enormous collection of French champagnes behind the barn in the wood!'

Two bottles of vintage Veuve Clicquot were taken up to the hayloft where they were polished off – 'in tall champagne glasses' of course, to the strains of *Dreigroschenoper* – the Threepenny Opera, written by Leipziger's old friend from Berlin, Bertolt Brecht. It was a tipsy, merry, memorable evening – *fantastich!'* as Leipziger exclaimed.

Huffener continued acting as a go-between for the Resistance and the Jews until the Germans finally caught up with him in March 1943 when he was arrested, imprisoned and interrogated by the Gestapo. Although they were not able to pin anything definite on him, he was in their clutches and, like thousands of other young men, was sent off for slave labour in the Ruhr area of Germany where he endured the usual sordid conditions which, in his case, he shared with Russian and Eastern

European prisoners. He was there during the famous Dambuster raid, witnessing the fact that it did not affect the industry in his part of the Ruhr. The Allied bombing raids were severe and terrifying, with no shelter for the slave labourers.

Not able to cope with the heavy labour, ever quick-witted and knowing there was a need for a typist in the factory he was working in, he appealed successfully for a clerk's job there, suddenly discovering typing skills. This made life much easier. At one point during his ordeal in Germany he contracted scabies, a dreadful, highly infectious itching disease, with suppurating sores, which spread from between his fingers and toes to his body. The contagious nature of this, together with some cheeky demands, helped to get him a two-week leave pass back to Holland. The train back was full of German soldiers returning to the Western Front and the Atlantic Wall. During the journey Huffener had the satisfaction of passing on his scabies parasites to the German soldiers with whom he was in close contact, regarding it as 'yet another contribution to the Allied progress because scabies not only deprives one of sleep, but nobody can scratch and shoot at the same time'.

Leaving the train at Utrecht, he was determined not to return to Germany, but obviously had no idea that there was 18 months to go before war ended. He never did return, but from then on was constantly on the move to escape detection from the SS. They had been looking for him during his time in Germany after a tip-off about his more serious underground activities, on one occasion searching the family home for him. He never discovered who had betrayed him to the Nazis. He was in poor physical shape when he returned from Germany, not only suffering from scabies but also from severe vitamin deficiency and gum disease. But with the war still ongoing, and getting effective treatment for his scabies, he was determined to resume his underground activities, but now as a 'nomadic fugitive'.

It was at this time that he was given a key to an apartment in Amsterdam which he understood to be empty. Life in the city had deteriorated rapidly since his last visit, with the population seriously malnourished. He described how 'Women with their children in tow and a few older men with handcarts, prams and wheelbarrows were straying further and further from home in search of food.' He found the apartment in the street situated where the Jewish ghetto began – the very street in which he had visited the Weinbergs two years ago; since then, they had been deported to Theresienstadt. He was surprised to find it occupied by a young Jewish couple in their late thirties, who had taken refuge in the bare, dismal place which contained just two mattresses on the floor covered with grubby bedclothes. Sidney and Marion, as he called them, were shocked when he appeared. They were in a pitiful state: lacking ration cards or any sort of food, they were on the point of starvation, and terrified with the round-ups and deportations still ongoing, and to Huffener's distress, told him that they had decided to use the cyanide pills they had been saving to end their misery. Huffener, still in a very bad way himself, was stunned and tried to persuade them that he would find a way to help, offering a stream of suggestions.

They were all paralysed with fear when the sound of hobnailed boots could be heard marching over the wooden bridge into the ghetto. They all knew the routine and soon heard other Jews in the street gathering their bundles of possessions and being herded off to deportation. When the rifle butts were heard smashing the door of the flat on the floor below from which music was playing, they were saved, incongruously, by a West African who was living there and had emerged wanting to know what was going on. The Germans were so surprised that – probably never having seen a black man before and perhaps thinking that he couldn't possibly be Jewish – they departed from the building without attempting to reach the floor above. After the shock of this, as darkness came, Huffener fell into a deep sleep on an old iron bed-frame he found in the next room. The following morning he crept into their room, opened the blackout curtains to peer out, then turned to the mattresses:

'Having a long look at the couple stretched out under their blankets I did not immediately recognise them. I went to Sidney and tapped him on his shoulder. He did not move but his eyes were not quite closed. Marion next to him was lying there with her mouth open without making any noise. Was I deluded? What I had feared all through our terrifying experience could not have happened. Why had they gone a weird colour?... My nerve had snapped. Encouraging them to wake up, to begin with, then frantically urging them to answer me produced no result. At last convinced that they were dead, I felt sick and devastated. Why? I paced the room no longer in charge of myself. Mechanically I opened the door and left the flat. I was no more of any use to them.'

His failure to help this young Jewish couple was a traumatic end to Huffener's wartime humanitarian work. Being in such a weak state after his ordeal in Germany, it was the last straw for him and he suffered a nervous breakdown. With the SS still after him, he went into hiding where he lived out the remainder of the war.

The entire Huffener family took enormous risks in their work for the Resistance and to save Jews. Huffener's younger brother Joep would raid distribution centres for ration cards and other resources whenever possible, as well as engaging in increasingly dangerous and risky sabotage. Towards the end of his life, Henk, in a letter to his eldest daughter, Clare, explained how anti-fascism was an important part of their motivation:

'Why we adopted early on a definite anti-Nazi stand was easy to explain. We hated fascism before the war. They were fraudulently marching on the Queen's birthday. Apart from the National Socialist flag, a variation on the swastika, they carried the Dutch national flag with the orange pennant. Fascist youths sported black caps with orange tops and all the time they were the Nazis friends and helpers – traitors. Friends of the family were in '42 militant anti-Nazis, later resistance fighters. I had proof of treason committed by high-ranking [Dutch] officers... The terrifying plight of German Jews was ignored because government and army spokesmen among the Allies said that it was irrelevant when it came to defeating the German army. After the expected victory Jews would be pleased to do as they pleased.'

After the war Henk Huffener, like many others in this book, turned his attention and efforts to helping the victims of the Nazis, working with UNESCO in Paris for a time in a large rehabilitation centre for displaced teenagers. In 1950, he decided to move to Britain, where preparations for the Festival of Britain were under way. Through a painter friend of his, he met the chief designer of the Covent Garden opera, Leslie Hurry, a major contributor to the Festival. But Hurry found that his commission was impossible to finish on time, and offered Huffener a half share, which was eagerly accepted. This was for painting scenery for the exhibits and the share for six months' work amounted to £1,100 – a very considerable sum at that time, enough to buy a good house. Soon after his arrival in Britain Huffener married Margaret, an Englishwoman. He and his wife had three children, Guy, born in 1952, and two daughters, Clare and Jo.

Part of Huffener's reason for moving to Britain was his dismay that so many Dutch collaborationists were back in government or other high offices. In Britain, Huffener continued his humanitarian work, albeit in a totally different sphere. Appalled with the racism and prejudice existing in Britain in the 1950s, he set up a Legal Defence Association which, on the payment of ten shillings [50p], gave families in need access to a solicitor in case of arrest, or of charges brought against them. The arts centre, Atlantis, which Huffener ran for ten years in a disused church in Bruton, Somerset, was open to people of all races who used the place to practise arts, craft, music and all manner of skills, many going on to rewarding careers.

Back in Holland, Joep Huffener married Lotty Veffer, a survivor of Auschwitz-Birkenau. Today, at 90 years of age, she is very well known in Holland and is to serve as an important witness for the prosecution, at the war-crimes trial of Ivan 'John' Demjanjuk, known by camp inmates as 'Ivan the Terrible'. The indictment relates to Demjanjuk's involvement in the deaths of 28,000 people from occupied Holland, killed in Sobibor in the summer of 1943. Lotty's parents and sister were among those murdered.

Henk Huffener was honoured with the Resistance Commemorative Cross after the war.

When Yad Vashem recognised him as a 'Righteous Among the Nations' in July 1998, he was told by the Israeli Ambassador, Dror Zeigerman, who presented the award in London on 3 February 1999, 'You are a shining light amidst the darkness of the Holocaust, your stunning bravery is a testament to all humanity.'

Henk Huffener died in 2006 and was among those honoured posthumously as Hero of the Holocaust in March 2010. His daughter Clare told me that her father would have been very honoured, but surprised at the award – 'he would have considered it a great joke to be considered a British hero since he was Dutch!'

June Ravenhall with her children. From left: Margaret, June Isobel and Ron. This picture proved a great comfort to June's husband, Les, throughout his internment in Tost camp, Upper Silesia.

'Treehill', the Ravenhalls' home during the occupation, where the Jewish youth, Levi Velleman, was given refuge during the war.

ELSIE JUNE RAVENHALL
1901–1984

'Mum would wonder what all the fuss is about.'

Elsie June Stickley was born in Kenilworth, Warwickshire, in 1901, the second child of Walter and Nelly Stickley. She never liked the name Elsie and was usually known as June. On leaving school, June worked in various places including Wyleys, the chemists in Coventry, often walking the daily six miles there and back to save money.

June met Les Ravenhall at a local musical evening and after a few years of courtship they were married in St Nicholas' Church, Kenilworth in 1925. Les was a local man who had moved to Holland in 1922 where he worked as the Dutch agent importing and selling motorbikes for the manufacturer Coventry-Eagle. The young couple started their married life in Kijkduin, a small village near The Hague. Their first child Margaret was born in 1928, June Isobel in 1930 and Ron in 1933. Before the war Les's business prospered and the family experienced a happy and good life. Les became well known, not only for his skills as an engineer, but as a successful and popular racing motorcyclist, competing all across Europe.

As war approached, June and the children were on holiday in England. On Friday 25 August 1939 five people were killed and seventy injured by an IRA bomb which exploded in the centre of Coventry. Ironically, June decided Coventry was too dangerous for her young children and cut short their holiday to return to The Hague. Les, on receiving her telegram that they were on their way back, telephoned a relative asking him to stop their return, but by this time, June and the children were already on their way. Ten days later the Second World War started.

The German invasion of Holland, on 10 May 1940, had started with a full airborne invasion in conjunction with ground forces, one of the first ever launched. The Ravenhalls' home was near the small airfield of Ockenburg and close to The Hague, so was in the initial attack zone. In all a total of 800 Germans landed or were dropped on the area. A Dutch counter-attack and bitter hand-to-hand fighting delayed the German seizure of The Hague for a while, but by 14 May Dutch resistance had been overcome and the country capitulated to the Germans. Two of the Ravenhall children remember the raid well. Ron recalled the parachutes falling, 'like gossasmer, thistledown, all different colours, at five am on a beautiful May morning…at the end of the one-day battle there were thousands of dead on the airfield'. June Isobel was frightened by the noise of the *Stukas* and, 'as the planes swooped down low, you could see the pilots in their cabins, the bombing and shooting was terrifying'. Les was known to the Germans for his motorbike-racing skills, having often beaten German teams, and so was soon arrested, and sent to an internment camp in Belfort, France. He was then moved with other British civilian internees to Tost in Upper Silesia where he was imprisoned until 1944.

June was not interned because of the children, but she was left to fend for her young family in very reduced circumstances and in a new area. They were evacuated from their comfortable home near the coast to Hilversum, further inland, where they were kept under surveillance, concern about spies being paramount. As June Isobel explained, 'The business went, the house went, the money went, we had fourteen days of clothes and nothing else. We left our home and everything in it. I had nothing of my childhood at all.' Eventually, after several house moves, each more squalid than the last, June managed to rent 'Treehill', a house at Boomberg in Hilversum. June Isobel described it as, '…ideal, it was the gardener's cottage on an estate, not very big but, oh, how we loved it!' But it was not an easy time for June: she was left in enemy territory without her husband, penniless, and a mother of three having to live on her wits. She received a small amount of help from the Dutch government and, as June Isobel explained, 'She earned a little money teaching English and cycled halfway round the Netherlands borrowing and swapping her few possessions for food, but she was never downhearted… It was here at Boomberg that the Jew came into our lives.'

On 10 January 1941, after the compulsory registration of Jewish people, the persecution and deportation of Dutch Jews started. One night Levi Velleman, a Jewish youth, known as 'Louis' or 'Lou', arrived, seeking refuge at their home. He had been betrayed in an earlier hide-out and was on the run; most of his relatives had been arrested and deported to concentration or death camps. His brother, who had decided to continue with his university studies, was taken by the Germans to Camp Vught and was reported as having died of pneumonia. The Dutch Resistance, with whom June was in touch, had sent Louis, asking if she could shelter him for a few days. Her house was an ideal hiding place as, rather like the Huffener home, it was situated in a small wood and near a tuberculosis sanatorium which the Resistance knew the German soldiers would not enter for fear of infection. Also, who would have expected an English family to risk everything to shelter a Jew? They had not reckoned on the compassion and courage of June Ravenhall. Not only did she give refuge to Louis for the rest of the occupation, but she also had a radio hidden behind boards in the attic. As June Isobel explained:

'We had a nightly routine. Mum and Lou listened to the BBC news. Lou was a reporter, he took notes, typed the information and in the night took them to people round and about. Mum loved to listen to *ITMA* (the BBC radio comedy *It's That Man Again*), I can see her happy face now. We soon picked up the latest tunes. One day Mum was in the city humming one of those songs and she was arrested. Luckily for her, thank goodness, the Dutch officer who arrested her was pro-English. I could go on and on with the danger facing us from day to day. I marvel that we came through all that misery.'

As we have seen from Henk Huffener's experience, men from the age of sixteen were taken for slave labour for the Third Reich. To avoid this many went into hiding: they were known as *onderduikers* ('underdivers', or those in hiding). Several were given refuge in the Ravenhall home. The German troops would stage sudden and terrifying raids on homes and work places, known as *razzias*, sealing off whole areas searching for *onderduikers*, moving through premises banging and shooting through walls during their search. Searching the Ravenhall home during one of these raids, the Germans missed the radio by a few inches when banging the board nearby the hidden compartment. After that the radio was buried in the garden for safety.

The risks June ran were certainly great: sheltering a Jew and other *onderduikers*, listening to the BBC, let alone hiding a radio in the home, were all punishable by death. There was also another serious risk. During the time Louis was given refuge, he was suffering with tuberculosis. This had given June pause for thought before taking him in as her mother had died of tuberculosis and her greatest fear, at a time when medicine and treatment were difficult if not impossible to obtain, was that her own children could become infected. But any qualms were overridden with her compassion for the youth, and she knew the country situation of the cottage was an ideal environment for a TB sufferer. June Isobel recalls how her mother kept a constant watch on Louis: 'He had his own room, slept out of doors mainly as this was the known cure then, he also cooked his own food which was provided by the underground.'

The Ravenhall children became fully aware of the Jewish situation. Ron described how a small Jewish school friend of his was affected:

'His name was Benjamin. One day a man came into the classroom, obviously Gestapo. He said to the teacher, "You must ask these children to give the Christian names of their fathers and grand-fathers." When it came to my turn I told them mine; and when it came to Benjamin's he said something like "Israel", and the next day he was gone because he was a Jew. We used to see them, first of all wearing the [yellow] stars and gradually they would disappear. We were not stupid, we knew what was going on. The under-ground knew, everyone knew what was happening.'

Steven Frank, a young Dutch Jewish boy, was just five when the German troops marched into Amsterdam. He experienced both Barneveld and Westerbork camps before being deported with his mother and brothers to Theresienstadt concentration camp in Czechoslovakia where, although in a terrible physical condition, they survived the war. Steven's father was gassed and cremated, a victim of the Final Solution:

'There was this "Barneveld List" with names of prominent people in Dutch society... Eventually three non-Jewish prominent men in the city, who had previously unsuccessfully pleaded clemency for my father, managed to get us on the Barneveld List. Barneveld was in the mid-southern part of Holland; we lived in the castle, situated in beautiful grounds, there were no guards or barbed wire. If you wanted to walk out, you could... People were very grateful to be there, a bit like a flock of sheep – you feel safety when you're all together...

'Suddenly, in September 1943, the German Army came into Barneveld camp and we had about half an hour to pack our belongings. We were being sent to Westerbork... This was a completely different place, suddenly we had this enormous number of people there from all walks of life, mostly Dutch but some Germans too. The camp was situated in eastern Holland, in heathland in a woodland clearing, surrounded by barbed-wire fence about six feet high and a moat with dirty turquoise-blue water in it. Outside the fence were sentry boxes on stilts with German guards and searchlights. Suddenly things changed completely; we were out of our privileged environment into the reality of what the Germans were doing to Dutch Jewry.

'Pretty soon I learnt to be streetwise. I remember once I was zipping around the edge of this building and I came face to face with two guards with an Alsatian dog. They let the dog off the leash and he came bounding up to me and started biting me. I put my arms up and was bitten on my arms and legs. I can still hear them laughing – they thought it was a bit of sport, then suddenly they got bored with it and called the dog off. After that if I got to a blind corner, I'd stop and look around it before proceeding. You learned to look after yourself.'

Levi Velleman was spared such ordeals, being well protected by the entire Ravenhall family, the children fully trusted and given great responsibility. They were told never to talk about 'the Jew'. June Isobel explained:

'Instinctively we knew not to. We saved his life often, for little ears hear voices, cars and lorries coming to our quiet area, and we'd warn him and he'd move off and hide in the sanatorium or woods until all was safe... Really, after the war had started, we were no longer children... Everything that happened was all so everyday and normal for us kids.'

She recalled how one day she and her sister Margaret were walking in the woods when they saw a party of Germans approaching. Margaret was a very pretty girl, and to give June Isobel time to run off to warn her mother and Louis, Margaret sauntered up to the soldiers, telling them that she was English and flirting with them to hold them back. The soldiers had the task of seizing blankets for troops on the eastern front; but when they finally arrived at the house to meet a trembling June, passport at the ready, they didn't even bother to go upstairs and left the blankets with the family.

This had embarrassing consequences for Margaret. A little later, when walking in the town with her friends, two of the Germans approached her in a familiar, friendly way – not a good thing for the reputation of a young, pretty girl who could be accused of collaborating with the enemy. Margaret, of course, couldn't reveal anything to her friends due to secrecy surrounding the presence of Louis in their home. On occasions when other dangers were perceived, the family would place signs on the door suggesting that disease was prevalent in the home in order to deter unwanted visitors.

June Isobel recalls how the happiest moments for the family were when the Allied planes were overhead, off to bomb Bremen and other places in Germany. 'Mother would take us all into her big bed and we would all pray, "Please God bring those boys back safe." We were all very sad when we heard the noises of the damaged ones, their engines destroyed, limping back to England.' Her brother Ron described the dramatic occasion on 13 May 1943, when one of the British planes was hit, causing a huge explosion:

'My mother and two sisters ran out of the cottage and watched in horror as fragments of an aeroplane came down to earth, falling like hailstones. In the morning, small pieces of aluminium and human bodies littered the area, including gruesome finds like a boot containing a leg, a flying helmet with an ear in it, a knee and fingers. But my mother found an article that she treasured for the rest of her long life – a sixpence, bent almost double by the force of the blast, that came out of the pocket of one of her brave young fellow-countrymen... When my mother died the bent sixpence was buried with her.'

The food situation was often a great problem throughout the war years, and June found feeding a young family and their Jewish refugee challenging at the best of times. But things got even worse after 'Operation Market Garden' in September 1944, when the Allied attempt to breach the German defences at Arnhem failed. The Dutch government-in-exile had asked the train drivers to strike in order to further the Allied liberation efforts. The German authorities retaliated by placing an embargo on all food transports to western parts of Holland. When the embargo was partially lifted in November 1944, allowing restricted food imports over water, the unusually early winter had frozen the canals making them impassable to the barges.

The Germans had also flooded the fields making growing food impossible. Food stocks in the cities quickly ran out, as Huffener experienced when he returned to Amsterdam; this is when the population was reduced to eating anything they could lay their hands on including tulip bulbs and sugar beet in their desperate hunger – 'You name it, I've eaten it!' June Isobel told me. Ron explained, 'We weren't hungry, we were *starving*. It's difficult to explain to people who haven't starved: you're weak, you get boils, I used to get scabs all over my face, there were no vitamins at all.' A low point for the family came when June, who had saved some diamonds and jewellery, bartered these for a chicken and some porridge oats, only to discover when she opened the packet of oats that it was sawdust. 'It broke her heart,' Ron explained. June Isobel added, 'And then my mum cried. It was very sad.'

Christmas Day 1944 was a sorrowful day for June. Not only was she without presents for her three children, but there was nothing substantial to feed their bony frames; there was also no fuel to keep them warm. June Isobel remembers looking around the bare room and cold stove and saying:

> "It's not going to be a very festive Christmas, Mum." But unexpectedly, mother smiled and said, "Cheer up, I have a lovely surprise for you all. I hid it and managed to save it for Christmas!" and she took a tin of condensed milk from the top of the cupboard to three instantaneous shrieks of joy from us as we thronged excitedly round the small tin. Oh, it was so lovely, a really precious treat!'

On Christmas Day, 62 years later, June Isobel's children and grandchildren presented her with a beautifully wrapped tin of condensed milk, along with other gifts. As she explained, 'I was completely overcome. They had everything to give, but the most insignificant of their presents meant the most to me…'

The dire shortage of fuel meant that most of the trees surrounding the Ravenhall home were chopped down to burn, along with anything made of wood that people could find to keep warm. The denuding of the woods presented an added risk as they had previously concealed the family's day-to-day living from prying eyes; from then on, Louis was far more vulnerable to detection. As the war drew on some help came from Sweden, and from 29 April 1945 to the German surrender on 5 May, the German authorities in Holland permitted some air drops of food by RAF Lancaster bombers. In that final year of war – the *Hongerwinter* – 22,000 people died of hunger and cold in Holland. The legacy of the famine was felt for many years after war had ended, manifested with many health-related problems, some serious and long-lasting. June Isobel was the only child of the Ravenhall family to suffer serious illness. Back in England after the war ended, she was treated for bovine tuberculosis, undergoing surgery; for many years she was sickly and in pain and had five operations for various problems until she regained better health at the age of 27 years.

Although the Ravenhall children remember their mother as being very easy-going, they realise how hard the war years must have been for her. June Isobel recalls that she seldom cried or showed her distress, but the one thing she evidently couldn't control was trembling with fear every time the Germans came into the house. Also, 'She did miss Dad. We didn't have contact for months on end. When she did have news, she read the letters over and over again and we'd celebrate.'

During one night in early May 1945, under cover of darkness, the German troops departed and five long years of occupation came to an end. June Isobel recalls, 'We knew they were coming. We waited for days for the Canadian tanks and I finally saw them coming up the road. Everyone cheered. I just hid and cried – I just couldn't face it...' Ron continued the story: 'The soldiers, seeing starving faces, started to chuck food at them and that was a big mistake. When you have starved that long, rich food kills you.' It was then that old scores were settled with the same rough justice against collaborators that had so horrified Sister Agnes in France. Ron witnessed the shocking sight of men being strung up and women humiliated, having their heads roughly shaved in public.

During his four years of incarceration, Les Ravenhall had endured terrible conditions, especially during the long winters when temperatures fell to minus 40 degrees. He witnessed many suicides from desperate inmates. As he later told Ron, 'The place had previously been a lunatic asylum, it almost became one again.' However, he occupied himself in a variety of ways. He gave lectures on engineering, and carved beautiful wooden cases out of a bed leg for his wife and daughters – gifts still treasured today. He had been released before the war ended, in a prisoner exchange, and was actually back in England before his family returned on 25 August 1945.

Like all wartime reunions, it had its happy and traumatic sides. Les had left three young children of eleven, nine and six and was now faced with two daughters of seventeen and fifteen and a son of twelve years, all of whom had been fully involved in the rescue of Louis, bearing great responsibility and acting with maturity well beyond their years. Les was also reunited with a wife who had endured four years of extreme stress and privation, heroically holding the family together under incredible odds. June had coped as a single parent for so long and had become, as June Isobel remembers, 'A woman in her own right and so she wouldn't do everything that Dad told her.' She explained how there was also a huge culture-shock challenge for the children adapting to English life and language, as well as a total lack of interest, or understanding, of what they had endured during their years under enemy occupation.

Les had lost everything he had worked for in Holland and never received any compensation. For a couple of years he worked for the Allied Control Commission for Germany, giving technical advice on the destruction of the Nazi war machine. After that he returned to engineering in England, resuming a normal, happy family life. Margaret and June Isobel eventually married Englishmen, and Ron did his national service in the RAF before going up to Oxford to obtain a degree in English after which he became a schoolmaster.

Levi 'Louis' Velleman remained with the Ravenhall family until liberation. Velleman had a distinguished career in journalism and wrote a book, *My Real Name is Levi*, about his wartime experiences in which he wrote of June Ravenhall, 'A monument should be raised in Boomberg to that exceptional lady.' When a press reporter asked him how brave he thought June Ravenhall was, he said, 'The English are not brave, they are mad!'

Les Ravenhall died in 1960 at the age of 62. June died, at the age of 83, in 1984. Two years after his mother's death, Ron Ravenhall set out to have his mother recognised posthumously by Yad Vashem as 'Righteous Among the Nations'. In 2007, 23 years after his mother's death, he was presented with a medal and scroll by the Israeli Ambassador to the UK. It was on this occasion that Ron told the *Jewish News* what an historic event it was for the family, suggesting that his mother's actions were perhaps even more outstanding than those of Victoria Cross recipients:

'The VC acts for minutes, fully adrenalised, in the heat of battle as part of an army with a weapon in his hand and can survive the encounter with an enemy. She was an unarmed woman, alone, with her husband in a Nazi concentration camp and three young children to protect and her action was sustained and deliberate, lasting for years, during any second of which there could have been rifle butts knocking on the door. She would be shot. Her death was certain...'

June Isobel explained how Ron's speech brought tears to the audience of 200 and received a standing ovation:

'There were many death camp survivors in the distinguished audience and at the end of the proceedings my brother and I were mobbed by people who wanted to hear more of our eye-witness account of the Nazi occupation of Holland and the dangers associated with an English family hiding a Jew under the very noses of the Gestapo, with our father already in a German concentration camp.'

Asked what his mother would have thought about the honour, however, Ron replied, 'Mum would wonder what all the fuss is about.'

Above, two Dornier Do17 bombers fly over Athens and, left, the Acropolis on which the Nazi war flag is raised.

GREECE
1941–1945

As it is a Greek term, 'Holocaust' had a special resonance for Greek Jews. Starting in the spring and summer of 1943, it resulted in the annihilation of more than 85 per cent of the 80,000 pre-war community, two-thirds of whom lived in Salonika.

The Holocaust story of Greece is complicated by the division of the country among the three Axis powers, with Jews subject to variations of treatment in each area of control. Italian forces had crossed the Greek border from Albania in October 1940. Bulgaria, the lesser power, which had entered the war on the Axis side on 1 March 1941, crossed its borders into Greece on 24 April of that year. On 6 April 1941, German troops entered Greece from Yugoslavia and by 27 April had entered Athens, hoisting their war flag over the Acropolis.

When the occupation zones were established, German forces occupied the more important strategic areas such as Athens and Salonika (Thessaloniki), Central Macedonia and several Aegean islands, including Crete. North-eastern Greece, Eastern Macedonia and Western Thrace, with the exception of Evros prefecture, came under Bulgarian control. The remainder of Greece – the largest area – was occupied by Italy, including the Italian-speaking Jews of Corfu, Rhodes and other islands.

Before the Second World War, there were two main groups of Jews in Greece: the scattered, Romaniote Jews – the most ancient Jewish community in Europe, and the 53,000 Sephardic Jewish community of Salonika, which, from April 1941, found itself under Nazi control. For a while assurances were given by the Germans and the Greek Jews were unmolested. But once the decision had been made in Berlin for their elimination, the Nazis acted swiftly in their area of control: in February 1943 the Nuremberg Laws were introduced with the usual outcome of identifying, isolating and forcing Jews into ghettos. Mass deportations in packed cattle trucks started in March 1943 on the slow, long, agonising journey to Auschwitz where 85–90 per cent were gassed on arrival. By the summer of the same year, all the Jews of the German zone, with the exception of those living in Athens, were gone. Jews from the Bulgarian zone had also been deported and murdered over the same period, the majority gassed in Treblinka.

However, Italy did not share Nazi Germany's fanatical hatred of Jews and those living under Italian occupation remained in relative safety. After the fall of Benito Mussolini and the Italian surrender to the Allies in September 1943, the Italians, often after hard fighting, relinquished their zone of occupation to German control. The Germans soon turned their attention to the Jews of the former Italian occupation zone; and to the sizeable minority still living in Athens. Until then their anti-Jewish actions in the city had been restrained by the collaborationist Greek puppet government that had existed under its first two leaders, General Georgios Tsolakoglou and Konstantinos Logothetopoulos, and by their more moderate Italian allies whose priorities were other than the murder of Jews.

On 24–25 March 1944, the first night of Passover, the Jews in the mainland communities in the former Italian zone were arrested. In Athens just 800 Jews had registered on the orders of the newly arrived SS General Jürgen Stroop, now Chief of Police in Greece. The majority of these – mainly refugees from Salonika or the starving poor – were lured into the Athens synagogue with the announcement that matzo (unleavened bread) would be distributed there. Athenian resident Jews belonged mainly to the Romaniote community and were well assimilated into Greek society; they were therefore far less susceptible to Nazi propaganda, and more difficult to identify and single out from non-Jewish citizens, many of whom were Orthodox Christians. Also, there was impressive support from the Archbishop of Athens, Damaskinos, who ordered his priests to encourage their congregations to help Jews and, despite the terrible reprisals if caught, many did so. On many occasions, Greek police also ignored German instructions to hand over Jews. The Grand Rabbi of Athens, Elias Barzilai, rather than submitting a list of the names and addresses of the Jewish community demanded by the Germans, destroyed the records, saving the lives of thousands. He also urged Athenian Jews to flee and go into hiding, and was himself smuggled out of the city by members of EAM (*Ethnikon Apeletherotikon Metopon*, the National Liberation Front) to join the Resistance. Many more Jews escaped with the EAM's assistance and, like their Grand Rabbi, stayed on to fight the Germans.

Among those in Athens who hid Jews was Princess Alice of Greece, a great-granddaughter of Queen Victoria, and the mother of Prince Philip, the Duke of Edinburgh.

Princess Alice of Greece, wife of Prince Andrew and mother of Philip, the Duke of Edinburgh.

PRINCESS ALICE OF BATTENBERG
1885–1969

*'I suspect it never occurred to her that her action was
in any way special. She was a person with deep religious faith,
and she would have considered it to be a perfectly natural
human reaction to fellow beings in distress.'*

On 2 June 1953 the coronation of Queen Elizabeth II took place in
Westminster Abbey. It was an occasion with all the brilliance of magnif-
icent pageantry. Three million people lined the streets of London to
catch a glimpse of their new monarch in the golden state coach on her
way to and from Buckingham Palace, while another twenty million
watched the royal cavalcade and solemn rites within the abbey on the
one million new television sets sold just before the event – the first time
that a television audience almost doubled that of radio. Among the
8,000 guests in the abbey, all splendidly attired in ermine, velvet and
satin, with precious jewels glittering from coronets and throats, one
woman, dressed simply in a long grey flowing dress and cloak and wearing a nun's veil, stood out from the rest. This was Princess Alice who,
from the Royal box, watched her son, Prince Philip, kneel before his
newly anointed wife and sovereign to vow, 'her liege man of life and
limb'. Princess Alice was a woman who had lived through most of the
turbulent events of the 20th century: wars, civil wars, end of empires,
revolutions, exile and separations. She had endured personal illnesses,
and many tragedies. From early in her life she had devoted much of her
energy to charitable and humanitarian causes including the saving of a
Jewish family, the Cohens, who had been trapped in Greece during the
Nazi occupation of the country.

Princess Victoria Alice Elizabeth Julia Maria of Battenberg was born
on 25 February 1885 in the Tapestry Room of Windsor Castle in
Berkshire, England, in the presence of her great-grandmother, Queen

Victoria. Princess Alice, as she was called, was the eldest daughter of Princess Victoria of Hesse and by Rhine and Prince Louis of Battenberg. Her three younger siblings, Louise, George and Louis later became, respectively, Queen of Sweden, 2nd Marquess of Milford Haven and Earl Mountbatten of Burma. We learn much of her early life from Hugo Vickers' biography *Alice, Princess Andrew of Greece*, which as well as giving fascinating details of Alice's own life gives a wonderful picture of the *fin de siècle*.

It was noticed from an early age that Alice was congenitally deaf. With her mother's support and encouragement the young girl learned to lip-read and speak, first in English and German, and later, Greek. Princess Alice's childhood was spent moving between Germany, England and Malta, where her naval officer father was sometimes stationed. She was educated privately and spent most of her young life in royal circles. Alice had met Prince Andrew of Greece and Denmark at King Edward VII's coronation in 1902; they married in a civil ceremony in Darmstadt on 6 October 1903; two religious ceremonies were held the following day, one in a Lutheran Church, the other a Greek Orthodox ceremony. The wedding was one of the last great gatherings of European royal families before the outbreak of the First World War.

After their marriage the royal couple lived in Greece, with Prince Andrew continuing his career in the military and Princess Alice increasingly involved in charity work. By now they had started their family of five children: four daughters – Margarita, Theodora, Cecile and Sophie – were born between the years 1905 and 1914; seven years later, on 10 June 1921, their only son, Prince Philip of Greece and Denmark, was born.

When the Balkan Wars started in 1912, Princess Alice was quick to offer her services as a nurse, setting up field hospitals and assisting at operations. Sharing the privations and sufferings of war proved a decisive point in her life; from then on her concern to serve others less fortunate than herself remained paramount.

The First World War, which soon followed the Balkan upheavals, had a huge impact on the fortunes of the European dynasties, including the

Greek. In June 1917 King Constantine of Greece, Alice's brother-in-law, was forced to abdicate and most of the royal family were exiled in Switzerland. Soon afterwards, in 1918, two of Alice's aunts, Alix, Tsarina of Russia and the Grand Duchess Elizabeth Fyodorovna, were executed by the Bolsheviks during the Russian Revolution. This was particularly distressing for Princess Alice; in 1908, on a visit to Russia for a royal wedding, she had formed a close attachment to the Grand Duchess who was then about to enter a spiritual life. It was during the First World War that Alice's father, Prince Louis of Battenberg, anglicised the family name to Mountbatten. Although the German and Austro–Hungarian empires, like the Russian empire, had also disintegrated at the end of the war, King Constantine was restored to power in 1920 and Alice and her family returned to live on Corfu, where Prince Philip was born in 1921. Their return was cut short by political events when, once more, the royal family were forced into exile in December 1922, this time on the cruiser HMS *Calypso*, sent by King George V to rescue them. Prince Philip, then 18 months old, is reputed to have been carried to safety in a cot made of an orange box. It was only with the restoration of the Greek monarchy in 1935 that the royal family returned to its homeland.

It was during the period of her second exile, living on the outskirts of Paris, that Princess Alice became deeply religious and resumed her charity work. In October 1928, she entered the Greek Orthodox Church and spent much of her time helping Greek refugees. It was soon after this, in 1930, that she suffered a nervous breakdown and was diagnosed with paranoid schizophrenia. She was removed from her family and placed in the famous institution of Dr Ludwig Binswanger in Kreuzlingen, Switzerland. It was at this time that she and Prince Andrew separated. In the early 1930s her daughters all married German princes; Prince Philip went to England to stay with his uncles, Louis and George Mountbatten, and his grandmother, Victoria, the Dowager Marchioness of Milford Haven.

After she left Dr Binswanger's clinic in 1932, Princess Alice was transferred to a sanatorium in the South Tyrol, a far more relaxed environment which suited her well. It was here that she regained her health and began to lead a more normal life. During her years of illness, she had very little contact with her family, apart from her mother, until 1937 when she was briefly reunited with her husband and members of the family at the funeral of her daughter Cecile, her son-in-law, and two of their children who had been killed in an air crash. According to her daughter, Theodora, it was the shock of this tragedy which triggered Alice's recovery. After this, in 1938, she returned alone to Athens to undertake charity work with the poor, living in a small flat near the Benaki Museum. Prince Philip was reunited with her for a holiday in Athens when she tried, without success, to convince her brother Louis that her son should return to Greece. But during his years of separation from his mother, Prince Philip had become well assimilated into British society. He had been educated at British boarding schools – Cheam and then Gordonstoun – and had already entered the Royal Navy as a cadet.

During the Second World War, Princess Alice was in the unenviable situation of having family members on both sides of the conflict: sons-in-law fighting on the German side and her son an officer in the Royal Navy. While most of the Greek royal family went into exile in South Africa during the war, Alice and her sister-in-law Princess Nicholas of Greece remained in Athens. In the early days of German occupation, conditions deteriorated rapidly as food ran out in what is now known as the 'Great Famine' of 1941–1942 when an estimated 300,000 people died. This was caused by requisitions of food by the occupying forces as well as the Allied blockade of Greece. A report to Washington DC described how 'the people of Greece existed in a state of unparalleled suffering with mass starvation'. It was estimated that between 500 to 1000 people, mostly children, died every day. Conditions were particularly severe in Athens and its port, Piraeus. Alice worked indefatigably for the Red Cross, helping to organise soup kitchens, opening shelters for orphaned children and setting up a nursing system for poor areas of the city. On one occasion she flew to neutral Sweden to obtain medical supplies on the pretext of visiting her sister, Louise, who was married to the Swedish Crown Prince.

The German occupying force left her alone; after all, one of her sons-in-law was a member of the *Waffen-SS* and another had been invalided out of the *Wehrmacht* in 1940 having been injured in France. But she was by no means pro-German, and is reputed to have told a German general, who had asked if there was anything he could do for her, 'You can take your troops out of my country.'

By March 1943, with the ghettoisation and deportations of Jews in Salonika, the situation was getting desperate and details of their ordeal would have spread to those still living in relative safety in Athens. Janine Assael's family were sent to the ghetto in Salonika when it was opened. They were all arrested two months later. She gives a vivid picture of the treatment they endured:

'It was the first day of May 1943. I shall never forget that day. Two German soldiers and a Jewish functionary came to collect us and took us to the Gestapo. The first five hours we were made to stand with our faces against the wall, nobody said anything. We were not allowed to talk amongst ourselves. It was a very hot day. I looked sideways at my mother, whom I loved very much, and her face was very tense. I can remember to this day how a big stain of sweat was going all the way down her back and she looked as if she was going to collapse at any minute. Then five hours later a German officer came in and for no reason he pulled my father out and beat him to a pulp. My father was also a diabetic and it is very difficult for a diabetic to lose a lot of blood so we were very worried, but we were not allowed to move or tend him, or even look at him, our faces were against the wall.

'We were feeling very tired and I realised that this was the day when I would die. As my birthday was on 29 May I would have been twenty at the end of the month. I really didn't want to die. I thought it was very unfair. I realised how I'd never prayed to God in my life and I apologised to God for not praying and said, "If you really want to show me that you are listening today, show me a sign, get us out of here." I bargained with him, I am ashamed to say.'

The exhausted and terrified Assael family were sent back to the ghetto. With deportation imminent, they were rescued by a bold friend, Manolis Korniordos, and were taken to the home of Maria Voudouroglou, a Christian, where they were given refuge. Later they were betrayed, but managed to escape again and were given shelter by another Christian friend, Kostas Athridis. By the summer of 1943, the majority of Jews from the area had perished in Auschwitz. The Assaels were the only family in Salonika to survive as a whole unit. After the war, in September 1945, Janine married Harold Ingram, a British Jewish soldier who had served in the liberation of the area.

It was after the capitulation of the Italians to the Allies in September 1943, that the Jews in the former Italian zone and those in Athens began to experience the full impact of the Final Solution. The arrival of a section of the Gestapo responsible for deporting Jews to Auschwitz was an ominous sign for the Jews who were still living in the city.

As we have seen, the Greek Orthodox community's record in helping Jews is admirable: thousands of false identity papers were issued to help Jews escape, and many Athenians concealed Jews in their homes. It was at this time that Princess Alice gave refuge to a Jewish widow, Rachel Cohen, and two of her five children to save them from deportation to the death camps. This was an extremely risky undertaking in the close-packed streets of Athens where there was always the danger of spies and gossip.

The family was known to Alice. Rachel Cohen's husband, Haimaki, a property developer and former member of the Greek parliament, had given refuge to King George I and other members of the royal family, including Alice, during a flood in the province of Thessaly in 1913. In return the King had offered any service that he could give the family should the need arise. At the start of the German invasion of 6 April 1941, Cohen had moved his family from Tricala in northern Greece to the relative safety of Athens. He died in 1943 leaving Rachel his widow, who had been born a British subject, a daughter, Tilde, and four sons, Elie, Alfred (known as Freddy), Jacques and Michel. Once the danger became imminent after September 1943, the family had moved to a farm on the outskirts of Athens, under the protection of three elderly Protestant ladies called Chrisaki, congratulating themselves that they had found a safe refuge away from prying eyes. But their sense of security was shattered when a friend of Jacques Cohen told them that he had overheard a conversation in which it became clear that their where-abouts were known.

After their father's death in 1943, Freddy, a lawyer, took over the main responsibility of the family. He remembered the offer made by King George I and he decided to find Alice and appeal for help. In order to contact her he approached a well-known Athenian, Madame Nelly Iliasco, who knew Alice, asking her to approach Alice on the family's behalf. Madame Iliasco agreed, but Alice was cautious and told Madame Iliasco that she wasn't prepared to take the risk. She felt it more prudent to make her own arrangements to contact the family. She did this through a good and trusted friend, Madame Sophoulis. Very soon, on 15 October 1943, Rachel Cohen and Tilde moved into Alice's home where she was living what in royal circles would be considered a simple life, helped by her lady-in-waiting and a small staff. The staff were told that Mrs Cohen was the former governess to her children. They were given two rooms with a kitchen on the upper floor of the house. Michel, the youngest of the four brothers, joined them about a month later. The other brothers, relieved that the women and younger brother were safe, escaped across the Aegean, eventually making their way to the Greek forces in Egypt to join the Allied fighting forces.

Alice would call on her hidden guests in the afternoons, glad of their company and enjoying their conversations, mainly about Judaism and other religions. There were great risks, not least the position of the house – the front door faced the residence of Archbishop Damaskinos, which always had a German guard on duty outside. She was sometimes interviewed by the Gestapo and used her deafness to advantage, pretending not to understand their questions or what they were talking about. It worked and they soon gave up. Princess Alice honoured King George's promise and, thanks to her, the entire Cohen family avoided a traumatic ordeal and survived the war. Greek inmates of the Nazi camps endured special anguish. As well as suffering the brutality and degradation suffered by Jews of other nationalities, Greek Sephardic Jews whose vernacular is Ladino had the added torment of the prevailing antagonism of Yiddish-speaking Ashkenazi Jews to contend with. Maria Ossowski, a young Polish woman who was in Auschwitz-Birkenau when a deportation of Greek Jewish women arrived, witnessed other aspects of their suffering:

'The misfortune of the Greek girls was that they didn't know any other language than Greek; they couldn't speak Yiddish or German, and that made their life a double misery because you had to understand what all the shouting was about, and the shouting was all in German. I remember they were still quite lovely because they were fresh arrivals in May 1943 and they were singing beautiful songs. They didn't last long, not only the lack of food and hard work, but the climate took its toll and they perished extremely, extremely quickly. I remember how, once, one of those Greek girls out on a *Kommando* (work party) was so ill she had fallen somewhere in the ditch and nobody spotted her. The whole camp was standing for three hours or more because if one was missing on the *Appell* (roll call), the posse went out to search for the missing person. In the end they found her, they dragged her into the camp and set the dogs on her. And this is how she died.'

As the war was drawing to a close in the summer and autumn of 1944, the food situation on mainland Greece and on the islands was desperate; there was hunger and malnutrition everywhere and often starvation. In October 1944, as Greece was liberated, Harold Macmillan visited

Athens to negotiate the return of the Greek government. Louis Mountbatten had been worried about his sister and Macmillan agreed to visit her and Princess Nicholas. Of his visit to Alice he wrote that she was living 'in humble, not to say somewhat squalid conditions… When I pressed her to know if there was anything we could do for her, she admitted that she and her companion (an old lady-in-waiting) needed food'. Alice wrote to Mountbatten soon after to thank him for the arrival of provisions since Macmillan's visit, telling him, 'The last week before liberation I had only eaten bread and butter and the servants were half starved…'

Although the city had been liberated in October 1944, living conditions had not improved by December. Communist guerrillas were fighting the British forces for control of the city and the threat of civil war loomed. Then, on 3 December, Princess Alice was told of her estranged husband's death; although separated from him for many years, it was a terrible blow as the couple were hoping for a post-war reunion by then, not having met since 1939. During the street fighting, Alice continued her charitable work for refugees with her district nurses; it was not unusual to see her walking the streets of Athens, distributing whatever food she could gather for those in need, ignoring the curfew order. When warned that she could be shot by a stray bullet, she replied, 'They tell me that you don't hear the shot that kills you and in any case I am deaf. So, why worry about that?'

Princess Alice travelled to England in February 1945 to visit her mother; she returned to Greece in time to publicly greet King George II who was restored to the throne of Greece in September 1946. In April 1947 she was back in Britain to attend the wedding of her son, now Lieutenant Philip Mountbatten, RN, to Princess Elizabeth, George VI's heir, in November of that year. Some of Alice's remaining jewels had been used in Princess Elizabeth's engagement ring. During the service Alice sat at the head of her family on the north side of Westminster Abbey, opposite King George VI, Queen Elizabeth and Queen Mary, the whole joyful occasion a great contrast to the simple and austere life she had been living in Greece. Her daughters had not been invited, out of respect for the depth of anti-German feeling in Britain following the Second World War, especially for those known to be directly linked with Hitler's regime.

Returning to Greece, Alice's charitable work took a new turn when she founded the Christian Sisterhood of Martha and Mary, a nursing order of Greek Orthodox nuns inspired by the convent founded in 1909 by her late aunt, Grand Duchess Elizabeth Fyodorovna, in Russia. During the war Alice had found it practical to wear a nun's habit when working in the soup kitchen and doing her other charity work. In the summer of 1948 she decided to eschew civilian clothes altogether and from then on, although not an official nun, she was only seen wearing a simple habit. She found this form of clothing not only comfortable but very useful when raising money for her charities. Her mother seems to have been rather bemused by this and is known to have said, 'What can you say of a nun that smokes and plays canasta?' The aim of Alice's sisterhood was to send her trained nurses out into the world for humanitarian work.

When Alice heard of the death of King George VI, she flew to London to be with her son and the new Queen before returning to Athens to resume her charity work. The Queen's mother-in-law arriving in London wearing a nun's habit had created a quite a stir. But it was at the coronation, wearing her unadorned grey robes and serenely leading her family out of the abbey, that she created such a striking contrast to the panoply of splendour within its walls, leaving a lasting impression of elegance and simplicity.

Throughout her time in Athens Alice had lived through one political upheaval after another. The last came on 21 April 1966, when the king, then Constantine, was placed in confinement as the military seized power in his name in the 'Colonels Coup', announcing that the army had saved Greece from the Communists. Although the king soon regained his freedom, it was clear to Prince Philip and the Queen that eventually he – and Alice – would have to flee. Alice was invited by the Queen to live at Buckingham Palace. Having disposed of her few possessions, she left Greece for the last time in May 1967. Princess Alice's remaining years were spent at the palace, her days enlivened by visits from her grandchildren. She died in her sleep on 5 December 1969. Her remains are interred in a crypt below the church at the Convent of Saint Mary Magdalene in Gethsemane on the Mount of Olives in Jerusalem where her beloved and inspirational aunt, the grand Duchess Elizabeth Fyodorovna, was buried.

After listening to an account of what his mother had done in sheltering persecuted Jews, Prince Philip said, 'I suspect it never occurred to her that her action was in any way special. She was a person with deep religious faith, and she would have considered it to be a perfectly natural human reaction to fellow beings in distress.'

Adolf Eichmann, the Nazi SS officer in charge of Hitler's Jewish bureau, who directed the implementation of the Final Solution.

HUNGARY
1944

The tide of war against the Nazis had turned with the Allied victory, under General Montgomery and the 8th Army, at El Alamein on 23 October 1942, and the Red Army's encirclement and defeat of General von Paulus's 6th Army at Stalingrad on 22 November of the same year. By January 1944, the Nazis had been pushed back almost to the Polish border and in the summer of that year, the Red Army renewed its offensive in support of the Normandy landings in the west. By this time the extermination camps of Chelmo, Belzec, Sobibor and Treblinka in occupied Poland had completed their killing, leaving Auschwitz-Birkenau as the major death centre. Faced with the spectre of defeat on the Eastern Front, the campaign to root out Jews left under German control was stepped up. This was to have dire consequences for the Jews of Hungary.

Hungarian Jewry was the last Jewish community to suffer under the Nazis; the change from relative security to internment, degradation and despair happened more rapidly in Hungary than in any other country subjected to the Nazi 'Final Solution'. With Hungary's entry into the anti-Soviet war in 1941 on the Axis side, the government, which had incorporated racial laws against the Jews patterned on Germany's Nuremberg Laws, further tightened conditions. Although thousands of Hungarian Jewish men were sent as forced labour to German-occupied Russia where they suffered appalling conditions and sadistic treatment, the Hungarian Regent, Admiral Miklós Horthy, consistently resisted inclusion in the 'Final Solution', refusing Hitler's demands to deport Hungary's Jews. The situation changed rapidly in 1944: as the Red Army rapidly advanced towards its borders, the Hungarians sought to withdraw from its alliance with Germany. Since the Soviets were some distance from the Hungarian border, the Nazis invaded on 19 March 1944 and soon occupied most of the country, installing a government composed of Fascists and Nazi sympathisers led by Ferenc Szálasi, and his dreaded anti-Semitic Arrow Cross (*Nyilaskeresztes*) which he had founded in 1937.

Adolf Eichmann, with his *Einsatzkommando* (killing units), immediately set about dealing with Hungary's 760,000 Jews, nearly five per cent of the population. Although they had suffered the effects of anti-Semitic measures, they were still living in largely intact communities. But in a very short time they were ghettoised and prepared for deportation to the gas chambers and crematoria of Auschwitz-Birkenau for what was to become an infamous killing spree, with over 320,000 Hungarian Jews killed in less than two months. Before the year's end, when the gas chambers were finally blown up, some 400,000 Hungarian Jews had been murdered. The Swedish diplomat, Raoul Wallenberg, working for the American War Refugee Board in Budapest, along with other diplomats from neutral countries, rescued nearly 100,000 Hungarian Jews from the deportations of 1944–1945. The Scottish missionary, Jane Haining, proved to be beyond his reach.

JANE HAINING
1897–1944

*'If these children need me in the days of sunshine,
how much more do they need me in the days of darkness.'*

Jane Mathieson Haining was born at Lochenhead Farm in Dunscore, Dumfriesshire on 6 June 1897. She was the fifth child of a farming family and grew up attending the village school and the Craig United Free Church. In 1909, at the age of 12, she won a place to Dumfries Academy, an old and famous school, where she spent six happy and successful years. When she left the Academy she moved to Glasgow to train at the commercial college, Glasgow Athenaeum, after which she worked for ten years as a secretary at a threadmakers in Paisley. She continued living in the Pollokshields area of Glasgow where she also taught a Sunday School class at the Queen's Park West United Free Church. One of her pupils, Nan Potter, recalled her great knowledge of the Bible and outstanding teaching skills, as well as her kindness and generosity towards the children, treating them to cream buns at her own expense.

It was at this time that Jane's interest in foreign missionary work began: she had set up a missionary library in the church, and there was a missionary in her family, Margaret Coltart, who was working in India for a Canadian mission. The seeds of Jane's future work were already planted when she attended a meeting of the Jewish Mission Committee. She was so moved by what the Reverend Dr George Mackenzie said about his missionary work among the Jews of eastern and central Europe that she remarked to a friend who had accompanied her to the meeting, 'I have found my life's work.'

In preparation, Jane left her job with J & P Coats and entered the Glasgow School of Domestic Science for a year, gaining a diploma as well as a housekeeping certificate. She also went to evening classes to learn German. All these accomplishments, together with her love of music and skills at the piano, meant that she was very well qualified when the call came. It was in 1932, soon after her thirty-fifth birthday, that she set out for Budapest to become matron of the girls' home at a Scottish Mission school where she cared for 50 girls of the 400 pupils attending the co-ed school.

Jane had a very good introduction to Hungary. On arriving at the Mission she had the pleasant task of taking a small group of girls to the summer quarters on beautiful Lake Balaton, the largest lake in Europe. And she fell in love with Budapest from the moment she saw the city, with its wonderful buildings and the River Danube flowing between Buda and Pest. The Mission was a large, long-established one, famous in the history of Jewish Missions. Conversion to Christianity had been its aim since 1841, depending on the free will of those over 18 years of age who wished for this. Many of the children in the home were orphans. Although some were Christian, sent to the Mission because of the outstanding quality of education offered there, the majority were Jewish. All children, whether Christian or Jewish, were given a Bible lesson each day which included learning the New Testament.

Hungarian is not the easiest language to learn, but Jane quickly mastered it, speaking like a native within a couple of years, albeit with a broad Scots accent; this, together with her knowledge of German, was vital for communication with her charges. Jane had always enjoyed working with children and soon discovered the special challenges those in the Mission presented. She felt a particular tenderness for the many unwanted children and the discrimination they faced by being Jewish. Her letters reveal her love for them. In one letter home she wrote about little Eszter Balázs:

> 'Just last night I had a long talk with one of my children who finishes with us this year. She is a little unwanted one of Jewish blood who was adopted and brought up by a Christian family. The child has always been taught to look upon her foster parents as her real parents and did not know otherwise. Her longing was to be a teacher, but in the eyes of the law she is Jewish and may not be a teacher, so she has to be told the truth. Of course it was bitter to swallow.'

Jane Haining, the only Scot to die in Auschwitz-Birkenau.

Hungarian women and children picnicking in the woods of Auschwitz-Birkenau, unaware of the horrendous fate that awaited them.

© IWM HU90295

Another letter described a little orphan of six who was going to school for the first time:

> '...without father or mother. She is such a pathetic wee soul to look at and I fear, poor lamb, has been in not too good surroundings before she came to us... She certainly does look as if she needs heaps and heaps of love. One other is such a nice child. Her father is dead and the mother left for America in June to try and make a home and a living for them both there, and yet one never hears a complaint from her of loneliness, which is so different to another who cries herself to sleep every night.'

During the years 1938–1939, when the Nazi expansion into Austria and Czechoslovakia caused a flood of refugees into the country, the numbers of Jewish children seeking sanctuary in the Mission increased – these were children the *Kindertransports* had not reached. It was Jane's first contact with Jewish refugees and it moved her to great sympathy for them. By then, members of the Arrow Cross had started their anti-Semitic propaganda and hatred of Jews began to rise in Hungary. Jane showed great empathy with these terrorised children, hating the way their lives were made miserable with the thought that they were inferior to other children and must be kept apart; she sought always to restore their pride and confidence by reassuring them of the great race they came from. On one occasion, in utter despair, she exclaimed, 'What a ghastly feeling it must be to know that no one wants you and to feel that your neighbours literally grudge you your daily bread.'

In 1939, just prior to the outbreak of the Second World War, Jane returned to Scotland on a much-needed break with her Hungarian colleague and friend, Margit Prém. They attended meetings in Aberdeen, Galashiels, and a big one in Glasgow of about 150 people, including all the Jewish delegates from the district around. Jane was not a natural public speaker, but Margit more than made up for this, being a 'born speechifier', relishing the task. In this way they were able to spread news of the Jewish persecution they had witnessed. The women were enjoying a holiday in Cornwall when war was declared. Despite the misgivings of family and friends for her safety with Europe now in chaos, she immediately returned to Budapest on what she described as a 'nightmare journey', feeling that the children would need her more than ever. In a letter home she wrote, '…of the war it is best not to speak… Hungary is neutral and anxious to remain so, so we, who are enjoying her hospitality, are refraining from talking politics.'

By the following year, after the German *Blitzkrieg* across France and the Low Countries and with the whole continent in danger of being completely cut off, she was ordered home but refused to leave her children thinking that she ran no risk. The committee thought otherwise; another urgent cable was sent urging her to leave, if necessary taking the route via Istanbul to Palestine, but again she refused. At that time there were 315 pupils, 224 of them Jewish with 31 Jewish boarders. Writing to her sister she said, 'If these children need me in the days of sunshine, how much more do they need me in the days of darkness.' Personal details are scarce, but the next few years could not have been easy for Jane. Although Hungary was considered relatively safe for Jews until 1944, the Fascist Arrow Cross was ever more active with its strident anti-Semitic rhetoric and Jews were continuously harassed by its members. Jane would have been very aware of the precariousness of her position as well as the dangers for her Jewish charges.

During the war, the Mission came under the charge of the Hungarian Reformed Church, with Jane responsible for the negotiations with the Reverend Dr Louis Nagybaczoni Nagy on the day-to-day running of the place. News of Jane and the Mission arrived back in Scotland in various ways; it was known that she was well and very busy managing to procure what little food was available for her children. The BBC news, which she listened to on her wireless set, became a great comfort to her. In 1942 the Mission's conversion course for Jewish pupils was suspended; Jewish children who arrived were immediately given life-saving certificates to say that they had been baptised, in the hope that this would give them some protection if the need arose – the urgency and danger of the growing anti-Jewish measures made the suspension of free will inevitable.

The following years of increasing austerity and struggle culminated in the Nazi takeover in March 1944, when overnight the situation of Jews became much worse. All Jews were ordered to wear the yellow Star of David on their clothing, including her girls. This caused Jane great distress; it was a bitter time for her.

The committee in Scotland, aware of her vulnerable position, had alerted the Foreign Office and Swiss authorities to keep an eye on her situation. Their concern was confirmed when soon after the Nazi invasion and occupation, in April 1944, two Gestapo men appeared at the Mission, searched Jane's office and bedroom, and arrested her, giving her fifteen minutes to get ready to leave. She had been denounced by the son-in-law of the school cook, Schréder, a member of the Nazi Party whom she had reprimanded when he was caught eating the tiny amount of food intended for her girls. Her credentials, including the safe conduct issued by the Swiss legation, were ignored and her Bible was tossed aside by one of the Gestapo. Jane remained calm and is remembered by one of her colleagues, Otto Töth, going out of the building: 'As she passed she looked up, waved and smiled and called back, "I'll be back soon".'

Jane was taken to one of the 'Gestapo villas' on the Buda Hills. From there she was moved to the notorious Fö utca prison in Buda. Every effort to procure her release by the Reformed Church and the Swiss legation failed. Bishop Laszlo Ravasz had even approached the Regent, Miklós Horthy, on her behalf, only to find that Horthy also had no power to effect Jane's release. A fellow prisoner, Frances Lee, wrote, 'She endeared herself to all her fellow prisoners and everybody wept when she left.' The list of charges against Jane was long: that she had worked among the Jews; that she had wept when seeing her girls wear yellow stars; that she had not dismissed the housekeeper who was an Aryan (the law declared that an Aryan could not be employed where Jews lived); that she had listened to the BBC news; that she had many British visitors; that she was active in politics; that she visited British prisoners of war and sent them parcels. She admitted most of these, giving sound reasons, but not the charge of being active in politics which she declared was totally false.

Jane was then taken to the transit camp of Kistarca where, in May 1944, she and 90 other prisoners were put on a transport to Auschwitz-Birkenau. Although it is rumoured that Jane accompanied some of her Jewish children on her journey to the camp, there is no evidence supporting this. Nor is there any reliable evidence of what happened to them after her arrest. Gertrude 'Trude' Levi was among Hungarian Jews deported in the summer of 1944. Her account of the journey from Hungary through Poland to Auschwitz gives some idea of what Jane must have endured:

'The normal load for the trucks was 60–90 people, we were 120… We had two buckets for our human needs, we had to overcome our inhibitions to use them – men, women, strangers, children – but we used them and they weren't quite sufficient for 120! Anyway, with every jolt of the train the muck ran out so we were sitting in it and we couldn't do a thing about it. This was June 1944, a very hot summer and there was very little air in the truck. The two openings had barbed wire over them and the air became really unbearable. We were thirsty, we had a bottle of water to drink, most probably we drank it the first day, thinking that we could refill our bottles, but this didn't happen and we were getting thirstier and thirstier. In our normal life we talk about being thirsty, but thirsty there meant one's lips were parched, broken, hurting; you were hungry, you had a piece of bread in your hand but couldn't eat it because you couldn't swallow any more. It meant people went into hysterics, people went mad, people had heart attacks, and people died. And we had the dead, the mad, the hysterical and the screaming among us and we couldn't do a thing about it.'

Zdenka Ehrlich, a young Czech Jewess, describes the arrival at Auschwitz-Birkenau which Jane also must have experienced:

'The scene around was full of commotion, people were screaming, crying; there were children, there were dogs, there were guards beating everyone across the head and screaming, "Out out out!" When we all jumped out of the wagons we were put into a long, long column and told to march forward. It was not a station, no platforms, just these barracks, the barbed wire, nowhere else to go – it really was the end of the line. On the right were these crea- tures in rags, and naked women. I thought: what are they doing here? I will never be like them. Then, I saw some men on the other side in striped gear. And in between all you tried to do was avoid the guards, the sticks and the dogs. So you kept inside the column and marched. You were carried like a flood, it must have been for about a mile. Then, three men in uniforms; the uniforms were spotless, the boots were gleaming like mirrors. I'll never forget the impression of the man in the middle, Doctor Mengele. I just glanced at him; he was very good looking. Not a menacing face at all, rather…not benevolent, but not menacing. I remember his boots were so shiny, he was absolutely immaculate. He had white gloves on, not exactly like a traffic policeman, but a sign of distinction and importance. He lifted his hand as he looked at everybody who marched past him and just made a very slow gesture, a very light gesture, and said, "Right, left, left, left, right, left, left, right…"'

On arrival Jane was not directed to the line destined for the gas cham- bers and crematoria, as the majority of Hungarian Jews were, but was tattooed with the number 79467 and passed fit for work; this would have been heavy manual work to the point of exhaustion and death. Her death is recorded as 17 July 1944 which means she had two months of enduring the truly hellish conditions of Auschwitz-Birkenau. Maria Ossowski, an inmate when the Hungarian Jews arrived, gives some idea of what Jane Haining faced:

'In May 1944, when the Jewish population of Hungary arrived, they were burning 3,000 bodies a day. You have to remember that Birkenau itself was built on the lower lands near the River Sola and it was low, wet and horrible. So the air there was never fantastic, but given the addition of the smoke belching out of those five chimneys day after day, night after night, breathing in the camp was very unpleasant and it was difficult to do the hard work. I am ashamed to say that when I knew I was going away into another *Kommando*, six kilometres from Birkenau, what I was thinking was: thank God, no more smoke; because I left in the middle of the destruction of the Hungarian Jews.'

Jane was able to send a final official letter-form headed 'Konzenstrationslager Auschwitz' to her friend Margit Prém dated 15 July, post-marked Auschwitz 21 July 1944. This was characteristically full of concerns about the welfare of others and practical details of the school; it also revealed an indication of starvation with its thoughts of all manner of food. In this she wrote, 'Even here on the road to Heaven there is a mountain road to climb.' One wonders if this was a reference to the road leading to the gas chambers, known as the *Himmelstrasse* – the heavenly road.

Among the 400,000 Hungarians murdered in Auschwitz-Birkenau was this Scotswoman who had refused to leave the children in her care when ordered to do so. Due to her British citizenship the Church of Scotland was sent her death certificate which states, 'Miss Haining, who was arrested on account of justified suspicion of espionage against Germany, died in hospital July 17 of cachexia brought on by intestinal catarrh.' Exactly how or where Jane Haining died no one will ever know for sure. But it is generally accepted that she died in the gas chambers with a large group of Hungarian women. She was 47 years old, the only Scot to die in Auschwitz-Birkenau.

Kitty Hart-Moxon was a young Polish Jewish woman working in the *Kanada Kommando* at the camp, where the possessions stolen from the incoming Jews were sorted and stored. From there she could observe what was going on at the crematoria after the arrival of the Hungarian deportations:

'From one of the windows from my barrack I could see a person walking up a ladder wearing a gas mask and he would empty a tin into an opening, a sort of skylight, at the top, and he would run down the ladder very quickly. You couldn't hear a lot, other than a muffled sound; sometimes you could actually hear screams. After a pause you could see smoke coming out of the chimney of the Crematorium 4, and a while later activity could be seen at the rear of the crematorium; ash was being dumped at the back into a pond... The capacity of the crematoria at that stage could not cope with the arrival of three-quarters of a million people, so many of the executions took place at the back of the wood in pits. We saw men gathering brushwood where they had to make a big fire. We couldn't take it in for a long, long time. But of course we were there for eight months and we saw it day in day out. Also the huge amount of clothes gave an idea of how many people were being killed.'

On 22 August 1944, a member of the Gestapo handed over a bundle of Jane's personal effects to the Scottish Mission in Budapest and reported her death. Some time later a letter was received, written by Anna, one of her former Jewish pupils. She tells of how Jane had comforted her when she arrived at the school heartbroken and in tears at leaving her mother:

'I could not see anything except a couple of beautiful blue eyes and I felt a motherly kiss on my cheek...from that moment I loved her with all my heart... I still feel tears in my eyes and hear in my ears the siren of the Gestapo motor car. I see the smile on her face when she bade me farewell. I never saw Miss Haining again, and when I went to the Scottish Mission to ask the Minister about her, I was told she had died. I did not want to believe it, nor to understand, but a long time later I realised that she had died for me and others. The body of Miss Haining is dead, but she is not alone, because her smile and her voice is still in my heart.'

Another of her former pupils, Ibolya Suranyi, at a service in Budapest in 1997 to mark the centenary of her birth, said, 'It was almost natural in that terrible age that she became a martyr. Not only a Scottish martyr but the martyr of the Hungarian people. She died because she cared for the life of others.'

Jane's half sister, Nan O'Brien, made a pilgrimage to Auschwitz in 2000. At the time she recalled, 'It was no surprise that she refused to come back...she wouldn't have had a moment's happiness if she had come home and left the children.'

Although Jane never married nor had children, her cousin, Dorothy Aalen, explained how her personality traits live on in the family:

> 'Generally speaking we are a bit of a "soft touch", no rows and definitely no temper tantrums, no loud or anti-social behaviour. But, when it comes to fighting for principle which we believe in, we do so with vigour and will not go until we feel we have at least been heard. We are stubborn, hate discrimination, hate injustice of any sort, and will not stay quiet, but will fight for justice.'

The Church of Scotland has said that Jane's life was 'Typical of all that is best in the Scottish tradition of missionary service, she gave the best years of her life to enhancing that tradition, and at the last gave life itself.' Jane Haining's story is truly one of selfless heroism, of personal sacrifice and bravery which emerged only many years after her death. When she was granted the honour of 'Righteous Among the Nations' by Yad Vashem in 1997, the Reverend Alexander McDonald, Moderator of the General Assembly of the Church of Scotland, said in his tribute to Jane, 'She aimed at proclaiming the love of God to all. This is the real meaning of mission... This award is a timely reminder of a life lived faithfully both in service and sacrifice.'

Auschwitz II-Birkenau, the main murder site of the huge camp complex, where evil reached its apogee.

AUSCHWITZ III, BUNA-MONOWITZ
BRITISH PRISONERS OF WAR
1944–1945

'What went on in Auschwitz-Birkenau showed what
happens when a principle of evil is harnessed to up-to-date
technology in an atmosphere denuded of humanity.'
(Rabbi) Hugo Gryn, Holocaust survivor

Of all the Nazi camps, none is more infamous than Auschwitz. A conglomerate of forty sub-camps, it was both a concentration camp and an extermination camp. As well as Jews and gypsies, it housed a variety of groups: prisoners of war (POWs), political prisoners, Polish and other European intellectuals and convicted German and Austrian criminals. Jews were transported there from all parts of Europe and four out of five of them were sent immediately to the gas chamber and crematorium, only the fittest being selected by an SS doctor – from 1943, often Dr Mengele – who decided who should live and who should die. Temporary survival meant having as much work as possible squeezed out of them before they succumbed to weakness and, ultimately, their journey down the *Himmelstrasse* to the gas chamber. It has been estimated that as many as 1.1 million victims were gassed in Auschwitz from February 1942, Jane Haining among them. Ninety per cent of those murdered were Jews; of the 23,000 gypsies sent there, 21,000 perished. The Nazi campaign to exterminate the Jews and gypsies was pursued systematically, methodically and vigorously; its uniqueness lies in the industrial scale on which it was organised and implemented.

The three main camps were Auschwitz I, II and III. Auschwitz I was used from June 1940 to house Polish political prisoners; later the prison population became a mix of nationalities. Auschwitz II opened two kilometres away, at Birkenau in 1942. It was much larger and housed mainly Jews and became the main murder site. The third main camp, Auschwitz III or Buna-Monowitz, was the industrial part of Auschwitz and added a further dimension to the camp. This was built in January 1941 by the I G Farbenindustrie chemical company which invested 70 million Reichsmarks, the equivalent of US$1.4 million, in the site. Zyklon B, the main poison gas used in the gas chambers of all the extermination camps, was manufactured by an I G Farben subsidiary, Deglesch.

I G Farben was not a nationalised company, but it willingly cooperated with supporting the needs of Goering's Economic Four-Year Plan which, once it became clear that the war would not be over quickly, required a Buna – synthetic rubber – plant to be built in the East for the war effort. The process involved putting coal through a process of hydrogenation, when hydrogen gas was passed over it at high temperature. The Auschwitz concentration camp in Silesia was an ideal location with its resources of coal, lime and water as well as a developed transport system and, crucially, a large work force. The firm also had the cooperation of Himmler and the SS. Operations started in May 1942 and from this time I G Farben exploited the slave labour of thousands of Jews as well as other groups of forced labourers from all over occupied Europe, including British POWs, who built and operated the synthetic rubber and liquid fuel plant at Monowitz, which became known as Auschwitz III.

Most of the POWs had already been incarcerated for anything up to three years before their transfer to Auschwitz. Many had been sent from camps in Italy after its capitulation to the Allies in September 1943. Initially the POW camp was located some distance south of the chemical plant's perimeter fence, which meant a march to work every day. There, about 1,400 Allied POWs shared space with civilian forced labourers from states occupied by the Nazis such as Poland and the Ukraine. Then, in mid 1944, 600 British POWs were relocated to a work detachment of *Stalag* VIIIB which was under the control of the *Wehrmacht,* in a location adjacent to the plant and opposite the concentration camp for Jewish slave labourers just a short distance away. Being in such close proximity, and after working on the same *Kommandos*, the POWs could see and hear what was happening to the hapless and wretched Jews.

By August 1944, the Red Army was at the gates of Warsaw; simultaneously, the Anglo–American forces were liberating large parts of western Europe. As well as trying to obliterate all evidence of crimes in the western Soviet Union and Yugoslavia, the Nazis acted to ensure that no living witness would fall into Allied hands. As battlefronts approached the concentration camps, these were liquidated and inmates forced out on death marches deep into the Reich. In the spring and summer of 1944, the camps in eastern Europe were the first to be dismantled with the inmates driven in a westerly direction, away from the approaching Red Army.

As the noose around the Nazis began to tighten in the winter of 1944–1945, inmates by the thousands – Jews, and non-Jews like Harold Le Druillenec from Jersey – were sent on forced marches in various directions to concentration camps such as Dachau, Buchenwald, Mauthausen, Sachsenhausen, Ravensbrück and Bergen-Belsen. Even this was not the end of the agony, as the newly arrived inmates in many of the now overflowing camps were pushed out again on further ordeals of marching as both Western and Soviet forces drew closer. Long columns of inmates from different camps trudged along, merging, separating, merging again in sluggish columns of increasing misery, leaving corpse-strewn paths behind. In the last two months of the war, 250,000 prisoners were sent on death marches which continued until the last day of war in Europe, 8 May 1945.

Of the 66,000 Jews evacuated from Auschwitz from 18 January 1945, 15,000 died on death marches. Soon after the Jews had left, on 21 January, British POWs from Auschwitz, although not part of the death marches as such, were sent out on similar long 'hunger marches' away from the advancing Russians, sharing the ordeals of Hitler's Jewish victims as they trekked through the frozen lands westwards. Among them were two British POWs, Charles Coward and Denis Avey.

Charles Coward gives testimony to the I G Farben case at the International Military Tribunal, Nuremberg, November 1947.

CHARLES COWARD
1905–1976

*'England can be very proud of these men… who really
proved that even in Auschwitz humanity could prevail.'*

Charles Coward grew up a self-sufficient, resilient boy in the tough
district of Edmonton, north London, during the First World War and its
immediate aftermath. Although, like other working-class boys of the
day, his formal education had ended early, he was an intelligent lad with
a keen interest in football and boxing. He enlisted in the army at the
age of 16 and served in India until 1924, returning to civilian life in
Edmonton. He married Florence, and fathered four children during the
inter-war years. For a time he managed a shop, but when that proved
unprofitable in the difficult years of the 1920s, he worked as a gas-fitter.
He had continued in the Territorial Army, and, when war clouds were
gathering in the late 1930s, was among the first to be recalled into his
old regiment, the Royal Artillery. Initially he served as an instructor, but
when the British Expeditionary Force left for France, he went out as
Quartermaster Battery Sergeant Major with the 8th Reserve battalion,
Royal Artillery. When the German *Blitzkrieg* reached France in 1940, he
fought alongside his men in a desperate rearguard action, his unit suffering heavy losses. He was wounded in the head and leg at Calais and was
captured soon afterwards. A high point of his captivity came when, lying
wounded, tucked under blankets in a German field hospital, undistin-
guished from other German patients, he was awarded the German Iron
Cross by a visiting German general.

From the moment of his capture, Coward's main aim was to escape,
make it back to Britain and rejoin the war. He had made two attempts
even before he was 'put in the bag' for the first time and had attempted
more daring escapes before being sent, in October 1943, to Auschwitz, a
name that meant little to him at the time. He ended up in work detachment known as E715 near the I G Farben chemical industrial plant and

the concentration camp of Monowitz. The British POWs called themselves 'Kriegies', a jokey reference to the German *Kriegsgefangenen* (prisoners of war).

The I G Farben complex was a wired compound in grid formation about two miles long and a mile deep, a hive of activity. It was dominated by a large industrial plant with four tall chimneys which the Kriegies soon named the *Queen Mary*. Railway lines threaded along the different blocks kept the hundreds of building sites supplied, all with the aim of expanding the work for the German war effort.

The Geneva Convention ruled that officers could not be compelled to work and NCOs could only be ordered to supervise the men in their charge. It allowed compulsory labour for enlisted POWs, provided that the work was not war-related or dangerous. It could be argued that the POWs' work – manufacturing rubber, synthetic oil and methanol installations – did contribute to the German war effort and certainly many POWs complained about the war-related aspect of the work they were forced to do, but to no avail. The only thing they could do was to slow productivity by sluggish labour and by engaging in sabotage whenever possible.

By the time of his arrival in Auschwitz, Coward had a fair command of the German language. He also brought with him a reputation of daring, determination, efficiency and what the Jewish inmates would have described as *chutzpah* (brazen nerve or cheek) – all qualifications for his appointment as Red Cross liaison and trustee – a *Vertrauensmann* (a 'man of confidence' or spokesman) – for the POWs in E715. His main function was related to the prisoners' welfare, such as the distribution of Red Cross food parcels and clothing. Coward exploited his role to the full, not only looking after the POWs' interests, but helping the Jewish inmates, taking advantage of the freedom the job offered to move throughout the camp as well as to surrounding towns. As time went on he became known as the 'Count of Auschwitz' for his smart appearance and the confident manner in which he went about his business. The role of trustee was not always a comfortable one and his relations with other POWs were not always straightforward. It required a certain amount of interaction with the Germans – the SS as well as I G Farben civilian staff – which some viewed as collaboration; but this was usually for bribing and persuading officials for his own ends.

British POWs were deeply shocked when they saw the emaciated, filthy and exhausted Jewish concentration camp inmates. Even in the most bitter winter weather, all the clothing they wore were wooden clogs and thin, striped pyjamas. It was when the POWs were put to work on various *Kommandos*, working in close proximity with the Jewish concentration camp inmates, that they witnessed at close range the harsh treatment meted out to the 'stripeys', as they called them. The German plan was obvious: to starve them, provide the most inadequate clothing and shelter that was not even fit for cattle and finish them off by working them to death.

Fred Knoller, an Austrian Jew, who had been in the French Resistance before his capture and deportation to Auschwitz, recalled his initiation into the system:

'An SS officer came and made a speech. He told us that we were going to work in a factory and the factory was to produce artificial rubber, they were building the factory and our job would be to carry cement, to build roads, to dig and to do anything to finish the factory so that they could produce the artificial rubber which is important for the war effort. We were also told that our life was nothing to them and if we did what we were told it would be fine, if not we were not going to live very long. It was a speech without any feelings and it was a speech full of contempt, an additional way to show us that our life was worth nothing, that we were sub-humans and if we wanted to stay alive not to put up any resistance whatsoever.'

John Fink, a Jewish youth and trained electrician, was a slave labourer working in Buna-Monowitz:

'I G Farben were making soap and other things from coal, but the main product was artificial gasoline, or petrol. The firm had to pay the SS for each slave labourer and naturally they only wanted people who could work. They worked us to death because how long could you labour with just the little bit of food we were given? I was assigned to a small electricians' *Kommando*. We were a small group, only twenty men. In fact there were only two real electricians, the others were what you would call 'Lager electricians' – they were smart enough to say that they were electricians in order to save their lives. I was a tradesman, used to a hard life, but there were professional people there – university educated people like doctors and lawyers who had lived very well in normal circumstances, but in those conditions, they couldn't stand up to it. If you couldn't work that was the reason to be beaten and taken away.'

The treatment of the Jews horrified the British men so deeply that many have been haunted by their memories of the suffering they saw ever since. Time and time again, they saw dead or dying bodies lying around the plant, often as many as thirty in one day. They saw the inmates treated as worthless *Untermenschen* – beaten, starved, punched and kicked senseless and whipped, even killed before their eyes. After the POWs were relocated nearer the plant, and being much closer to the concentration camp, they were often kept awake at night by shootings, shrieks and screams coming from the camp. They could also see the victims of regular hangings strung up inside the camp gates. One of the most sickening things for the POWs was the awful stench wafting over from Birkenau. They often wondered what had happened to some of the Jews they had worked with who suddenly disappeared, and began to realise that, like many of the new arrivals into Auschwitz-Birkenau, they had been 'sent to the showers' then 'sent up the chimney' – gassed and burnt. Their suspicions were soon confirmed by the Jews they worked alongside.

The POWs gave the Jews whatever help they could. Food obtained from the Red Cross parcels meant that they were not entirely dependent on the rations the Germans provided – which was better quality than what the Jews were given – and they would often place portions of this around to be picked up and eaten by the concentration camp inmates. Cigarettes were especially valuable as a barter currency for the Jews, and these would be slipped to them during working parties, sometimes with a piece of chocolate as a special treat. If caught, penalties were severe for both POWs and Jewish inmates, but the help continued. The POWs also gave away items of clothing that could be spared. At one time, Coward made an appeal to I G Farben management, offering to set up a clothing collection within E715 for the inmates of Monowitz concentration camp, but this was turned down.

Coward, in his role as camp trustee, also passed complaints to the plant management on behalf of the POWs. In the main these were about food and inadequate clothing for the heavy work they were doing. He always investigated the complaints himself and found them justified, but often he was put off by the German authorities and got no satisfaction. All POWs in detachment E715 agreed that whatever their privations, they were nothing compared with those that the concentration camp victims were suffering. They were able to keep relatively fit, were mainly adequately clothed and had their Red Cross parcels throughout their time in E715, until their evacuation in early 1944. They were treated better than any other national group at the Buna factory. Even so, some very unpleasant and brutal incidents occurred.

On many occasions, the POWs acted instinctively in helping Jews in distress, many of whom had become friends. Frank Harris, for instance, once spontaneously helped a young Jew, who had collapsed through weakness, to his feet, only to be rifle-butted in the face and see the youth shot before him. Corporal Reynolds, with another four men, refused to climb to the top of a treacherous, slippery girder, not having the proper boots or equipment, and was shot and killed on the spot. Another POW, Private Campbell, was stabbed in the back as he helped a young Polish woman inmate staggering along to the work site with a heavy load of food. Unlike Reynolds, he survived the attack. One of the most distressing things for the British POWs was how the cruelty and suffering they were witnessing lowered their morale during this stage of their captivity; they never got used to the horror they were witnessing daily. Coward was quick to notice this and complained to the *Wehrmacht* about the effects of this brutal treatment on the British prisoners.

Coward's own role in helping the Jews was considerable and the testimony he later gave on this was backed up by other POWs in the camp. A very important part of this was the way he determinedly sought to witness what was going on in Auschwitz-Birkenau as well as in Buna-Monowitz, sending details of what he had seen and heard to the War Office at the time it was happening. As the Red Cross trustee, Coward had extensive letter-writing privileges, and writing coded messages to his deceased father c/o 'William Orange' at his home address sometimes five or six times a week, he listed Jewish transports and the terrible state of the Jews upon arrival, giving dates on which he saw thousands arriving and being marched to the concentration camp at Monowitz. At first Florence, his wife, was puzzled by these weirdly addressed letters, but soon realised their meaning and passed them on to the War Office.

As well as Jewish transports, Coward sent what he considered relevant military information, as well as details of the conditions and treatment of the British POWs. He also described the atrocities committed towards the Jews, including what he knew of the gassings and crematoria in Birkenau. After the war he was commended for this work by MI9, the relevant British agency dealing with such matters. Coward also complained to the Swiss authorities, when they visited Buna-Monowitz on two occasions in 1944, describing the brutal treatment of the Jews, but gained the impression that they were helpless to do anything about it. Information about the gas chambers in Auschwitz-Birkenau was also passed by Coward to his counterpart at Stalag VIIIB who passed the information on to the International Committee of the Red Cross.

One of Coward's most daring exploits was when one of the inmates of the concentration camp passed him a note written by Karel Sperber, a Czech doctor who had been working on a British merchant ship, and who was interned there. Sperber asked Coward to inform a relative in Sunderland, England about where he was being held, and also to alert the authorities. (Under the Geneva Convention, Sperber should have been held as a POW.) Coward felt it imperative to meet him and bribed a *Kapo* (criminal camp guard) to allow him to swap uniforms with one of the inmates and to march into the concentration camp with them when they returned from work at night. He managed to do this, spending one of the most nightmarish nights of his life.

In his testimony to the I G Farben trial in 1947 he described the crowded, filthy, smelly barracks, the uncomfortable wooden bunks, and how, due to lack of space and crammed bodies, he spent the entire night in a sitting position, listening to the lamentations and groans of the pitiful inmates as well as seeing the occasional beating. He described how dead men were held up at roll call on entering the camp in order for others to grab their rations of watery soup, and how later he witnessed the inmates having to fight for their own meagre portion. After enduring all this, he was unable to locate the doctor in that particular barracks. It is not known whether he managed to contact the doctor's relatives. Needless to say, the inmate he changed places with had what must have been a blissful time: clean clothing, a neat barrack, good food and a peaceful night. Dr Karel Sperber survived the war and died in 1957.

One of the most macabre and ingenious escape schemes in the Second World War was also devised and executed by Coward helped by Yitzhak Persky, a fellow POW. Persky, a Palestinian Jew, had been captured while serving with the Royal Engineers in Greece in 1941 and met Coward during an earlier captivity. Coward had persuaded other prisoners not to reveal Persky's Jewish origins and he was living in E715 under the name of a deceased British Gentile POW. Together they worked out a plan to help a number of Jewish inmates escape. Coward had managed to 'buy' a number of dead bodies from the German in charge of body disposal, paying him with goodies from the Red Cross parcels. The plan was to swap the dead bodies with three Jewish slave labourers who were coming to the end of their working days and were destined for the gas chambers in Birkenau. A slave labour liaison man had been picked to prepare the selected escapees for flight when the signal was given. This was to happen on the way back to the camp at night.

Coward and Persky bribed themselves out of their camp and laid the three bodies in the ditch, waiting for the prisoners to come along the road with guards ahead and behind the line. The escapees would then be told to get into the ditch and lie down, the corpses would be distributed along the route in likely places where the prisoners had passed, and when the bodies were recovered, the numbers would tally. The escapees meanwhile would be given clothing and non-Jewish documents by Coward, and sent on their way, getting a chance to survive. Although hundreds of Jews are alleged to have escaped in this way, the total number rescued by Coward and Persky has yet to be confirmed.

There were also instances of sabotage that Coward and other POWs planned and helped execute within the Buna factory. They were not alone in this: many of the Jewish inmates committed acts of sabotage whenever possible, a far braver act for them given the severe beatings and death penalty they would receive if caught. Leon Greenman, a British Jewish inmate who was deported from Holland with his wife and child, found himself in Buna-Monowitz. He felt he had nothing to lose as he had witnessed his wife and child being led off for extermination as they arrived:

'When nobody was looking, I pushed my shovel into a bag of cement and it would pour open. I felt it was sabotage against them. Others did it too and the next morning when you came to the work place there were bags and bags and bags all broken on purpose. Bricks were broken for the same reason too.'

By mid 1944, I G Farben was within the range of the American Flying Fortresses. John Fink was working in the generating plant on 20 August 1944 when I G Farben was hit during a bombing raid on the factory:

Reichsführer-SS Heinrich Himmler carries out an inspection of the Monowitz-Buna plant at Auschwitz III, July 1942. From left to right, SS officer Rudolf Brandt, Himmler, Chief Engineer Max Faust (centre) and Camp Commandant Rudolf Hess.

'We went down to the basement and the foundations were shaking and when we came up after the air raid there was nothing left of Buna plant. A bomb fell into the prisoners-of-war camp too. They were English prisoners and I believe about 30 were lost. I think they were bombed by accident as they were very careful with their bombing. They didn't bomb the crematoria or anything in the Auschwitz camp, they were only interested in getting this artificial gasoline plant. We thought this was the end for us because they wouldn't need us for work any more, but lo and behold, next morning we had to march out again and start working to clean the place up. The water and gas were restored and once more the prisoners started working in Buna…'

The bombing took place when the end of the war seemed within sight. The deaths and mass burial of the British POWs marked a very low point for Coward and the rest of E715. They had not been allowed to use the air-raid shelter in the plant. Coward protested to Walter Dürrfeld, the director of the plant, about their lack of protection. He was dismissively and grudgingly told that a place could be used as a shelter in the future although a key would have to be obtained first. The Jews had no protection at all unless, like Fink, they were in a position to get into a safe place, and foreign slave labourers were taken into the fields for the duration of raids.

At last, suspected of sabotage, Coward was moved from I G Farben Auschwitz to the nearby camp of Teschen before the closure of E715 in January 1945. Destined for interrogation by the Gestapo, he had then been moved by the camp leader into a work group in the Bobrek mines. The hunger march that the E715 POWs were then forced to undertake is described later by Denis Avey. Suffice to say that Coward joined a similar march from his new workplace, experiencing the same hunger and exhaustion. With the freedom of movement he enjoyed while at I G Farben, Coward had ample opportunity of escape, but he had eschewed this due to the responsibility he felt towards the other POWs as well as the vast distance involved; but when arriving three months later in Hanover on the hunger march, he seized his chance and made off with another POW, Henry Allingham, eventually making it to safety in Brussels. From here he sent a cable to his wife Florence on 14 April 1945: 'Darling, escaped from Germany arrived here by plane will be home about 4.00…'.

Like the majority of those who had endured traumatic experiences during the course of the Second World War, the returning POWs often found it impossible to communicate what they had experienced in Auschwitz – who could possibly understand, let alone believe, the horror they had witnessed? The British authorities also urged them to forget the war and get on with their lives. Most tried, albeit with great difficulty; the exceptions were those who had been traced and agreed to give witness at the Nuremberg Trials, but even this was in an official capacity, rather than sharing their experiences with family and friends.

Much of the evidence for the humanitarian help given by British POWs to Jews in Buna-Monowitz emerged from the testimony Coward and seven others from E715 gave to the I G Farben case, in November 1947, at the International Military Tribunal at Nuremberg and another lengthy, powerful statement made by Coward in 1947. The firm was accused of becoming a participant in forced population settlement, slave labour and mass murder in pursuit of its business interests. It is reckoned that by the time it became operational in October 1942 until the evacuations of January 1944, between 23,000 and 25,000 forced labourers had been murdered in various horrific ways, including gassing, or worked to death by sheer exhaustion.

The trial lasted from 27 August 1947 to 30 July 1948. The evidence provided by Coward and other British POWs helped secure the conviction of senior I G Farben personnel for their involvement with the crimes committed there. As Coward testified, 'I am sure Dürrfeld, who was always walking around the factory, knew about the gassings and burnings… Everybody knew, from the civilians to the top dogs. It was common talk… Farben was responsible for its inmates and could not help knowing what was happening to them.' In the event, of the 24 defendants arraigned, 13 were found guilty on one or more charges of plunder, spoilation of private property in German-occupied territories and other war crimes. Their sentences ranged from eighteen months to eight years, including time already served.

In February 1953, Coward and Robert Ferris, another POW from E715, flew to Frankfurt to give evidence in a very notable civil action against I G Farben on behalf of Norbert Wollheim, a Jewish Monowitz inmate who was demanding compensation from the firm. Wollheim, who had worked on the German *Kindertransport* before the war, had volunteered to work as a welder on the building site in order to contact the British POWs. He exchanged news with them, becoming one of their main informers, and became particularly close with Reginald Hartland who informed Wollheim's family in the United States of his situation. The evidence provided by Coward and Ferris proved vital to Wollheim's case which he won, being awarded 10,000 marks. The judge mentioned the importance of the evidence given by the British men and paid tribute to other British POWs who had helped the Jews of Buna-Monowitz, saying, 'The fact that a British prisoner of war had to show the German defendants what moral courage involved is a matter of regret to a Chamber of a German court.' Wollheim added to this with his tribute which included other British POWs, 'England can be very very proud of these men…who really proved that even in Auschwitz humanity could prevail… The British extended the…hand of solidarity of man.'

After the verdict, a letter arrived from the Association of British Refugees:

'We feel urged to point out to you how deeply we were impressed by the humane spirit and courageous attitude displayed by you and Mr Ferris during your imprisonment in the Monowitz camp. We know only too well from the reports which have transpired since the end of the war what our people had to endure in the camps. Apart from physical sufferings the worst for them was certainly the fact that they were helplessly exposed to the cruelty of their persecutors. It will therefore have helped them to retain their belief in humanity if their burden was eased by men like you and Mr Ferris.'

After the war Coward and his family continued living in Edmonton. Another child was born after his return. He obtained work with Harris Lebus furniture factory, working as a timber porter. When the factory closed in 1969, he worked as a despatch clerk for an Oxford Street department store. His love of football continued, as did his support for Tottenham Hotspur. He became a freemason in 1955 joining the Camberwell Old Comrades Lodge, and is remembered by Charles Stancer, one of the brethren from another Lodge, as 'a remarkable hero, a modest self-effacing man'.

It wasn't until the publication of the book by John Castle, *The Password is Courage*, that Coward's story became public. A Metro-Goldwyn-Mayer film of the same title starring Dirk Bogarde as Coward followed. This was a derring-do, light-hearted account of Coward's escape exploits from the time of his capture in France with the briefest reference to the time he spent in Auschwitz and his rescue work there.

This was rectified in 1960 when the BBC programme *This Is Your Life* celebrated Coward's remarkable story, including his I G Farben Auschwitz experience, reuniting several of his old comrades and Norbert Wollheim. Ten years later, in 1970, Coward was honoured with the award of the 'Righteous Among the Nations' by Yad Vashem, when a tree was planted in his honour in the Avenue of the Righteous. He had given testimony to the museum when Yitzak Persky – then known as Gershon Peres, the father of Shimon Peres, a foreign minister and prime minister of Israel – confirmed his role in helping Jews escape. Another POW, G J Duffree, verified that an escape plot took place in E715.

In 2003 an English heritage blue plaque with the words, 'Rescuer of Prisoners from Auschwitz lived here 1945-1976', was put on Coward's home at 133 Chichester Road, Edmonton, where he had lived until his death at the age of 71.

DENIS AVEY
1919–2015

*'My trouble in Auschwitz is that part of me died there,
without any doubt at all. You were under-ridden by this ghastly
twenty-four hour stench from the ovens and the chimneys – twenty-
four hours a day this sickly smell. And do you know, to this day I
can still taste it. And then these dreadful situations with the political
prisoners and the stripeys. It was ghastly, absolutely ghastly.'*

Denis Avey's background was a great contrast to that of Coward's: he
was born and raised on what he described as a 'horse farm' in the Essex
village of North Weald. The farm was successful and his boyhood was
idyllic; he rode horses from an early age, first in a side-basket when his
legs were too short to straddle his mounts. The family lived off the land,
growing their own food and wild game was shot in the nearby woods for
the larder. He grew up a healthy, independent lad enjoying a 'marvellous
village life; there was always a season for it – tops, bikes, climbing, paper
chases into the forest with my own little gang'.

His was a close and happy family and he grew up greatly admiring his
grandfather and his father, a 'fine Christian', who served in the First
World War, both men important role models who 'gave me a great
respect for animal and human life'. He had always enjoyed tinkering
with any machinery on the farm, including cars and motorbikes, so it
was a natural progression when a free scholarship took him to Leyton
Technical College in East London. This, in turn, led to employment as a
student apprentice with Tate and Lyle the sugar firm. When war started
he enlisted in October 1939 into the London Rifle Brigade for 'the sheer
hell of it, for the adventure', little suspecting 'how much hell there
would be'.

After training with the 2nd Battalion of the Rifle Brigade, Acting
Corporal Avey left Liverpool on the troopship *Otranto* in August 1940, a

keen, confident 21-year-old 'red-headed soldier with a temperament to match'. He had gained a reputation as a crack shot and was bound for Egypt to join the Allied forces in the war against the Italians in the Western Desert. The Italians had entered the war on the Axis side on 10 June 1940. By the time Avey went into action against them they had reached Sidi Barrani, 65 miles into Egypt from Libya, which was then an Italian colony.

Very soon his battalion was off to join the 7th Armoured Division, the Desert Rats, at Mersa Matruh, where the Allies had built a base expecting a further Italian advance. During the next few months Avey was to see a great deal of action chasing the Italians out of Egypt into Libya, engaged in action in Bardia and Tobruk. With his shooting skill he was sent out on night patrols behind enemy lines on numerous occasions, once, near Tobruk, going right through an Italian base of some 200 men, unchallenged and undetected. Each patrol was 'a battle for survival', as he found the Italians were certainly 'no push over'. It was during such a patrol that he was forced to kill a man with his bare hands. The Allied forces hardly had time to congratulate themselves at defeating the Italians when Rommel and his *Afrika Korps* entered the desert war, pushing the Allies back to Cairo. At this time Avey was taken seriously ill and hospitalised with sandfly fever and malaria and did not go into action until 'Operation Crusader', with the aim of relieving the beseiged Tobruk, was about to begin.

It was during this operation in the 'forgotten battle' of Sidi Rezegh, that the Bren gun carrier that Avey was driving was ambushed. Les, the commander of the carrier, was killed and Avey was wounded, with the added horror of having Les's blood and gore mixing with his own. He was dragged out of the carrier into captivity and taken first to an advanced dressing station, and then a very basic hospital near Benghazi where he received very good treatment. Soon, with the British advancing on Benghazi, and recovered from his wounds, he was taken to Benghazi docks and put into a cargo ship, two holds down, with about 100 other prisoners in crowded, ghastly conditions.

Denis Avey with his sister Winifred during his embarkation leave, August 1940.

The following evening, the ship was torpedoed. The imprisoned men, trapped beneath the waterline, were thrown into panic. Avey managed to hoist himself up a rope out of a partly-opened hatch and jumped over the side into the water. Those who made it into the sea then faced the danger of being mangled by an Italian sub-chaser manoeuvring at speed back and forth in the water searching for the Allied submarine that had fired at the ship; any hapless survivor in its path would be ruthlessly mangled. In ever-increasing horror, depth charges against further submarine action were dropped causing huge thuds from below, followed by giant spumes of water churning the sea. With the light fading, and the ship gone, Avey managed to scramble on to a wooden crate and to stay afloat, fading in and out of consciousness for about twenty hours. The tide eventually washed him to the edge of a rocky cove, in what he later discovered was southern Greece. By then he was very weak and in a terrible state: 'I was as black as the ace of spades, with fuel oil all over my face and hair, and was found and cared for by a very small Greek farmer before being captured by the *carabinieri*, the Italian police.'

He was taken to a series of 'hellish' makeshift camps, first in the Italian-occupied area of Greece and then in southern Italy, ending up at his first established camp, Prisoner of War Camp PG 65, near Altamura in southern Italy. At the first chance, when sent outside the wire on construction work, Avey escaped hoping to make his way towards neutral Switzerland. But after about three days, weak and hungry, he was captured and returned to the punishment cell in the camp. Life-threatening dysentery, which was a feature in all the camps, was rife and it was in the lice-ridden PG 65 that he endured the torment of scabies which he suffered for months. As he summed up in his book, 'That year in Italy was hellish. Many of the lads died of disease and neglect.' When the time came to leave the camp, 'The best any of us could muster was a slow, listless walk to the lorries.'

The journey to his next destination, Austria, in crowded cattle trucks was equally sordid with the men sitting in their own excrement which had overflowed from the single bucket provided for the journey. Later, Avey learned that theirs was the same route used to deport Italian Jews to the concentration and death camps. From this time he passed through a number of prisoner of war camps. The worst by far, a rat-infested one which also housed Russian POWs in an even worse state than other Allied prisoners, being worked and starved to death. It was in this camp that Avey, working down the mines alongside Russians without helmets or protective clothing, witnessed the extent of Fascist sadism, this time against Russian POWs.

One of the barefoot Russians had dared to improvise some protection from the sharp rocks by cutting strips of rubber from a disused conveyor belt in the mine, and had been detected. Avey, with nine Russians, was shoved against the tunnel wall facing five soldiers with lifted rifles. Five were shot alongside Avey, who was eighth in line: 'What happened in that satanic hole shook me more than anything before or possibly since.' Avey, along with the remaining Russians, was accused of sabotage, marched to a train and thrown in with some other prisoners. He took a chance when the train stopped, jumped out and ran into the nearby fields. He was soon caught, questioned, beaten up a bit, and sent to a punishment camp at Graudenz in northern Poland, as a habitual troublemaker – he had previously got into trouble for failing to salute a German officer in the camp. Eventually, he was put under guard on a train, and was on the move again, this time to Auschwitz.

By this time, with all he had endured, Avey was battle-hardened, had seen a great deal of brutality and death, including many of his best mates. He had killed a man with bare hands, and performed a mercy killing on a dying Italian soldier during the desert war. He had endured starvation, illness and had faced execution; he had also learned to be wary with trust, and above all, to be self-reliant. In short, he was as prepared as anyone could be for Auschwitz.

From Auschwitz station Avey was taken to E711, a former Hitler Youth camp, which accomodated 150 British POWs:

'I thought I'd landed in fairyland, we had wonderful barracks, running water, bunk beds, blankets – that was really first class. There was a big area where we could exercise, and the walk every day two miles to I G Farben Monowitz to work, not bad. We were there for one month. Things changed when we were moved to E715...

As for overall control, the main Stalags were responsible for various work places around; there was no such control for E715, I G Farben Monowitz. We had a "man of confidence", Charlie Coward. The Count of Auschwitz we called him – if ever there was a con man he was. He was for us and against us if you like. He worked very well with the Germans, but nevertheless he did help quite a bit in talking to those in charge.'

Avey and the other POWs soon realised that I G Farben was no ordinary labour camp, that it was, 'Hell on earth, Hell on earth. There was no grass, no greenery of any sort, just mud in winter, dust in summer... I never saw a butterfly, a bird or bee the whole time I was there.'

Avey had always been keen on sport and was a good boxer. One day he recognised Victor Perez, the world champion flyweight boxer, among the Jewish prisoners in I G Farben. He managed to talk to him briefly, telling him that he remembered his big fight against Johnny King in Manchester. Avey was horrified by Perez's emaciated, stooped appearance, a great contrast to the photographs he'd seen of the athletic young fighter in his heyday. Later, he heard that Perez had been forced to box on the *Appelplatz* (roll-call area) of the camp by the SS who laid their bets on the matches. Perez was shot in 1945.

The all-pervasive inhumanity of the SS and other camp authorities never ceased to appal him. One day he saw a Jewish prisoner rummaging in a dustbin for something to eat. Then, without time to warn him:

'This SS woman got hold of this poor stripey, he was Polish, and she had leather gloves and she struck him around the neck and put him right down on the floor, she screamed at him, stood astride him, picked a rock up above her head like that, and smashed his head to smitherins, that was the sort of thing going on there...'

The British POWs were working an eleven-hour day on a seven-day week basis, with an occasional Sunday off. It was hard physical work although, all admit, nothing as hard as what the Jewish forced labourers were doing. Avey was one of the five selected to go and make the case that the work they did was in breach of the Geneva Convention. But nothing was achieved. The POWs had no option but to return to work, but they were more than ready to subvert the work they were forced to do. Avey made friends with a young Ukrainian, Paulina, who worked in the office of a German engineer in I G Farben, and she was willing to help. When special shipments of machinery were expected, she tipped the POWs off in time for them to arrange some form of sabotage. Her information was vital, as was Avey's prior engineering experience in their 'slow-burn' sabotage activities. As he wrote, 'The ground for the Buna rubber plant had been prepared in April 1941... Not a single batch of rubber was ever produced in that plant and I'd like to think we played our part.'

During his time in I G Farben, two Jewish prisoners stood out from the rest and became particularly significant for Avey. These were 'Hans' and 'Ernst'. No other names were exchanged, and Avey was always known as 'Ginger', never his proper name. Avey had met Hans when they were both working in a building under construction. Hans, a Dutch Jew, had asked Avey for a cigarette. Their meeting was necessarily brief, but Avey had gained the impression that there was something special about Hans, who seemed an interesting, educated chap. Over the weeks Avey saw more of him and now and again they managed to speak – by then Avey had picked up some German and was able to communicate with prisoners, like Hans, who spoke the language. At night they returned to their different camps, the Jews to Auschwitz III, Monowitz, and Avey to the relatively better conditions of E715.

Increasingly, and with growing anger at the way the Jews were treated, Avey became obsessed with the need to know more about the whole work and killing system and the conditions the Jews were living under. Over the weeks he worked out a plan for an exchange whereby he would enter the Jewish camp for a night, and Hans would spend a night in the British camp where he could have more rest and better food. Between them, in the odd moments they could speak alone, they worked out the details. They realised that a limited number of others had to be involved if the exchange was to be successful; cigarettes were the means to this end. Fortunately, Avey had built up quite a stock. Two British POWs, Bill Hedges and Jimmy Fleet, were let into the secret and their part was to hide Hans in Avey's bunk in E715, with the story that Avey was sick. Two of Hans's workmates, who shared his bunk, were also rewarded with cigarettes, their task being to guide Avey throughout the swap from the moment work was finished to getting into the camp then the barracks, and out the next day.

Avey took great pains in planning the exchange, knowing that it was a matter of life or death for him and Hans. He studied the Jewish prisoners closely, imitating their stoop and their listless and shuffling manner of walking. He traded more cigarettes for a pair of wooden clogs and, wrapping rags around his feet, practised shuffling around in them. The riskiest part of the whole enterprise was bribing one of the less brutal *Kapos*, essential for the plan. As the day of the swap drew near, Avey hacked off his hair and then shaved his head and when the time actually came, smeared his face with dirt to give the appearance of exhaustion.

The swap went as planned in the assigned place, with Hans leaving as a British POW and Avey in Hans's bug-infested, filthy striped pyjamas and clogs, being guided into the middle of the column returning to the camp. After the drawn-out counting and re-counting the column trudged off, the sight of the bodies of the newly dead littering the roadsides. As they approached the camp Avey noted the barbed-wire fence, the electric current wire, the watchtowers. Hearing the loud barked commands of the SS guards, he knew he had to stand erect, whip the cap from his head and look as if he could do another day's work. At last he could see the layout of the camp, and witness the 'sweet, ghastly smell of the distant crematoria'. The lifeless body hanging from a gibbet gave a grim warning. He knew that if he was identified as an impostor, he was finished. Then, standing on the *Appelplatz* for yet more counting, he heard the surreal strains of classical music – the camp orchestra was welcoming the wearied workforce back. Anita Lasker-Wallfisch, a Jewish inmate, was a member of the orchestra:

'Our job was to play marches in the morning and in the evening at the camp gate as people went out – there were lots of factories around there: Buna and I G Farben – and thousands marched out to work, and they marched to music. So we did that in the mornings and in the evenings, and in the day we went back to the block and all sorts of music was obtained and we had a whole team of people copying out the music after it had been orchestrated – that's how a whole group of people were saved, through being copyists. And then we learnt these pieces and played for the amusement of the Germans…especially after selections, when they were quite worn out from their efforts of selecting people to go to the gas chamber.'

At the end of roll-call, Avey spotted one of the men involved in the plan and followed him into the barracks, gagging on the fetid air within. Arriving at the bunk he met both of his Jewish helpers, a Pole and a German with whom he could communicate. The bunk was just over five feet in depth and the three of them lay crosswise to the frame in order to fit in; Avey was between the others, with his head away from the corridor. He worked out that there were 100 to 150 men in the barracks and noted the trading going on for pitifully small items such as a single button or piece of thread. When the evil-smelling soup arrived, he declined to join the queue because, 'Now I was gasping for air alongside them amidst the stench of faeces and sweat. It smelt of death there and no mistake. It was sickly and overpowering.'

Avey learnt that about 16 female prisoners were used as prostitutes in the *Frauenhaus*, mainly as a reward for the *Kapos*. Despite all he was observing, and the information he was memorising about the perpetrators, he soon realised that the barracks was but one part of a huge, monstrous machine, and that he would learn nothing specific about the selections and the gas chambers from there. Like Coward, he had a nightmarish night, kept awake throughout by the cacophony of groans, shrieks and screams: 'It was like nothing else on earth; it was hell on earth. This is what I had come to witness but it was a ghastly, terrifying experience.'

The following morning, having picked up his meagre slice of black bread which, again, he found impossible to eat, he shuffled out with the rest to the *Appelplatz* to endure the interminable count and re-count before being marched out to work. At the worksite he was relieved to spot Hans among the British POWs, and the swap was executed swiftly and successfully, albeit with much trepidation. Later Avey was upset to hear that the extra food Hans had eaten and enjoyed so much in the British camp had made him ill. It took Avey a while to reflect on the harrowing experience, but in his book he concluded that what he had seen was the worst thing you could do to a man: 'Take everything away from him – his possessions, his pride, his self-esteem – then kill him slowly. Man's inhumanity to man doesn't begin to describe it. It was far worse than the horror I'd faced in the desert war.'

Weighing up the experience, although he was glad that he had gained some names and information and had a much better idea of what went on in the camp, he was disappointed that he had learnt nothing about the extermination programme that went on elsewhere. Although he realised the whole escapade had been foolhardy, he was determined to go in again and did so, with a few changes of plans, a few months later. By then, the weather had changed and he found the cold very difficult to bear; he also noticed the declining health of his two companions in the bunk. Avey tried a third time, but was thwarted by a guard snooping around the place in which the swap was to occur.

Avey was obviously taking an enormous risk in entering the Jewish camp. If caught the penalty would have been, 'shot out of hand, there and then, without any doubt'. But he told me how important it was to have a cause:

> 'My experience in the desert, my capture and the subsequent tough experience meant that it was no big deal getting into the concentration camp; I had done worse. I was just so angry, indignant at the injustice of it all and the appalling inhumanity I witnessed...'

The other slave labourer Avey befriended was Ernst, a German Jew. They met while working in the same area of Buna-werke. Avey had noticed Ernst looking at him intently; as with Hans, there was something different about him that attracted Avey: he seemed more alert than the other inmates. They exchanged names, and Avey slipped him a cigarette. A few days later working in close proximity, Ernst whispered to Avey that he had a sister living in Birmingham, England, who had emigrated in 1939 on a *Kindertransport*. Avey asked for her address which Ernst gave him when they next met and Avey memorised. Avey decided to make the contact through his mother in a childhood code he and his sister had used. In his letter he urged his mother to write to Susanne, the sister, telling her that he was with her brother in the British camp, that her brother was OK, but if she wanted to help him, sending cigarettes by post via Avey would be the most useful way. He made obscure references to 'camps' and 'Jews' and asked her to pass the information on to the War Office, by referring to a local man known to them who worked there.

Avey had little expectation that his plan would work, but after some months he received a letter from Susanne which although it began 'Dear Ginger' was clearly intended for Ernst. In the letter she promised that cigarettes would be sent. A little later he received the parcel of cigarettes sent by his mother, confirming the contact had worked. Ernst was overjoyed at being in touch with his sister and even happier when he received the first batch of cigarettes and a precious bar of chocolate.

Avey smuggled in the rest in instalments over time to avoid detection. He well knew the importance of cigarettes as the main camp currency and realised also how they could bring advantages for Ernst and an increased chance of survival. The rest of the cigarettes were fed to him over the weeks, although Avey had no idea how they were used.

There were numerous gross human rights abuses that Avey witnessed in Auschwitz which continued to haunt him long after the war ended. One occurred when he was ordered to go to the nearby town of Katowice by train to load up supplies and return. Waiting on the platform for his train, he saw prisoners arriving and being lined up, women and children separated from the men. One woman held a crying baby in her arms. An SS guard passing down the line roughly demanded she should stop its cries, which she could in no way manage to do. To Avey's shock and rage, the irate guard marched back to the woman and punched the baby hard in the face, killing it.

Another terrible scene that he not only witnessed, but was involved in, happened during one of his work shifts alongside the Jewish prisoners. The British POWs were in a muddy trench laying electric cables from a heavy wooden drum which was on the ground above the trench. The drum had stopped rolling for some unknown reason. 'We stood looking and one of the SS approached this prisoner – a young stripey – immediately above me. They always had to stand to take their caps off and stand to attention, which he did, and the SS hit him right across the face.' The boy was then killed before the horrified eyes of the POWs. Avey, shocked and enraged beyond fear, shouted at the SS accusing him of being a *'verfluchter Untermensch!'* (damned sub-human) – the worst insult anyone could give a German, linking them with the inferior much despised Jews, gypsies and Slavs they had named as such. For this Avey was whipped hard across his face with a Luger, resulting in him losing an eye after the war.

'My trouble in Auschwitz is that part of me died there, without any doubt at all. You were under-ridden by this ghastly twenty-four hour

Barrack accommodation for prisoners at Buchenwald (taken after liberation). Elie Wiesel last face, second row from bottom. This is the type of accommodation and bunks that Charles Coward and Denis Avey would have experienced during their time in Auschwitz-Monowitz.

stench from the ovens and the chimneys – twenty-four hours a day this sickly smell. And do you know, to this day I can still taste it. And then these dreadful situations with the stripeys. It was ghastly, absolutely ghastly... And this happened day in and day out...

'And they said that the people of Germany didn't know what was going on! The people of Auschwitz itself complained bitterly about the smell from the crematorium. And all these people coming in daily! There must have been hundreds and thousands of Germans who saw them and yet they said, "Oh no, we didn't know anything that was happening." That's ludicrous. It's a fact: old people and children were killed. The best of the menfolk were allowed to live [to work]. The rest were burnt daily, daily, daily...'

Like Coward, Avey showed little respect for the Red Cross in their visits to E715 and I G Farben, Auschwitz, although they did correctly report the unfit drinking water and insufficient latrines; but, on the whole, as he explained in his book he found them 'highly gullible':

'Some of their reports into conditions of the camp I saw later bore little resemblance to the truth. They suggested we had been able to play football whenever there were enough guards. It was utter balderdash. One Red Cross report claimed that the work was not hard and that there were no complaints about it. They said we had hot running water, and even more ridiculous that they had seen inmates playing tennis...'

When the big Allied air raid, earlier described by John Fink, occurred on 20 August 1944, Avey managed to get down into a massive culvert with about 40 civilian workers and guards:

'They had these fog-makers to conceal the works from the air, the wind took the fog from our side of I G Farben. The American bombers came over and bombed hell out of the factory. One stick of bombs fell on the crude air raid shelter the POWs were in... I organised the shifting of the blocks of concrete and got the bodies out. 38 were killed – all British POWs... I got one of our men out from the very bottom, a miracle survival. He complained that I dropped water on his face as I gave him a drink! I helped with the burial of the bodies, the grave was hit two months later by US *Superfortresses*. They were reburied and their remains were later reburied [in an official war cemetery in Krakow], there were four-teen missing, no bodies for these.'

On 18 January 1945, with the level of gunfire signalling the approach of the Red Army to Auschwitz, the slave labourers, the majority of them Jewish, were evacuated from the camp to embark on their notorious 'death march'. John Fink, the Jewish slave labourer from Monowitz, was among them:

'When we were marched out of Auschwitz-Birkenau, we didn't know where we were going. The only ones left behind were the sick prisoners, about eight, nine hundred of them, including Primo Levi; we thought they would all get killed because we couldn't imagine that they would let anybody live.

'So we marched. Well, the weather was terrible and anybody who dropped back was shot in the back by the SS; so many. They were just left lying there, and there were already dead people lying there who had marched before us. These were the people who couldn't really do it because most people didn't even have shoes; they only had wooden clogs and you couldn't march in those in that terrible frost and snow. I had a pair of shoes but the right and the left weren't the same. When you could keep your feet in order you had a chance of life; so many died because of their feet, many got water in their knees and the pus would come out of their bodies.

'Anyway, we marched through the night and in the morning they put us in an empty tyre factory. We rested there for a while and then we were ordered to march again. In the afternoon we must have reached the former German border. We marched through the streets of Gleiwitz, there were street cars running and civilians about. The SS weren't around us there and we were so desperate for food that we asked people where there was a concentration camp – can you imagine the mentality! We stayed for two days in an overcrowded camp; no order there, nothing.

'After a day or two we were ordered to the railroad yards. We were put on an open train; every car was filled with prisoners, you couldn't sit down. We went on through days and nights, the train would stop every so often because of the bombings. People died. We would just throw the dead out of the cattle cars to make room to finally sit down. We came through Czechoslovakia and at the railroad stations we would have to take the sick out and leave them on the platforms where the Gestapo would kill them in front of the civilians of those towns in Czechoslovakia and Austria. They took us to Mauthausen. By then the camp was so overcrowded that its *Kommandant* refused our unloading, so the train went on and on.

'Suddenly we came to Berlin. I knew Berlin, I saw the famous radio tower – that was 28 January 1945. We were unloaded in the big, old concentration camp of Sachsenhausen. Then back on the train again to Flossenburg, another overcrowded camp. Since the Americans were coming from one side, the Russians from another, and the British from up north, the noose was tightening. But they never got rid of the prisoners for some reason, except those who got killed or died on the way. Then I was loaded on another train and now we were sitting on the dead. We weren't human any more, we weren't supposed to be human anyway. That's how I came to Belsen around 8 March 1945.'

A few days after the slave labourers had left, on 21 January 1945, with E715 disbanded, the British POWs set off for what for them would prove to be the nearest they ever got to sharing the full horror of the Jewish Holocaust experience: if not at the extreme end of human suffering, touching it. Their situation had deteriorated sharply from December 1944 when Allied bombing of the German transport system had blocked Red Cross parcels from arriving. But now, in near-Arctic temperatures, they set out on what developed into a hunger march, a nightmarish journey that was to last for three months through western Poland, through Czechoslovakia, into Bavaria. Depending on the few crumbs of German rations that were spasmodically provided, they began to experience the symptoms of starvation and weakness they had earlier noted in the concentration camp victims.

The march was haphazard with guards having no idea of where they were heading except away from the Russians in the east towards the west. Nights were spent shivering in frozen fields or icy barns, most of the men suffering with frostbite. Already distressed with the inhumane treatment of the Jews they had seen during their time in I G Farben Auschwitz, they were now confronted with their numerous skeletal frozen bodies lining the part of the route the slave labourers had staggered along before them. Avey thought of his friends Hans and Ernst, feeling sure that they too had perished.

When the marchers reached Pilsen in Czechoslovakia, Avey decided that, rather than starve to death as seemed more than likely, he'd take a chance to escape alone from a lightly guarded barn they were sleeping in for a night. He set off for the German border stealing whatever food he could, and made it to Regensberg. From there he headed towards Nuremberg, still on foot, and had almost reached Bamberg when he ran into an American tank unit and liberation. He estimates the march from Auschwitz to this point was 900 miles. He was then driven to a small abandoned airstrip watching and waiting for planes. Eventually he was joined by a group of Americans including some former POWs. Two days later, seeing an RAF Dakota land he ran out, with dozens of other men from other parts of the field's edges, and clambered in. They were flown to Brussels where he was taken to an army camp and given food for the first time in weeks. The following day he was taken to an airfield and put into a Lancaster bomber for a low flight over the Channel which was strewn with the detritus of war. But it was his beloved English country-side that he was most struck by:

> 'I had never seen such greenery in my life – there wasn't anything like the green of England. This was two days before VE Day; I made my way home, jumped ship, I didn't have a penny on me, no ticket. I was known at the local station, there was a coal lorry in the coal yard and there were some nice expletives from the driver, a chap I knew. My mother wasn't expecting me and when I knocked on the door I've regretted ever since what I said when she opened it, "Mother you do look old".'

Denis Avey had left home in 1940 as a young man thirsting for adventure. He returned an older, broken man, suffering from what today would be called Post-Traumatic Stress Disorder (PTSD). As he put it, 'I was Harpic – clean round the bend!' He had risked his life twice to enter the hell of Auschwitz III–Monowitz, to share a night with the Jewish prisoners, in order to bear witness to the sadistic treatment they were enduring under the Nazis. The irony was that he had risked his life in order to tell the world what he had seen, yet when he returned, like so many others, he found it impossible to talk to anyone about it, not even to his parents. Even if he tried, he would always receive 'the glazed-eyed syndrome'. When he reported back to the British Army authorities, they showed no interest in the fact that he and other British POWs had been used as slave labour, working an eleven-hour day, for seven days a week, against the terms of the Geneva Convention.

That wasn't the worst of it for Avey. Soon after his return, the traumas started, terrible nightmares in which the sight of the baby beaten to death and the young Jewish boy's bloody, bashed-in face would vividly return. 'I know I was a mess, a complete and total mess.' His nightmares reached a climax later when married to his first wife, Irene: he woke up in the terror of one of his nightmares about the Jewish camp, with his hands around her neck trying to strangle her.

Avey had suffered ill health throughout the war from the sandfly fever and malaria in the desert, to the debilitating scabies and dysentery in the series of terrible POW camps in which he'd been incarcerated, and then the drawn-out ordeal of the hunger march. With his friends either dead or having moved on, finding that life at home was no longer the same, he moved to Manchester. It was there that he was diagnosed with systemic tuberculosis in the throat, lungs, stomach and intestines and hospitalised for eighteen months in Manchester Royal Infirmary, having major surgery on his intestines which took months to heal. And then, in Baguley Sanitorium, enduring the tough, uncomfortable 'fresh air' treatment for TB at the time which, in winter, with external doors and all windows open, often meant that snow drifted on to his hospital bed.

During these months of illness, as the Nuremberg Trial of I G Farben was being prepared, Avey was not tracked down to give evidence; had he been able to give his witness this might have acted like a catalyst and provided the satisfaction of being heard. But he was in no condition to do so. Eventually he returned to engineering where 'work became my crutch', and he built up a successful career as chief engineer of an engineering business. This enabled many years of fast living, 'seeking a constant adrenalin rush', desperately trying to forget his war years. He also used a way of coping which had started in the camps:

'With all the inner pain I was feeling and with the nightmares, I found a way of coping. I was able to get above things. I managed to get an alter ego: that it wasn't happening to me – all the pain I was going through and the hunger and mental problems, they weren't happening to me, but happening to this facsimile of me, and I could get above the pain threshold – can you believe it? I didn't consciously work it out, it just came on to me and then I realised what I was doing. I'm still able to do it, I can get above pain until I get tired or a bit dejected over something and then the pain comes back.'

It was to be more than sixty years before he found it possible to speak at any length about his experiences: this was during an interview he gave me for the Imperial War Museum – his 'first step'. By then, as we have seen, the Eichmann trial had transformed the situation: the Holocaust was to be remembered not forgotten. The 50th and 60th anniversaries of the liberation of Auschwitz opened up the topic still further and the world began to pay serious attention. It was the BBC journalist and writer, Rob Broomby, who took the interview further and revealed the whole story, which eventually developed into the bestselling book published in 2011, *The Man Who Broke Into Auschwitz*.

It was through Avey's collaboration with Broomby that he met Susanne, Ernst Lobethal's sister, who told him that Ernst had survived the war and had managed to emigrate to the United States making a rich and satisfying life for himself, his name changed to Ernie Lobet. Furthermore, in a video recording Ernst had made for the Shoah Foundation, he had mentioned the 'fiery ginger soldier' and how the cigarettes 'Ginger' had obtained for him had been like being given 'the Rockefeller Center', as he could barter some for a stout pair of soles for his shoes which proved essential for surviving the death march, and the war. Avey was upset to learn that Ernst had died a few years earlier. All that he heard about him had confirmed the great affinity he had felt with him in the camp; but watching the video he was 'emotionally turned over' to know that he had saved Ernst's life; it had all been worthwhile. Now he could talk and people were prepared to listen.

Avey is now in his 93rd year, a tall, charismatic man, still travelling around the country talking about his experience to all manner of audiences, from students numbering 500 in the Cambridge Union to small school groups. Finally, after all those years, he has achieved his aim of bearing witness to what he saw, heard and endured in I G Farben Monowitz, potent evidence against Holocaust deniers. He is one of the two living men among the 27 honoured as 'Heroes of the Holocaust' by the British government, receiving his award from Gordon Brown in March 2010, who, like everyone else who meets Avey, was evidently greatly charmed by him. Although he is now keen to talk, Avey is still very modest about the part he has played, and it is enough for him that his witness has been given and accepted. His fervent hope is that it will encourage people, especially the young, to stand up and 'do something positive and active in our unsettled times'.

Sara Hannah's reunion in 1972 with the men who saved her life. Left to right standing: John Buckley, Roger Letchford, Bill Scruton, Bert Hambling, Willy Fisher. Left to right seated: Stan Wells, Tommy Noble, George Hammond, Bill Keeble. Alan Edwards arrived after the photo session.

THE RESCUE OF SARA MATUSON BY

STAN WELLS   ALAN EDWARDS
GEORGE HAMMOND   ROGER LETCHFORD
TOMMY NOBLE   JOHN BUCKLEY
BILL SCRUTON   BERT HAMBLING
BILL KEEBLE   WILLY FISHER

*'In 1973 when they were honoured in London, they were
asked, "Why did you do it?" And they said, "We are British."
And I think there's such a pride in that, and very telling.'*

It was towards the end of December 1944, that Sara Matuson with her
sister, Hannah, and her mother started on their 'journey to hell' from the
labour camp Torn (Thorn) near Stutthof, in the Baltic.

Sara was born in 1928 and raised in Shavel, Lithuania, the youngest
daughter of Samuel-Lieb and Gita Matuson. Theirs was an affluent,
cultured and observant Jewish family and Sara had a privileged, happy
childhood with her elder sister Hannah and a wide circle of friends. All
this changed dramatically with the Russian invasion of 1940–1941 when
her father, a wealthy leather manufacturer, was arrested on a trumped-up
charge and imprisoned for six months. Things were difficult enough for
the family living under the Russians, but with the German invasion after
22 June 1941, conditions became even worse. Samuel-Lieb was arrested
again, but this time, after being forced to dig his own grave, he was shot.
Of the 300,000 Jews in Lithuania, only four per cent, 12,000, survived
the war.

Soon after the arrival of the Germans, all Jews in the area were
moved into nearby ghettos which had been formed; Sara and her family
went into the Kavkav ghetto. It was in that ghetto that Hannah was
raped by a drunken German guard. Berelowitz, the man who had taken
them into his home in the ghetto, had saved his own daughter, by sending the German, who was demanding a young girl, to Hannah. Sara was

not told of this at the time; when she heard about it much later, it helped explain 'the unbearable sadness that Hannah carried with her even before the terrible events of the death march'.

In 1943, when the Kavkav ghetto was closed, the family were moved to Traku ghetto. Then in July 1944, when the Germans were being pushed back by the advance of the Red Army, the inmates were moved out of the ghetto on a five-day journey in crowded, filthy cattle wagons to Stutthof concentration camp in the Baltic. It was from a sub-camp of Stutthof, on 21 January 1945, that 6,000 to 7,000 Jews were taken on a death march, driven into the Baltic Sea at Palmnicken and machine-gunned to death. But before then the Matuson family had been sent as forced labourers to four different camps, the last one, Torn (Thorn). They were kept on the point of starvation, doing back-breaking manual labour, digging trenches and deep foxholes with picks and shovels for German troops to defend the area against the advancing Red Army. As Sara has written:

'December came and it was bitterly cold. People exhibited meanness to each other, because people were trying to survive in conditions that made life impossible... I have thought many times of this time in the camps and I find that the memories are buried, so very deep. I know that there were other people around, but I rarely spoke with them. My mother and sister were the centre of my life and all I could do was get through each day with the numbing cold, the ceaseless hunger and the all-consuming fear. But I also had hope for an end to this nightmare... Then we were suddenly told that we would be moved to "save us" from the Russians. And so the final march deeper into Germany began.'

In December 1944, wearing only the thinnest rags and clogs, the 1,000 women began their long march which, by January 1945, was truly a death march, their numbers then down to 300. By the time they reached Gross Golemkau (Polish *Golebiewo*) in Poland, they were literally dragging themselves along, filthy, lousy and starving, guarded by SS men with whips and guns which they turned on the women at the slightest provocation. Sara was then just 16 years of age.

It was during the last months of the war that those living and working in the areas that the death marchers straggled through became aware, often for the first time, of the terrible state of concentration camp victims and the sadistic treatment they endured. A group of ten British POWs from Stalag 20B, working on farms in the area of Gross Golemkau, were shocked and horrified at what they witnessed. In his diary, William 'Willy' Fisher gave a vivid description of the state of the death marchers as they trudged through the town, on 26 January 1945:

'God punish Germany… I have seen today the filthiest, foulest and most cruel sight of my life…at 9 this morning a column straggled down the road towards Danzig – a column far beyond the words of which I am capable to describe. I was struck dumb with miserable rage, a blind coldness which nearly resulted in my being shot. Never in my life have I been so devoid of fear of opening my mouth.'

At this point Sara was seriously worried about her mother's deteriorating state; she could hardly stand, let alone stagger on. Sara begged her for the diamond ring which had belonged to her father and had been concealed on her mother's body throughout their ordeal so that she could escape from the march and buy bread to take back to them. 'I would never let you go by yourself', her mother told her as she parted with the ring, 'but now…may God be with you.' Sara explained what happened:

'I ran out of the line into a barn and I waited there, and someone came in – a Polish kid – and I said to him "Here's a diamond ring, bring me some bread." And he said, "OK." But he came back with the police and they took me to the police station and the policeman said, "What are you doing?" I said, "I came for bread," and the policeman said, "Don't you realise you are dirtying our *Judenrein* town?" I ran and they started chasing me… I managed to get away and hide in another barn. So I lay down in a trough and a man came into the barn and I said to him, "Are you Polish?" and he said, "No I'm British." He was a British POW working on the farm, Stan Wells, and one of the first things he did was to go and get me something to eat… We spoke in German. He was already four years in Germany, taken prisoner in 1940. Stan said, "I have nine comrades and we will see what we can do to hide you." And then he left. But he had told me that Mrs Miller usually came to check the cows and chickens there; but there was a kerosene lamp and he said, "The only thing I can do is to hide it so she won't see you." And sure enough, late at night, I was sitting in the trough and leaning against the wall. I must have fallen asleep and somebody was shaking my leg and saying, "Who is there? Who is there?" I didn't move. I think at that point I really gave up because I could have gone outside so that she wouldn't see me if she came back with the lamp. She didn't come back…'

A day later, Fisher's diary records, 'More Jewesses in similar condition to yesterday. Stan comes to me after dinner and tells me a Jewess has got away and he has her hiding in the cows' crib.' Stan Wells had returned to his camp to discuss the situation with the other British POWs. They decided to get Sara over to their room, part of Stalag 20B; it was in a barn that was locked at night and the windows were barred. But the rest of the barn was used to house about ten horses; it also had a hayloft and this seemed ideal for a hiding place for her in the straw, near the chimney for warmth. They usually hung their laundry to dry in the barn, so this would be a good cover when they sneaked food to the starving girl. Willy Fisher was given the task of getting Sara into her new hiding place. He gave her a big army coat and described their journey to safety in his diary. He wrote:

'27 January. Wait 'til nearly dusk to go to Stan's farm. He hands over the girl. I tell her to walk five paces on the other side of road

Prisoners on a death march in the Dachau area, secretly photographed by a German civilian, April 1945.

and speak to no one. She is crippled, too frightened to understand me, grabs my arm. I am a bit windy as the Gerries will stop us as it is definitely a "crime" for a prisoner to speak or walk with women… No trouble at all! No refugees [fleeing the advancing Russians] in yard. One of our own lads (another POW) – who has escaped from Marienburg and is now staying in our camp under the guise of being with a refugee family down the road – has had a good fire going all day and brick chimney is hot. Hot water soap towel – old clothes, stacks of food rushed up to her… Take all clothing off kid, give her paraffin for lice in her hair and bid her goodbye. She grabs my hand and kisses it – and tries to thank me, calls me Herr, I say roughly, "Drop it we are comrades, only doing what we can." Had no chance to have good look at her, judge her to be about 25 years of age.'

The following day he wrote:

'Everyone brings in food for our escapee! Hundredweight peas – ducks, hens, best part of a pig. Bread by loaves – and believe me she ate 3 loaves today and 5 bowls of soup… She's ill now – sick, diarrhoea. Suggest only milk for a few days.'

One evening she was taken to the POWs' room to meet the rest of the group of ten POWs who were involved in the rescue: Alan Edwards, Bert Hambling, Bill Scruton, George Hammond, Roger Letchford, Tommy Noble, John Buckley and Bill Keeble. They had sawn through the bars on their window and she was pushed through. They knew her as 'Sonia', a name Sara felt sounded less Jewish. They spoke in German; each of them welcomed her and gave her a small gift – 'a bit of string or something' – as she explained. They revealed their plan to hide her should the horses and hay be taken away; how they would create a false wall for her to hide behind. Fisher noted:

'We had a good look at her. Her eyes are large as is usual with star-vation, sunken cheeks, no breasts. Hair has not been cut, body badly marked with sores caused by scratching lice bites. Head still a bit matted and lice still obviously in. I got my forefinger and thumb round the upper part of her arm quite easily... Feet blue and raw with frostbite, the right heel is eaten away by frost and constant rubbing of badly fitting clog. We have stolen clothing and a pair of shoes off the refugee wagons to replace hers which are marked with the Jew star. She sat making a new hat from material and sewing and talking. She will keep harping on about her mother and sister and the concentration camp, but we forbid her to mention them. She says it is lonely and the time passes so slowly in the daytime. We arrange for fellows to pop in and out during the day. (Discipline is loose – now everyone is apathetic and just wait-ing for the Russians to come!)'

Sara stayed under the POWs' protection for three weeks. They were taking great risks: the police station was nearby and the danger great. She explained, 'If I had been discovered, I would certainly have been shot together with the ten men. They all had families at home, I had no one and no one would have known that I had been killed. I would have been just another of the six million, but they had so much to risk, it was close to going home – they could touch freedom.' Many years later, when Tommy Noble was asked why they had risked all to rescue her, he replied, 'Why not? She was only a young girl, a very nice wee thing; she'd been badly treated like us – they were cruel pigs.'

Gradually Sara was nursed back to health, her injuries treated by Bert Hambling, the medic among them, who made her 'feel almost human again'. It was Alan Edwards who was able to visit her most regularly; this was usually in the late afternoons, taking her supper and staying to chat and comfort her. Realising her acute anxiety over the fate of her mother and sister, Edwards even went to Praust, the camp where the remaining death marchers had been interned. But typhus had broken out and it was quarantined. Later Sara heard that both her sister and mother had died in the camp on the day of liberation, her mother of starvation and Hannah of typhus and starvation; their bodies were thrown into its mass grave.

As the Russians approached Gross Golemkau, the POWs were evacuated. They had offered to take Sara with them, shaving her head and dressing her as a man, but, with all she had been through, she was reluctant to risk this. With their departure, she felt bereft, they had become her surrogate family, especially Alan, to whom she had become greatly attached. Before leaving, they had arranged for a young Polish co-worker to offer her a refuge. But although this plan failed, Sara managed to find work for a German farmer, Binder, with 'Annie' another young worker who had no idea that Sara was Jewish. One day she was horrified to hear Annie say, 'You know, we lost the war, but we did win the war against the Jews. We killed them all!', realising that anti-Semitism was as virulent as ever.

When the Russians arrived in Gross Golemkau, Sara was in hiding with a group of young Poles, all former slave labourers, in a cellar at the end of the town. Although she had been warned by her father that Russians were every bit as bad as Germans, she still hoped they'd be sympathetic, impressed with her survival and that she would be liberated and free. She was soon disillusioned and, as she started to move away from the town, was arrested by them as a spy, accused of 'consorting with the enemy'. Terrified, she underwent many interrogations, always at night; and was told that they had witnesses who had worked with her and would attest to her being a spy. The fact that she spoke excellent German and Russian was considered an important factor.

Eventually she was released although they still refused to believe her story, telling her that no one could have survived the experiences she had described, that she 'ought to write fiction'. On her release, she was shown into a place to sleep for the night which was occupied by men whom she had been warned as 'having been reduced to the level of animals'. She managed to spend the night in an outhouse and escaped the following morning, making her way back in the direction of what she hoped would be Lithuania. At a train stop, she was invited by the station master into his room to look at maps to show her the route back. But he had other plans, and immediately pushed her on a couch where he started roughly to undress her. Her screams and shouts, as she fought him off, caused two men in nightshirts to enter saying, 'First the whores come and then they scream.'

Having extricated herself out of this frightening situation, and feeling there was safety in numbers, she teamed up with two other young girls and they travelled together for a few months before finally reaching Bialystock in Poland. Throughout the journey Sara was continually shocked by the behaviour of the Russians. She described witnessing: 'A free-for-all – men lined up in front of a barn, where they raped a girl until she died – and this occurred time and time again.'

It took more perilous months before she was able to reach Germany, where she was traced by family members living in New York. Sara finally emigrated to the United States in 1947 to join relatives there, going through a marriage of convenience to Yakov Ginzman, a rabbinic student, in order to get the required visa. On arrival in New York they went their separate ways, although the marriage took a year and a half to dissolve, due to Yakov's objections – he had evidently fallen for Sara during the brief time they were together. But Sara made a good and satis-fying life for herself, completing high school and becoming a registered nurse. In 1952, she married Bill Rigler who later became a New York Supreme Court judge. Sara added her sister Hannah's name to her own to honour her memory, she has since been known as Sara Hannah. All of the POWs eventually made it home safely to face the usual challenges of adapting to civilian life.

We learn something of the POWs' end-of-war experience from a letter Sara received years later from Alan Edwards, when contact had been resumed. He explained how, when the POWs were evacuated from Gross Golemkau, they were taken to a British POW camp in Danzig where they slept in the open all night. Next morning about 2,000 of them were marched westwards towards Germany, halting the night in the Polish town of Kartuzy. Four of them – Alan Edwards, Willy Fisher, John Buckley and Roger Letchford – decided at this point to try to escape before crossing the frontier into Germany. As they approached within ten kilometres of the border, they slipped off in the dark into the woods by the roadside, making their way to the nearest Polish farmhouse where, without questions, they were sheltered in their barn by the family.

Three weeks later, the Russian 'liberators' arrived. The men's high hopes of freedom were short-lived as they were treated with hostility as spies, interrogated and pushed from one village to another. They managed to get away on several occasions, and during one escape, when Edwards refused to answer questions at a Russian police post, he was shot from behind as he made off on his bicycle, breaking a leg in two places, spending two months in hospital. He was nursed back to health by the Polish family that had sheltered him, and later married Wanda, the daughter. It was not until November 1945 that Edwards was able to return to England with his new wife.

More is revealed from Willy Fisher's diary which had been written up while travelling on a Russian train from Brest-Litovsk to Odessa from notes he had made on the back of photographs and odd scraps of paper. At the time Fisher was a communist, although he was weakening in his commitment, shaken by the behaviour he witnessed by the advancing Russians. His diary, 10 March 1945, gives some idea of this:

'We spoke with Polish people. All women had been raped – all watches and rings found stolen – all radios destroyed. Hens, horses, pigs had been taken... The amount of Russians on the roads was amazing... Alan got whipped in the face by a Russian, many believed that we were SS serving with the Germans... 20 March 1945 – we have visited Germans over the border, 7 cases of suicide, women from 15–65 being raped nightly, all valuables removed, all pigs, cows and horses. One woman, 3 months with child, raped 32 times the first day... A father had shot his 15 year old daughter who had been tied to a wagon wheel and raped innumerable times.'

Despite growing misgivings, Fisher had decided that his future was in the Soviet Union. He had managed to get a place on a train full of returning slave labourers, bound for Odessa; he noted how the repatriated Soviets were petrified about going back, some of them committing suicide when a chance presented itself; and when he saw the rest being killed on arrival, he quickly changed his mind about entering the 'workers paradise' deciding to return to Britain, eventually making his way back by July 1945.

It wasn't an auspicious homecoming for Fisher. He arrived to find his house bombed and his wife living with another man. Two brothers had been killed in the war and on the night of his return his father died in his sleep. After a spell in hospital Fisher had a variety of jobs, finally settling down as an industrial engineer. He never remarried. His new partner, Margaret Heap, of whom he said, 'She is the nicest thing in my life,' refused to marry a divorced man.

For her part, living a new and exciting life in the United States, Sara never forgot the men who had saved her life, always hoping that somehow they would meet again. As she explained in her memoir, they had been one of the most important connections of her life: 'Ten men from a different culture, different religion and certainly of a different generation.' But tracing them wasn't easy. They had given her some papers, addresses and photographs when they were evacuated, but these had been lost by someone she had entrusted them to. It was a postcard from the War Office in London in 1963 that led to their reunion and subsequent correspondence. Sara had been desperately trying to trace the men since her marriage in 1952 and had written to the War Office trying to trace Alan Edwards, explaining that she wanted to express her thanks to him and the other nine POWs for saving her life. Her letter found Edwards, who replied on 1 September 1964, expressing his delight at being in touch again and to hear that she was safe and well: 'When we were compelled to leave Gross Golemkau at short notice that night, and we had to leave you, I must admit that I felt very apprehensive about what might happen to you. I feared the worst, whether you were discovered by the Germans or the Russians...'

Edwards mentioned that he was still in touch with some of the other POWs and that they had often talked about her. He went on to say, 'I only tried to be kind to you and cheer you a little, please don't give *me* the credit for saving your life, although I must admit I prayed for you that night we left, so maybe it helped a little.' In 1967, when Sara and Bill arrived at London Airport on a stop-over en route to Israel, she met Edwards for the first time after 22 years, a meeting which she described as 'very emotional'.

Edwards gave the story to a reporter, Ken Graham, who published it in the Sunday newspaper *The People* on 14 May 1968. The story rang a bell with a friend of Willy Fisher, who gave Fisher a copy. His reaction was ecstatic and in a letter to Sara written a few days after publication, explained how it had the effect of making:

'...the miserable cold day into perhaps what was the sunniest and certainly one of the happiest of my life. I am by nature pretty hard and insensitive, but I must confess I do know now what "tears of happiness" mean. My joy at your being alive and well, and being transformed from that tragic waif I once met, into what your photograph shows, a very beautiful and obviously happy woman, in some measure made up for all the guilt I felt at being unable (or perhaps too cowardly) to do or risk more for you than we did, for I have never got over the feeling that we, perhaps, should have taken you with us...'

Fisher, who had lost contact with Edwards, was now determined to get in touch with him again as well as Bill Scruton. In fact it was from this time that the men all met up again and, to their great joy, with Sara also, in 1972. This was at the Portman Hotel in London with their wives and partners when, as Sara put it, 'They toasted their little sister who had found a special place in their hearts – and the stoic British cried.'

Sara also learned that she was not the only Jewish prisoner Fisher and other POWs had helped. Fisher told her what had happened in Reisenburg in the winter of 1940–1941 where British POWs were working in sub-zero temperatures, on eight-hour shifts, loading wagons of frozen sugar beet and manhandling wagons into position. Among the British POWs was a young man of obvious Jewish appearance and terrified out of his wits of being noticed by one of the guards. This eventually happened, and from then on he was picked for the worst jobs. There was little the other POWs could do except to complain to the British sergeant in charge. The sergeant at this time was engaged in trafficking with one of the guards, swapping soap which had been received for the use of POWs, for cigarettes and schnapps which he kept for his own enjoyment. This coincided with the issuing of new clothing for prisoners. Fisher and the others discovered that the sergeant, under orders from the *Kommandant*, was deliberately not issuing anything to the young Jewish lad, who was in great need. On the next roll call, one of the POWs stepped out of line, threatening the sergeant that they were going to report the trafficking to the officer in charge of *Stalag* XXI, and that he would be reported through coded messages to the authorities in the UK unless the Jewish lad got his share of warm clothing and boots. It worked: not only did the Jewish soldier get equal treatment from then on, but no Jewish soldier was sent out to work again, but was kept within the POW camps for the rest of the war. The sergeant was sentenced to two years' imprisonment after the war. In the same letter to Sara, written in 1975, Fisher told her that, even with this experience, none of the POWs he spent the war with had any full knowledge of what was happening to the Jewish people until the day he met her on the death march.

When Willy Fisher died in December 1976, Margaret, his partner, wrote to Sara informing her of his death and adding, 'The only names he mentioned were his mother and your name.'

Considering the miracle of her survival, Sara explained:

'When people ask me how I survived, I say, "I was lucky, lucky, very lucky. My survival was a miracle, it was a miracle!" All the men were involved in saving me. It had to be a unanimous decision. If anything had happened, all of them would have suffered... They brought me back to life and to health and they were very nurturing and caring. I was, as George Hammond once said, "a little sister..." And you know many times I have said to myself, "Would I do it? Would he do it?" In 1973 when they were honoured in London, they were asked, "Why did you do it?" And they said, "We are British." And I think there's such a pride in that, and very telling. It wasn't something altruistic – "Oh, we're so noble!" They were just good, *good* people. When you think of it, all those except for Stan, and maybe Alan, probably hadn't met a Jewish person before. And for them to take such a risk, is so admirable... I owe them my life. Something like that you can't forget.'

ABOUT THE MEDAL

The creation of the 'Heroes of the Holocaust' award was the result of many months of vigorous campaigning by members of the Holocaust Educational Trust, who were determined to gain official recognition for the men and women whose stories are revealed in this book, and to increase national awareness of their brave, humanitarian deeds. Karen Pollock, the trust's chief executive, explained that until the presentation of the award, and apart from an occasional plaque in their home towns, 'They went unnoticed... We realised that the only way to get that recognition was through government.' Pollock and her team were heartened to find a 'listening ear', not only in the Government but among cross-party MPs too. This was apparent in a House of Commons debate, 29 April 2009, a day after the Prime Minister Gordon Brown's visit to Auschwitz. It was a good, if unusual, occasion for British politics, with the House easily reaching a consensus across party lines.

Gordon Brown had already paid tribute to some of these men and women in his book *Wartime Courage* and had learned a good deal more of the risks taken by the wartime British rescuers during discussions leading up to the presentation of the award. The visit he made to Auschwitz left him deeply moved by what he had seen and heard, ever more convinced of the courage of those who had held out the hand of rescue.

The Department of Communities and Local Government, responsible for faith and cohesion policy, was designated to deal with planning and implementing the award. Sixteen of the recipients had earlier been declared 'Righteous Among the Nations' (*Hasidei umot Haolam*) by Yad

Vashem, Israel's Holocaust Museum and Memorial in Jerusalem. In order to qualify as a 'Righteous', it has to be proved that recipients are non-Jewish; have helped to save a Jewish life at proven risk to their own; that there were no rewards in any form; and that they performed deeds above and beyond what can be considered ordinary help.*

The British award is an entirely separate project, based on different, less strict criteria, defined by its organiser Fiona McElroy as, 'Those who through extraordinary acts of courage and selflessness put themselves in harm's way to save another person's life. And those whose actions went way above and beyond the call of duty in the most difficult circumstances, because they felt intervention was necessary.' This more inclusive criteria meant that those who had done so much to rescue Jews and others endangered by the Nazis, yet did not equate to Yad Vashem's criteria, could justifiably be granted the British honour.**

Readers may wonder why other British men and women mentioned in these stories of rescue were not also awarded the Hero of the Holocaust award. But Fiona McElroy explained how the list was by no means definitive and is still open to suggestions. She pointed to Margaret Reid, Frank Foley's assistant in Berlin, who worked alongside him when things became so desperate in the late 1930s; and Robert Smallbones who saved many Jews in Frankfurt, both as deserving cases. Although there has been no formal announcement of plans to award more 'Heroes of the Holocaust' medals, it is hoped that the list of those recognised will be expanded in the future.

---

* Those deemed to have matched Yad Vashem's criteria were: Ida and Louise Cook (1965), Charles Coward (1970), POWs: Stan Wells, Alan Edwards, George Hammond, Roger Letchford and Tommy Noble (1989), Sister Agnes (Clare) Walsh (1990), Princess Alice of Greece (1993), Jane Haining (1997), Sofka Skipwith (1998), Henk Huffener (1998), Frank Foley (1999), Albert Bedane (2000), June Ravenhall (2007) and POWs: John Buckley, Bill Scruton, Bert Hambling, Bill Keeble and Willy Fisher (2012). With the exception of Ida and Louise Cook, Henk Huffener and Charles Coward, all were posthumously awarded.

** These include: Denis Avey, Bertha Bracey, Harold le Druillenec, Ivy Forster, Louisa Gould and Sir Nicholas Winton.

The award ceremony at Number 10 Downing Street on 9 March 2010 was, by all accounts, an emotional and joyous occasion, with relatives, friends and others who had helped bring the project to fruition, celebrating the bravery of the men and women whose stories are told in this book. The awards were presented by John Denham, the Secretary of State, and Sahid Malik, the Minister for Cohesion and Faith, with the Prime Minister, Gordon Brown, paying a special tribute for their 'selfless humanity'. The presence of Holocaust survivors, as well as providing 'a wonderful binding factor', gave their endorsement to the accolade 'Heroes of the Holocaust'. Roman Halter, who had suffered great pain and loss during his experience as a young boy in the camps and as a slave labourer, and had himself been given refuge by an elderly German couple towards the end of the war, paid tribute to those honoured: 'There are so few heroes and the deeds of these people were extraordinary. They provide a role model for today's children; when they hear of their brave deeds it will light a flame in their souls.'

LYN SMITH lectures in International Relations and Human Rights at the Webster University (USA) in London. Over the past 30 years she has worked as a freelance interviewer for the Imperial War Museum Holocaust Sound Archive, and was specially commissioned for the IWM Holocaust Exhibition, which opened in 2000. She is the author of the bestselling *Forgotten Voices of the Holocaust*.

Also by Lyn Smith

*Pacifists in Action: The Experience of the Friends'
Ambulance Service in the Second World War*

*Forgotten Voices of the Holocaust: A new history
in the words of the men and women who survived*

Young Voices: British Children Remember the Second World War

Voices Against War: A Century of Protest

SOURCES AND FURTHER READING

Avey, Denis, with Rob Broomby, *The Man Who Broke Into Auschwitz*, Hodder and Stoughton, London, 2011

Bailey, Brenda, *A Quaker Couple in Nazi Germany*, William Sessions, York, 1995

Bardgett, Suzanne (ed) and Cesarani, David, *Belsen 1945: New Historical Perspectives*, Valentine Mitchell, 2006

Braham, R. L. and Miller, S., *The Nazis' Last Victims: The Holocaust in Hungary*, Wayne State University Press, 1998

Brown, Gordon, *Wartime Courage: Stories of extraordinary courage by exceptional men and women in World War Two*, Bloomsbury, London, 2008

Browning, C. R., *Nazi Policy, Jewish Workers, German Killers*, Cambridge University Press, 2000

Castle, John, pseud, (R. C. Payne and J. W. Garrod) *The Password is Courage*, Souvenir Press, London, 1954

Cesarani, David and Levine, Paul A. (eds.), *Bystanders to the Holocaust: A Re-evaluation*, Frank Cass, London and Portland, 2002

Chadwick, William, *The Rescue of Prague Refugees 1938–39*, Matador, Leicester, 2010

Cohen, Frederick, *The Jews of the Channel Islands during the German Occupation 1940–45*, Jersey Heritage Trust, 2000

Colvin, Ian, *The Unknown Courier*, William Kimber, London, 1953

Cook, Ida, *Safe Passage*, Harlequin, USA, 2008

Emanuel, Muriel and Gissing, Vera, *Nicholas Winton and the Rescued Generation*, Valentine Mitchell, 2009

Fogelman, Eva, *Conscience and Courage: Rescuers of Jews during the Holocaust*, New York, Anchor Books, 1994

Friedlander Saul, *Nazi Germany and the Jews: The Years of Persecution, 1933–39*, Wiedenfeld and Nicholson, London, 1997

Friedrich, Otto, *Before the Deluge: A Portrait of Berlin in the 1920s*, Harper and Row, New York, 1972

Gershon, Karen, *We came as Children*, Victor Gollancz, 1966

Gilbert, Martin, *The Holocaust*, Fontana, London, 1987

Gilbert, Martin, *The Righteous: Unsung Heroes of the Holocaust*, Black Swan, 2003

Gilbert, Martin, *Beyond The Call of Duty: British Diplomats and other Britons who helped Jews escape from Nazi tyranny*, The Holocaust Educational Trust, 2008

Grunwald-Spier, Agnes, *The Other Schindlers: why some people chose to save Jews in the Holocaust*, The History Press, Port Stroud, Gloucestershire, 2010

Hayes, Peter, *Industry and Ideology I G Farben in the Nazi Era*, Cambridge University Press, 1987

Hinsley, F. H., *British Intelligence in the Second World War* (abridged ed.) HMSO, London, 1994

Hitler, Adolf, *Mein Kampf*, Hutchinson, 1969 edition

Jackson, Julian, *France: The Dark Ages*, Oxford University Press, 2001

Janner, Greville, *To Life! The Memoirs of Greville Janner*, Sutton Publishing, Stroud, Gloucester, 2006

Lacquer, W., *The Holocaust Encyclopedia*, Yale University Press, New Haven and London, 2001

Lafitte, Francois, *The Internment of Aliens*, Libris, London, 1988

Land-Weber, Ellen, *To Save a Life: Stories of Holocaust Rescue*, Urbana and Chicago, University of Illinois Press, 2000

Leverton, Bertha and Lowensohn, Shmuel (eds.), *I Came Alone: The Stories of the Kindertransports*, Book Guild, 1990–1996

London, Louise, *Whitehall and the Jews 1933–1948: British Immigration Policy and the Holocaust*, Cambridge University Press, 2000

McDougall, Reverend David, *Jane Haining, 1897–1944*, Edinburgh, Church of Scotland World Mission, 1949 (updated by Ian Alexander, 1999)

Ofer, Dalia, *Escaping the Holocaust: Illegal immigration to the Land of Israel, 1939–1944*, Oxford University Press, 1990

Paldiel, Mordecai, *Saving the Jews: Amazing Stories of Persons who Defied the 'Final Solution'*, Schreiber Publishing, Rockville, Maryland, 2000

Pike Rubin, Evelyn, *Ghetto Shanghai*, Shenfield, New York, 1993

Rees, Laurence, *Auschwitz, The Nazis and the Final Solution*, BBC Books, London, 2005

Rigler, Sara Hannah, *10 British Prisoners-of-War Saved My Life*, Jay Street Publishers, New York, 2006

Sander, Paul, *The Ultimate Sacrifice – the Jersey islanders who died in German prisons and concentration camps during the occupation 1940–1945*, Biddles, UK, 2004

Sander, Paul, *The British Channel Islands under German Occupation 1940–45*, Jersey Heritage Trust: Société Jersiaise, 2005

Silver, Eric, *The Book of the Just: The Silent Heroes Who Saved Jews from Hitler*. Wiedenfeld and Nicholson, London, 1992

Skipwith, Sofka, *The Autobiography of a Princess*, Rupert Hart-Davis, London, 1968

Smith, Michael, *Foley: The Spy Who Saved 10,000 Jews*, Michael Smith, Politicos, 2004

Staub, Ervin, *Overcoming Evil: Genocide, Violent Conflict and Terrorism*, Oxford University Press, 2011

Vickers, Hugo, *Alice, Princess Andrew of Greece*, Hamish Hamilton, London, 2000

White, J. R. *'Even in Auschwitz…Humanity Could Prevail': British POWs and Jewish Concentration-Camp Inmates at I G Auschwitz, 1943–1945*, Oxford University Press, Holocaust and Genocide Studies, vol 15, N2, 2001

Zinovieff, Sofka, *Red Princess – a Revolutionary Life*, Granta, 2007

IMPERIAL WAR MUSEUM: DEPARTMENT OF DOCUMENTS AND SOUND

Documents:

Bayliss, Muriel, unpublished memoir 'Miss M Bayliss 96/49/1'

Warriner, Doreen, *A Winter in Prague*, unpublished manuscript, 04/14/9, June 1939

Interviews:

Where relevant, the contributor's name below is followed by their maiden name. Maiden names are used where relevant to period within the text. Reference numbers relate to where accounts are kept in the Imperial War Museum.

15441	Alexander, Norna
22065	Avey, Denis
16901	Bailey, Brenda (Friedrich)
4648	Bracey, Bertha
14205	Cadbury, Tessa (Rowntree) 14205
8942	Ehrlich, Zdenka
16594	Fink, John
16835	Greaves (Catchpool), Jean
17183	Halter, Roman
23830	Handler, Arieh
16632	Hart-Moxon, Kitty
19918	Huffener, Henricus 'Henk'
18671	Ingram, Janine (Assael)
9092	Knoller, Fred
4498	Krebs, Hans (Sir)
11914	Lasker-Wallfisch, Anita
10715	Le Sueur, Robert
17558	Levi, Gertrude 'Trude'
33356	McElroy, Fiona

19856 Mitchell, Warren
18814 Ollendorff, Berta
19794 Ossowski, Maria
33353 Pollock, Karen
9937 Riches, Frederick
33354 Rigler (Matuson), Sara Hannah
17469 Schaufeld (Löwyová), Vera
18572 Silberman, John 18572
10066 Sinel, Leslie

Courtesy of Clare Haddad (Huffener)
Unpublished manuscript, *Friends and Fugitives*, by Henk Huffener
Letter Henk Huffener to Clare Haddad

Public Records Office (PRO) – for Foley's reports to London
FO 371/1991
FO 371/16721
FO 371/18861
FO 371/24079
FO 371/24079
FO 371 TNA 371/21637, Sir George Ogilvie-Forbes report to London 16/11/1938

Nuremberg Trial, affidavit, Charles Coward, 24.7.47 T-301/96/NI-11696/664

United States Holocaust Memorial Museum, Department of Oral History
RG-50-486-0009, Gudrun Kübler

INDEX

Page numbers in *italics* refer to photographs